GW01339446

THE LIVING BOAS

Brazilian Rainbow Boa, *Epicrates cenchria cenchria*. Photo by J. Merli

JERRY G. WALLS

TS-278

In memory of Smudge, Kelly, Pip, Spock, Punkin, and all the others who provided such joy in their brief lives.

Drawings by John Quinn unless otherwise noted.
Edited by Thomas Mazorlig.

t.f.h.

© by T.F.H. Publications, Inc.

Distributed in the UNITED STATES to the Pet Trade by T.F.H. Publications, Inc., One T.F.H. Plaza, Neptune City, NJ 07753; on the Internet at www.tfh.com; in CANADA Rolf C. Hagen Inc., 3225 Sartelon St. Laurent-Montreal Quebec H4R 1E8; Pet Trade by H & L Pet Supplies Inc., 27 Kingston Crescent, Kitchener, Ontario N2B 2T6; in ENGLAND by T.F.H. Publications, PO Box 15, Waterlooville PO7 6BQ; in AUSTRALIA AND THE SOUTH PACIFIC by T.F.H. (Australia), Pty. Ltd., Box 149, Brookvale 2100 N.S.W., Australia; in NEW ZEALAND by Brooklands Aquarium Ltd. 5 McGiven Drive, New Plymouth, RD1 New Zealand; in SOUTH AFRICA, Rolf C. Hagen S.A. (PTY.) LTD. P.O. Box 201199, Durban North 4016, South Africa; in Japan by T.F.H. Publications, Japan—Jiro Tsuda, 10-12-3 Ohjidai, Sakura, Chiba 285, Japan. Published by T.F.H. Publications, Inc.

MANUFACTURED IN THE
UNITED STATES OF AMERICA
BY T.F.H. PUBLICATIONS, INC.

Contents

ACKNOWLEDGMENTS

INTRODUCTION 6

BOA FAMILIES AND GENERA 10

BOA STRUCTURE AND A CHECKLIST 23

THE TRUE BOAS: BOIDAE 37

THE BURROWING BOAS: ERYCINIDAE 152

THE DWARF BOAS: TROPIDOPHIIDAE 206

BOA CARE 256

BREEDING BOAS 270

FURTHER READING 276

INDEX 286

Acknowledgments

Any large book is the result of more than just personal experience. It is based on a mixture of what has been published in the past, what you can learn from other people, and your own experiences and interpretations. Much of what has been written before is included in the bibliography (and the bibliographies included in many of these works), though there never has been a single comprehensive modern review of the boas and their related forms. My personal experience has been largely observational, and I've seen and handled a good percentage of the species of boas recognized here (except of course many of the forms of *Epicrates* and *Tropidophis* that are practically unknown in the hobby). I must admit right at the beginning that I have never kept the larger boas because they are not compatible with my home life (a small house, small dogs, and other small pets), but this has not prevented me from enjoying them in the literature and as the pets of others.

I am greatly indebted to Dr. Darrel Frost and Margaret Arnold of the herpetology department at the American Museum of Natural History, New York, for allowing me access to the departmental reprint file and showing me the ins and outs of the Museum's library. Darrel also allowed me quick and dirty hands-on experience with some of the rarer boas housed in the collection of the American Museum. My thanks also to Dr. Ken Williams, Northwestern State University, Natchitoches, Louisiana, for helping solve a couple of technical points. The contributions of Drs. Samuel McDowell, Garth Underwood, and Arnold Kluge to the complex concepts of relationships among the boas have been essential reading for this book, though I must admit that I have followed in detail none of their classifications. The extensive work by Drs. Robert Henderson and Blair Hedges, as well as the late Albert Schwartz, on the boas of the Caribbean has filled in many of the gaps in our knowledge of the isolated forms.

Paul Gritis, John Johnson, and Donald Hahn are just three of many book dealers who have provided numerous important papers and books making this particular book possible. Dick Bartlett provided answers to a few hands-on questions and gave of his usual encouragement.

I can't even begin to mention the many hobbyists and breeders who let me "take a look" at their snakes and answer a multitude of questions about their methods of keeping and breeding. A few of the many who stand out include Byron Barnes, Steve Ennis, Larry Kenton, Steve Mitchell, Steve Osborne, Dwayne Richard, and

ACKNOWLEDGMENTS

Jim Tracy. My wife, Maleta, took many photos of boas at the various herp shows we attended in the Northeast, some used here but many even more important in supplementing the literature for details of scalation and color patterns.

The general hobbyist, in the zeal of attempting to add to the collection or perhaps breed a species for local sale, sometimes forgets just how important commercial breeders and dealers are to the herpetological hobby. Few hobbyists could afford the truly elite species and varieties of boas, but thanks to many men and women who devote countless, often thankless and low-paid, hours to making specimens available at reasonable prices any hobbyist can gather a diverse collection of fine specimens. I hope that you will remember your local breeders and dealers as you pursue your hobby. And remember, captive-bred always is the best way to go.

A NOTE ON THE PAINTINGS

The color paintings of anterior, midbody, and ventral views of each boa were done by John R. Quinn from the best descriptions and illustrations available, but they are still intended to be schematics, not scientifically detailed portraits. Boas as a rule are highly variable snakes, so it is to be expected that individual specimens will differ to some extent from any painting or photograph.

Dumeril's Boa, *Acrantophis dumerili*. Photo by V. Jirousek

Emerald Tree Boa, *Corallus caninus*. Photo by I. Francais.

INTRODUCTION

At the moment, the giant snakes, the larger species of pythons and boas, are perhaps the most popular group of snakes among terrarium hobbyists. Commercial breeders are finding several species of boas and pythons easy to produce in good numbers, and captive-bred boas and pythons today are being bred in large quantities, though not yet equaling the numbers of kingsnakes, bullsnakes, ratsnakes, and Corn Snakes bred each year. The signs all point to continuing popularity of at least the small to medium sized species, though the large and giant species are increasingly the target of restrictive legislation because of problems related to safely handling the large pythons and boas.

This volume is half of a pair covering the pythons and boas of the world. They treat a series of families that traditionally have been considered part of the large and unwieldy family Boidae with numerous subfamilies. I have taken the liberty of recognizing smaller units of this so-called family as full families. In the pythons volume I covered the true pythons (**Pythonidae**), the Calabar Pythons (**Calabariidae**), the Neotropical pythons (**Loxocemidae**), the sunbeam snakes (**Xenopeltidae**), and—perhaps unexpectedly—the Round Island split-jaws (**Bolyeriidae**).

The pythons were defined in a broad way as generalized snakes that lay eggs and have a varying combination of primitive and advanced characters including, in many of the species, the presence of the postfrontal bone in the skull, sensory pits within the labial (jaw) scales rather than between the scales, almost universal presence of hind limb remnants (spurs), and minor characters such as narrow ventral scales and generally divided subcaudals.

The boas, as treated here, are the live-bearing groups of the generalized booid snakes. Like the pythons they display a mix of primitive and advanced characters that relate them to both the pythons in the broad sense and the colubrids or advanced snakes. All the species in this volume fit with some ease into just three families that appear to be at least somewhat definable. These families are the **Boidae** proper for the arboreal and ground-dwelling booids of the New World, Madagascar, and the New Guinea—Solomons area; the **Erycinidae** for the burrowing boas of the Northern Hemisphere (barely crossing the Equator in Africa), and the **Tropidophiidae** for the strictly tropical American dwarf boas or wood snakes and their allies. These three families display different levels of distinction from each other and from the pythons, with the Boidae very similar in structure and ecology to the Pythonidae, the Erycinidae being close to the Calabariidae and perhaps the Loxocemidae, and the Bolyeriidae and Tropidophiidae showing a level of advanced characters approaching the colubrids.

As usual, the leading anatomists and systematists disagree with each other as to the exact relationships of the different booid groups. The technical classification of the snakes is in a constant state of flux at all levels, and many familiar names have become so confused as to be worthless. The hobbyist should not allow the confusion to detract from enjoying the terrarium hobby. Remember that there is not necessarily any single correct name for a species of snake and that traditional families and genera may be meaningless. Just as there is no single correct way to pronounce a scientific name, only a zealot would today suggest than there is only one "correct" scientific name for a snake. The concepts of genera, species, and subspecies are being attacked from all sides for many different reasons, and the words no longer mean the same things to all herpetologists. In fact, because of all the confusion hobbyists might be understood better among themselves if they just used common names and descriptive phrases for the familiar species and varieties rather than scientific names.

I will provide a checklist of scientific names and suggested common names for the boa species recognized in this book, and you will find that both lists deviate a bit from traditional lists. For one thing, I've recognized more species than most previous authors, following my version of the evolutionary species concept, which requires that isolated and distinguishable forms be recognized at the species level rather than subspecific level. Additionally, I have recognized few subspecies because I doubt that most traditional subspecies can be defined to truly represent how a species is showing variation over its range.

For each family covered I will discuss the genera in alphabetical order and then the species of each genus. Because there are over 60 species of boas to describe in this book, the descriptions are largely comparative and not as exhaustive as in the python volume. This also is in keeping with the generally low level of distinction of species in the large genera, *Epicrates* and *Tropidophis*, which are mostly island forms that are

Few scientists agree on how many subspecies of Rosy Boas, *Lichanura trivirgata*, should be recognized. Photo by K. Switak.

INTRODUCTION

distinguished by geography and very minor differences in scalation and color. I'll also give a brief summary of what is known of the natural history of the species and also any oddities of their captive care and breeding. Also along the way will be a few comments on the taxonomic history and any changes in the taxonomy of the species and genera. After the taxonomic chapters are short chapters on the general keeping and breeding of boas and a beginning bibliography to introduce you to the literature of the boas.

We have attempted to illustrate all the species and many of the varieties (subspecies and cultural forms) and to make this book as accessible to hobbyists as possible. This should not be considered a technical review of the group, though there are a few changes introduced here for the first time. Just think of it as a somewhat more technical book than the average hobbyist book and be sure to read the next chapters on the taxonomy of the boas and their structure. We've tried to design this book, and its companion on pythons, to be user friendly and answer any questions you might have about boas and their care.

Central American specimens of *Boa constrictor* are placed in the subspecies *imperator*. This is the most common boa in the hobby. Photo by J. Merli.

Boa constrictor, the Red-tailed Boa, is one of the most frequently kept and sold of all snakes. Even many non-hobbyists can recognize it. Photo by I. Francais

BOA FAMILIES AND GENERA

Boas cannot be defined as any distinct entity at the family level. They are instead several parts of a large group of rather primitive snakes often called the booids, and they represent a level of development rather than a group of probably related animals. By trying to shoe-horn all the various types of boas and pythons and their allies into one family we are hiding the fact that there is nothing that shows they are related to each other except for the retention of characters common to all primitive snakes.

Distinguishing a boa from a python, a common preoccupation of many authors on these snakes, is a waste of effort because neither is a real group. Hobbyists, and many herpetologists, for that matter, should try to stop thinking of boas and pythons as entities. Telling a boa from a python is like telling a frog from a toad—it is all a matter of definition. The living snakes can be seen as occupying several levels of structure, each level with a mixture of primitive and specialized characters. The wormsnakes or blindsnakes (Typhlopidae, Leptotyphlopidae, etc.) have many strange characters not found in the other living snakes and occupy the bottom level. Above them comes a level that contains not only the boas and pythons but the shield-tails, pipe snakes, and perhaps a few other groups (such as the wart snakes, Acrochordidae). The colubrid or true snakes and their allies the vipers and cobras occupy the upper level. The booid level contains a variety of species that range from primitive snakes to those that are almost indistinguishable from the colubrid level of development, but most booids are relatively primitive, with many rows of scales around the body, narrow ventral scales, often primitive skull structure that may be modified extensively for adaptation to burrowing, and generally the presence of two lungs (colubrids usually have only one developed lung). They also tend to have a number of variable characters of the skeleton and soft parts that mark them as a relatively primitive level compared to the colubrids, including the presence of a coronoid bone in the lower jaw (absent in colubrids) and a lack of spines in the hemipenial ornamentation. The booids also tend to lack distinct keeling on the scales of the back (very variable in the colubrids) and have multiple head scales, but these are very variable characters. All the booids have vertically elliptical pupils of the eyes, generally considered an adaptation to nocturnal hunting but a character of the entire level in this case. The majority of booids are constrictors of their prey, but this activity varies considerably depending on size of the snake and its prey.

FAMILIES

This book and its companion volume on the pythons attempt to cover several groups of snakes at the booid level of development. Because I feel that recognizing just a single family, Boidae, with several subfamilies for the boas and pythons gives a false feeling of confidence of relationships, I've chosen to recognize many smaller and more uniform families that probably represent actually related species sharing a common ancestor. It is almost impossible to show that any single family is more closely related to any one of the other families or that they evolved from a common ancestor. By recognizing each of these distinctive groups as a full family, the groups are put on a more even footing and there are no illusions about relationships that are not provable.

On this basis I recognize the booid level as containing about ten families:
Pipe snakes:
Uropeltidae
Aniliidae
Boas:
Boidae
Erycinidae
Tropidophiidae
Pythons:
Pythonidae
Calabariidae
Loxocemidae
Xenopeltidae
Bolyeriidae
The wart snakes, Acrochordidae, have variously been considered to belong to the booid level and the colubrid level or to fit at some unique level between the two groups. They are not treated here, and neither are the pipe snake families, which are rare in the terrarium hobby and unlikely to be run across by the average hobbyist.

This volume treats the three families of boas, allied by giving

The Horned Spiny Boa, *Trachyboa boulengeri*, is a member of the family Tropidophiidae. It is a very poorly known species. Photo by R. D. Bartlett.

BOA FAMILIES AND GENERA

live birth, lacking teeth on the premaxillary bones, and lacking the postfrontal bone of the skull. Though these three families (plus the Old World Bolyeriidae, here considered pythons) traditionally have formed the core of the mostly New World Boidae, the boas of most books, I have strong doubts that they are more closely related to each other than each family is related to another group in the pythons. The Calabariidae and Erycinidae are very similar in many respects, either through true relationships (i.e., sharing a common ancestor) or more likely through extreme adaptation to burrowing, and it even has been suggested by Kluge (1993) that *Calabaria* is a synonym of *Charina*, one of the most extreme over-interpretations of data to philosophy in modern herpetological literature. The Tropidophiidae and Bolyeriidae often have been considered to be closely related because they have several features of internal anatomy that approach the development of the colubrid level, but the two groups also differ in many aspects and probably have reached this "advanced" level of structure independently from different ancestors. Recently, in fact, it has been suggested that the four genera in the Tropidophiidae form two unrelated groups that should be recognized at the family level.

GENERA

The genera of the Tropidophiidae are four in number and fairly easy to distinguish. There has been little tampering with generic definitions of late.

Sometimes combined with *Acrantophis* or even *Boa*, most scientists and hobbyists place the Madagascan Tree Boa in its own genus, *Sanzinia*. Photo by M. Burger.

Even the very large genus *Tropidophis* is hard to interpret as distinct species groups, and no one recently has suggested breaking it into subgenera or genera.

In Erycinidae the generic groupings are cloudier. *Eryx* is certainly distinctive in structure and scalation as well as its Old World range, but there is some question as to whether two genera should be recognized, with *Gongylophis* as a full genus for *E. conicus* and perhaps a few related species. In the two species of Erycinidae in the New World, the Rubber and Rosy Boas of western North America, the generic limits always have been questionable, with the genera *Charina* and *Lichanura* recognized on flimsy scalation characters that are greatly exceeded by variation among the species of *Eryx*. For this reason I considered following (in part) Kluge's 1993 paper synonymizing *Lichanura* with *Charina* (though I consider *Calabaria* to belong to a separate family). The differences between the Rosy and Rubber Boa are largely those of degree of variation in head scalation, length of the tail, and color pattern. The two species occupy adjacent but barely overlapping ranges and are adapted to different habitats. It seems to me that the differences are at the specific level rather than the generic level. However, *Lichanura* seems primitive or not as specialized in skeletal characters as is *Charina*, which in many regards is very similar to *Eryx*. Using this rather flimsy basis, I continue to recognize *Lichanura* and *Charina* as distinct though very similar genera.

Within the more diverse family Boidae the genera are harder to define and there has of course been more controversy. There seems little doubt that the genus *Xenoboa* is very closely related to *Corallus*, and I follow Kluge (1991) in considering it a synonym, though there are quite a few distinctions in the anatomy of the two groups. *Candoia* and *Epicrates* are fairly well-defined, as is *Eunectes*. However, the relationships of *Boa*, *Acrantophis*, and *Sanzinia* long have been questioned. Kluge (1991) synonymized the three names as *Boa*, but there are some interesting differences between the two Madagascan groups (*Acrantophis*, *Sanzinia*) and the New World *Boa* in both internal anatomy (hemipenes, musculature) and chromosomes, and *Sanzinia* differs from both other genera by the extreme development of the labial pits. Though acknowledging that the three groups probably share a common ancestor, I feel that they have been distinct long enough, as indicated by the degree of internal differences as well as external ones, to be recognized as full genera, and thus I continue to recognize the three traditional genera familiar to hobbyists, *Boa*, *Acrantophis*, and *Sanzinia*.

Why are there continuing arguments as to the validity of the different boa genera and which species go into which genera? If you are aware of the current controversy between the tradi-

BOA FAMILIES AND GENERA

The burrowing boas of the family Erycinidae have been synonymized into one genus, Eryx, a move not accepted by many herpetologists. Here, Rosy Boas are left in the genus Lichanura. Photo by K. Switak.

tional philosophy of taxonomy and classification and the relatively new methods of cladistics or phylogenetics, you might understand why there are so many different opinions in the scientific literature about families and genera of these snakes. In cladistics the aim is to construct a classification that shows the relationships of the animals contained in it, each category in the classification containing only animals derived from a common ancestor. A worker using the cladistic method records the degree of development of many characters or states, often between 50 and 100, including features from the skeleton, soft anatomy, superficial appearance, and biology of the animals. These states are rated by giving them numbers such as 0, 1, 2 (depending on presence, absence, or degree of development), and then fed into a computer program that compares the characters to each other and produces several to many branching charts or "phylogenetic trees" called cladograms. The researcher evaluates the cladograms and determines which is more likely to be "the" correct one. This cladogram then becomes the basis of further discussions of relationships.

Cladists feel that their analyses are the only correct ones, but I personally cannot accept this position. In the first place, cladists feel that evolution acts in a direct and simple way, so the best cladograms are the ones that take the fewest steps to get from group A to group B. This is the principle of parsimony, the belief that nature always takes the shortest way to solve a problem. Unfortunately, the world around us shows that this is not correct, and nature often seems to take very round-about ways of producing new animals. Additionally, by coding all characters of an animal in a simple fashion, all characters are treated as though they were of equal significance. I just do not believe that this is a correct interpretation of nature; some characters are more important in determining relationship than are others. In the boas, especially the erycinids, for instance, the scales or shields of the head are notoriously variable and cannot be used to define groups above the specific level unless accompanied by other characters, yet in several cladistic classifications head scales are given equal value to features of the skull and skeleton in determining relationships. Finally, a computer program may produce literally dozens to hundreds of differing cladograms from the same information, and it is the researcher, with all his or her acknowledged or subconscious biases, who in the end tells us what is the "correct" cladogram. To the computer all the dozens of cladograms are equally correct interpretations of the data, and it finally is the beliefs of the researcher in interpreting the cladograms that determine what genera are recognized.

The more traditional methods of taxonomy were more practical, using analyses of structure and distribution to produce groups of

The Argentine Boa, *B. c. occidentalis*, is the most distinct of the subspecies of *B. constrictor* and may in fact be a separate species. Photo by S. Kochetov.

BOA FAMILIES AND GENERA

similar-appearing animals. If there was a gap in the characters setting one group apart from another, the groups were termed genera and assumed to be composed of related species. Differences and gaps formed the basis of the classification. When species were discovered that bridged the gap between established genera, the genera were reassessed and usually one was made a synonym of the other (though occasionally a new genus was erected for the intermediate species). The traditional system was "relationship neutral" in that you could use the classifications without worrying about how the animals had evolved and without having to answer the questions about which groups were related to or derived from which other groups. This made it a practical system that made identifications easier.

I tend to follow the traditional philosophy because I believe that classifications at the generic level must be practical; they must make it possible to more easily identify animals. The entire Linnean system was developed to make identification easy and practical, and I feel that still should be its purpose. Complicated philosophies of relationships and evolution are not necessary when constructing a taxonomy of a group, and they probably are wrong as well because there never is sufficient information to really know for sure how an animal evolved. The fossil record of snakes, for instance, consists mostly of vertebrae that, regardless of what the experts

Considerably different from the other members of the genus, the Rainbow Boa, *Epicrates cenchria*, **arguably could be split off into its own genus. Photo by A. Both**

opine, almost certainly cannot be used to trace relationships, just modifications of a single rather simple structure. Genera are artificial groups, at least in my philosophy, and they do not evolve; only species evolve.

SPECIES

What is a species? Frankly, I don't know and neither does anyone else. Definitions have been given for over 300 years and still don't answer the basic question. Older definitions that once were standard, including those that required lack of interbreeding between related species, largely have gone by the board. In fact, some biologists believe that hybridization or intergradation either in nature or in the laboratory is meaningless in determining relationships, and they probably are right. (In this philosophy the ability to interbreed is of course a primitive character, and one cannot base classifications on primitive characters.)

In this book I've tried to follow or at least give lip service to my interpretation of a rather new but very simple concept of species that also is quite practical. (See Wiley, 1978, for the first full discussion of the evolutionary species concept.) Basically, a species is defined as **a population of similar animals that are isolated (geographically, behaviorally, or biochemically) from other populations, are differentiated at some level, and have their own evolutionary history.** Differences between species may not always be visible to the human eye—after all, we cannot hear, see, and smell what a snake thinks to be of importance in defining its own kind. We know that there are distinct species of treefrogs that can be distinguished only by calls, species of insects that are separated by differences in timing of the life cycle, and many different animals that differ in minor details of breeding biology, including hormones and scent secretions. With new biochemical techniques it is possible to determine the genetic similarities—and differences—of two groups of animals to a very fine point. In the near future it should be economically realistic to conduct biochemical tests on numerous individuals from throughout the range of each possibly distinct population of boa (especially in the genera *Boa*, *Epicrates* and *Tropidophis*) and actually see how closely related each is to the other. Until then, we just have to look at the structure and distribution and take an educated guess.

In practical terms, a species of boa is any isolated group of animals that no longer seems to be sharing genes with its close relatives and thus has begun on its own evolutionary path, **and** has progressed far enough down this path to show distinctions of some type. Simple isolation on an island or on the opposite side of a busy highway, for instance, is not sufficient to indicate that the animals are a species. There is no reason to automatically assume that island populations are actually isolated (snakes can swim

BOA FAMILIES AND GENERA

Many localized variations of the Round-nosed Island Boa, *Candoia bibroni*, exist. It is possible more than one species is actually involved. Photo by I. Francais

and also can be carried great distances in logs and masses of floating vegetation). They must show signs that they have not shared genes with other animals long enough ago that they have begun their own history. This may be strongly indicated by differences in color pattern or scale counts as compared to the close relatives.

On the other hand, if two distinctive-appearing groups of boas are not isolated and appear (from the nature of their variation) to be sharing genes, they are not species no matter how distinctive they may seem to human eyes. Remember that humans are visually oriented—we *see* differences; most animals, including boas, probably *smell* differences. If we try to apply human-made distinctions to non-visually oriented animals we probably will be wrong.

A final word on hybridization. The fact that two well-differentiated species exchange genes over a narrow band or fragment where their ranges overlap is not an indication of less than specific status. Such limited hybridization may be a natural way of actually increasing the distinction between species, the hybrids serving as a barrier to prevent spreading of genes further into the parent populations. Many very different animals hybridize regularly in nature (for instance, the very different Mallard and Pintail ducks) and certainly are full species, often in different species groups. Natural hybridization must be carefully considered before its importance can be evaluated. Man-made hybrids, as in forced matings in the laboratory or breeder's terrarium, are meaningless and supply no information of significance in determining relationships of species. Hybrids between different genera, however, may be strong indications that the genera are not at all

Many subspecies of the Hispaniolan Slender Boa, *Epicrates fordi*, are recognized. They are hard to distinguish and possibly represent a cline in characters rather than true subspeciation. Photo by R. D. Bartlett.

valid, because by definition the species in different genera should be so distinctive that they cannot exchange genes at all. Remember, species are real, genera and families are artificial human constructs or pigeon-holes.

SUBSPECIES

As a general rule, I will not recognize subspecies for most boas unless they are deeply entrenched in the literature. I also don't like to use distinctive common names for the subspecies that are recognized. Subspecies are doubtful groups of doubtfully distinct animals. If they were distinct and isolated they would be species. By definition a subspecies is sharing genes with a close relative. Any species with a broad range may contain dozens, perhaps hundreds, of slightly distinct local populations that, at least for a few decades or centuries, can be distinguished from their close relatives. However, since these populations still are sharing genes, they are constantly changing genetically and cannot be defined. The subspecies is a transient concept at best and a misleading one at worst. Hobbyists and breeders often grab on to a subspecific name without understanding what it is and refuse to give it up. They force many different types of variations into a few subspecific names and then feel happy that they are breeding pure subspecies lines. This mis-

BOA FAMILIES AND GENERA

Probably extinct, Hoge's Boa, *Corallus cropani*, was once referred to its own genus. Now, it is considered a member of the genus *Corallus*. Photo by M. Walls, courtesy of the American Museum of Natural History.

conception may actually prevent hobbyists (and scientists) from really appreciating the full variation of a species. Applying common names to these poorly conceptualized subspecies makes them even more real to hobbyists and perpetuates the error and problems. The several subspecies recognized in the Rosy Boa, *Lichanura trivirgata*, for instance, seem to hide literally dozens of minor populations that are distinct and at least somewhat isolated at the moment but certainly not worth naming with formal Latin nomenclature.

It would make much more sense if instead of subspecies, which are entrenched in a formal system of Latin nomenclature, each deviation from the "norm" of a species (the norm would be the appearance of the species at its type locality) were given a short but descriptive name that referred to either the locality or the variation (i.e., "Striped," "Mexican," "Guyana," "Cottonwood Mountains," etc.). Such names could be given informally and cataloged by interested hobbyists and herpetologists just like scientific names. They would have the advantage of not being fixed (the variations themselves are not fixed) and not being controlled by archaic rules and systems developed before we even knew that animals evolved.

Please, do not use subspecies unless there is a good case for recognizing them. Most boas are much more variable than indicated by the presence of a few described subspecies. Subspecies are, in most instances, not real. Defined as distinct but geographically isolated portions of a species that still are at least theoretically capable of interbreeding with other members of the species, they usually are relicts of an antiquated way of interpreting variation. One artificial subspecies may contain dozens of quite distinct, still interbreeding variations each as deserving of a name as the formally recognized subspecies.

Only the species is real, and even it in many cases has been badly misunderstood in attempts to force it into narrow human-made boxes. I feel that practicality must come before obtuse philosophical arguments or else taxonomy is a trite and useless endeavor of interest only to a handful of specialists. Hobbyists need names that they can apply without worrying too much about the philosophy that went into producing the name. You don't have to agree with me, and I suspect that many will not, but that is the basis of this book.

The author believes that the subspecies of the Kenyan Sand Boa, *Eryx colubrinus*, are indistinct. Many intermediates exist, and there seems to be a gradation rather than subspeciation. Photo by K. Switak.

Boa Structure and a Checklist

FINDING YOUR WAY AROUND A BOA

Because this book is focused heavily on identification, much of it consists of descriptions of boa structure, especially the scale patterns on the body, the scalation. I have used many terms that, though standard in herpetological literature, may not be familiar to the average hobbyist. To go into detail on the structure of any snake would require a full book, one that admittedly has never been written and is sorely needed. The following quick summary will, I hope, give you sufficient information to be able to follow the descriptions and understand what are the important features in identifying a boa.

In case you don't know the basic scientific directions, **anterior** refers to going toward the front, **posterior** means going toward the back, and **lateral** going toward the side. **Dorsal** refers to the back or top of a structure or body, while **ventral** refers to the bottom or undersurface (belly) of a body or structure. The different directions can be combined, as in dorsolateral or posterioventral. Distal refers to a direction away from the origin or base of a structure, while

Many species of boas have heat-sensitive pits between the scales of the lips. The arboreal boas, like this Madagascan Tree Boa, *Sanzinia madagascariensis*, tend to have many pits that are grossly enlarged. Photo by R. D. Bartlett.

proximal refers to going toward the base.

The Skull

The bony supporting structure of the head of a snake is of course the skull. Technically, what usually is called the skull is the cranial skeleton, consisting of the lower jaws or mandibles and the upper jaws and braincase, the skull proper. If you look at the skull of a typical boa from above, the rather T-shaped bone that is at the front of the skull is the **premaxillary**, formed by the fusion of a left and a right element. Behind the premax the paired and rather elongated bones forming the central part of the skull are the **nasals**. They are flanked by large **prefrontals** on either side. The nasals and prefrontals may be fused. The prefrontals join the anterior edges of the **frontal** bones, which may be paired and occupy the center of the skull. To either side of the frontals are the indentations for the eyes, the orbits. The tops of the orbits usually are covered by a hooked bone called the **postorbital**. Unlike the typical pythons, the small **postfrontal** bone is absent in all the families here treated as boas. The bones of the top of the skull behind the level of the eyes are the **parietals**. The long bone that allows the jaws to expand, the **supratemporal**, is attached by ligaments to the parietal on each side. The other bones of the back and interior of the skull don't feature in the descriptions used in this book and are not mentioned here.

When you look at a skull from below, you notice that there are several rows of teeth, usually two on each side. Unlike the typical pythons, the premaxillary lacks teeth in all the boa families. Around the outside of the skull is the row of **maxillary teeth**, which usually contains over a dozen teeth, the anterior ones typically long and curved backward. The other rows of teeth are on two

Lateral view of the skull of *Epicrates cenchria* showing the major bones. Based on Frazzeta, 1959. *Bull. Mus. comp. Zool.,* 119(8).

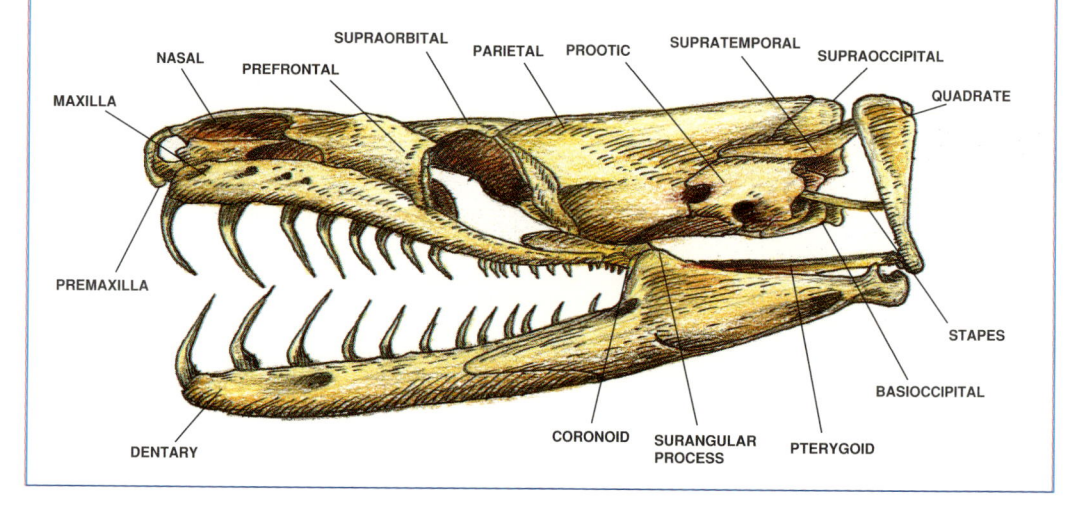

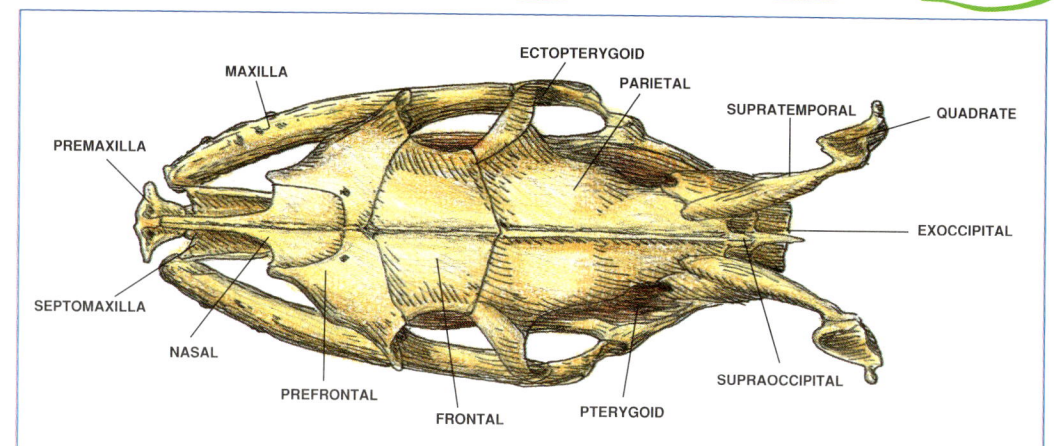

BOA STRUCTURE AND CHECKLIST

Dorsal view of the skull of *Epicrates cenchria* showing the major bones. Based on Frazzeta, 1959. *Bull. Mus. comp. Zool.,* 119(8).

separate bones that are joined and run in rows closer to the center of the skull. These teeth are on the roof of the mouth, and without cleaning off some tissue, appear to be one continuous row on each side. Actually, the longer anterior teeth are on the **palatine** bone, while the shorter ones to the back are on the **pterygoid**.

The lower jaw is the **mandible**, a composite comprising three major bones visible from the outside. The mandibular teeth are borne on the **dentary**. The back part of the mandible is the **surangular**, while the **coronoid** bone is a small bone on the "hump" near the center of the jaws. The surangular attaches to the supratemporal bone by the **quadrate** bone, allowing great expansion of the jaws to swallow prey.

Head Scales

Boas, like the pythons, are more variable in scalation characters than are most "advanced" snakes, but the scales of the head and body still are of extreme importance in identification. The

Ventral view of the skull of *Epicrates cenchria* indicating the major bones. Based on Frazzeta, 1959. *Bull. Mus. comp. Zool.,* 119(8).

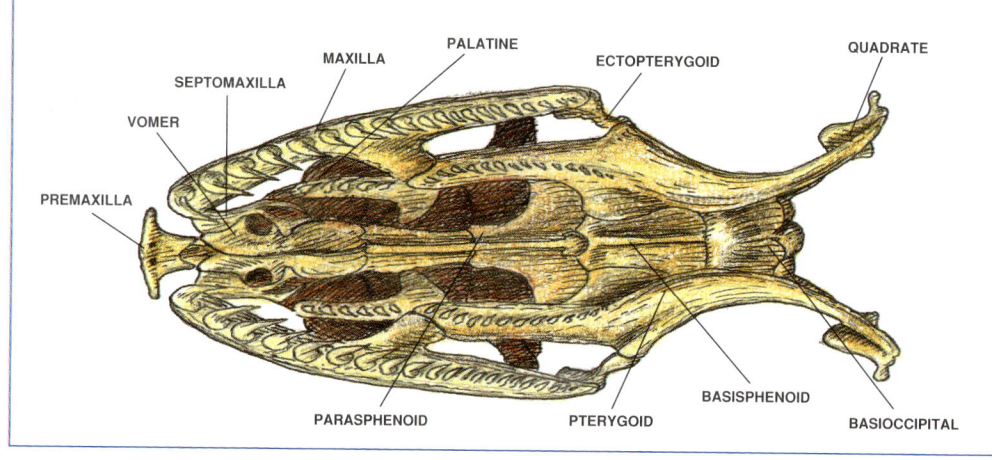

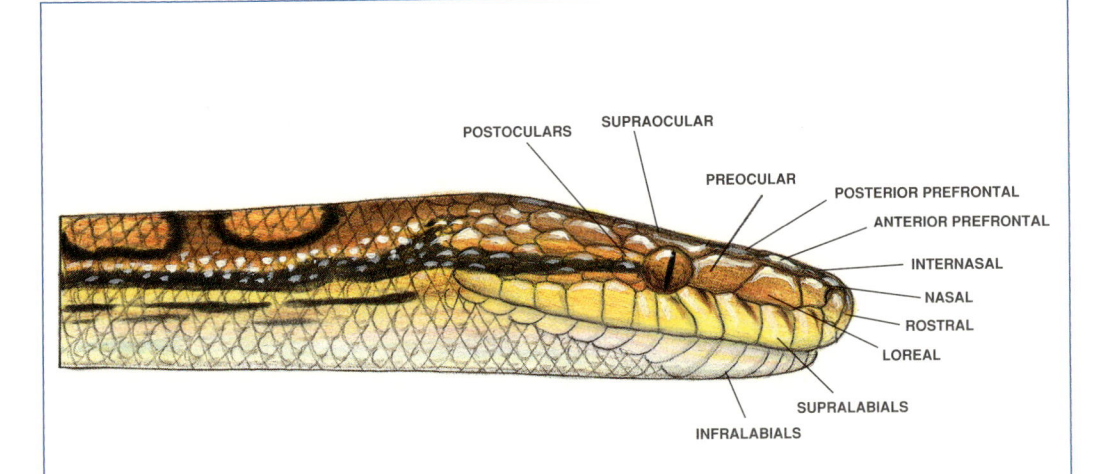

Lateral view of boa head scalation. Notice that this animal has no subocular scales.

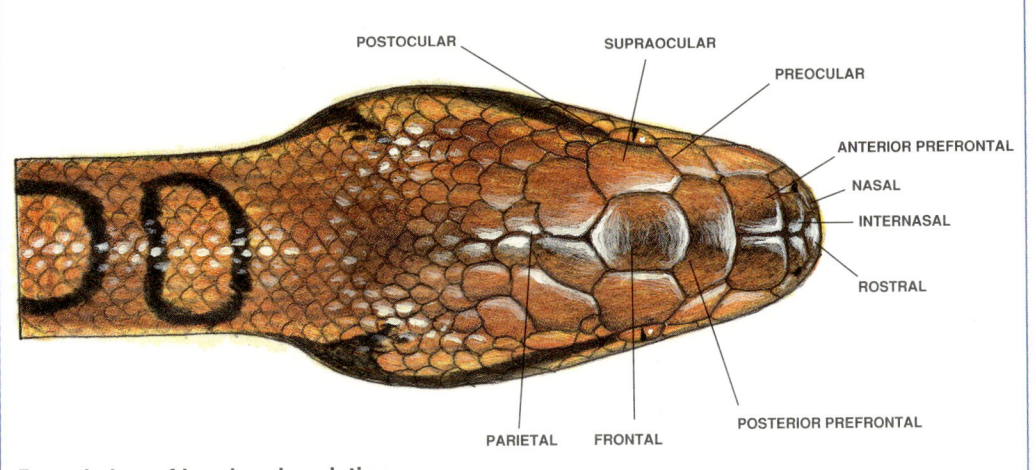

Dorsal view of boa head scalation.

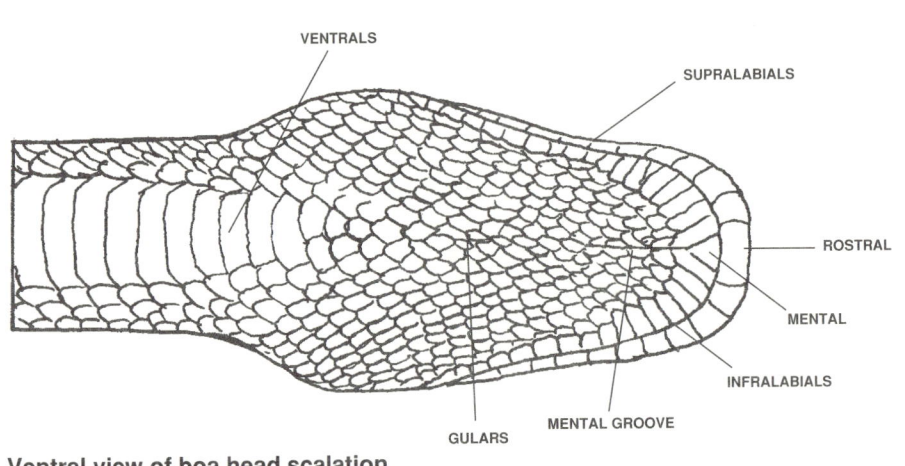

Ventral view of boa head scalation.

BOA STRUCTURE AND CHECKLIST

Head scalation of a Yellow Anaconda, *Eunectes notaeus*. *above*: Dorsal view. The nostrils of this mostly aquatic species are placed more dorsally than those of most boas. *below*: Ventral view. The mental groove is well developed. The chin of this specimen is very brightly colored which is not true of all Yellow Anacondas. Both photos by M. Walls, courtesy of Steve and Rini Mitchell.

enlarged scales on the head often are called shields to distinguish them from the body scales.

The top of the snout is covered by the **rostral** shield. The nostrils are located in the **nasal** shields, which may be a single scale or divided by short seams into two or more distinct scales. Between the nasals at the end of the snout are the squarish to trapezoidal and rather small **internasals**. Behind the internasals are the usually paired **prefrontals**, which vary greatly in development, but usually only the anterior pair is large. Between the eyes across the top of the head commonly are three shields. In the center is the **frontal**, which varies from triangular to round or many-sided and may be split into two or several distinct shields. On each side of the frontal over the eyes are the **supraoculars**. In the probably primitive boas the supraoculars may consist of a single large scale over each eye, but more typically there are several smaller shields. The front edge of the frontal contacts the prefrontals, while the back edge commonly contacts a pair of enlarged scales called the **parietals**. There may be several pairs of parietals or just small scales like the others on the nape of the neck.

From the side, the nasal shields are prominent. In front of the eyes are one to several large scales called the **preoculars**. Between the nasal shield and the preoculars are one to many large or small shields called the **loreals**. The loreals are bordered above by the prefrontals and below by the lip or labial scales. Behind the eye is a ring of one to several shields called the **postoculars**. The scales behind these are the **temporals**, which are not used in descriptions in this book.

The scales forming the edge of the upper jaw are the **supralabials**; those forming the edge of the lower jaw are the **infralabials**. It often is important to notice how many supralabials touch the lower edge of the eye. Such supralabials often are said to form the lower margin of the **orbit** or to enter the eye. From below, the infralabials on each side meet at the front of the jaw on each side of a single scale called the **mental**. In most boas there is a deep groove running down the center of the throat, the mental groove, that allows the jaws to stretch to swallow large prey. Often the groove is bordered on each side by one or two enlarged scales called the **gulars**. In most boas the gulars are small and not strongly distinguished from the other scales under the jaw; usually only one pair of gulars is strongly enlarged. In some boas the groove is absent or indistinct.

Body Scales

In boas the scales usually are small and in a great number of rows around the body that may be difficult to count. Typically they are counted in either a zigzag row (left-right-left-right, etc.) around the body or in a continuous oblique row forward to the central scale over the center of the back and then backward down the other side. The first scale row is the one bordering the widened ventral scales.

Commonly **dorsal scale rows** are expressed as just a single number to indicate the number of scales around the body at the midbody of the trunk (from the back of the head to the vent or cloaca). A slightly more complicated formula often is given that expresses the number of scale rows on the neck, at midbody, and before the vent. This gives an idea of how scale rows are added and dropped over the length of the snake to allow for the tapering of the body. The basic formula of perhaps 32-55-25 refers to counts made one head length behind the head on the neck (32), at midbody (55), and one head length in front of the level of the vent (as indicated by the anal scale) (25).

The scales on the underside of the body are very important in boa systematics. Basically, you are given a count of ventral scales and of subcaudal scales. The **ventrals** are widened, strap-like scales running down the center of the belly. Traditionally the first or anteriormost ventral was defined as the first one that was distinctly wider than long; today the first ventral often is counted as the first strap-like scale that is in contact with the lower rows of body scales, not separated from them by small scales. The scale that covers the opening of the **vent** or **cloaca** is the **anal scale**; it is not included in the ventral counts, but it may be important to notice if there is an oblique seam at its center dividing it into two pieces or if the seam is absent and the scale is entire. There may be a row of small scales in front of the anal scale that are not included in any scale counts. The **subcaudals** are the scales under the tail, those behind the cloaca. In most true boas the subcaudals

As a rule, boas have smaller ventral scales than the more advanced groups of snakes. Here, this is illustrated by a ventral view of a Brown Sand Boa, *Eryx johni*. Photo by M. Walls.

Hemipene of the Madagascan Boa, *Acrantophis madagascariensis*. Based on Branch, 1981. *J. Herpetology,* 15(1).

Hemipene of the Garden Tree Boa, *Corallus hortulanus*. Based on Branch, 1981. *J. Herpetology,* 15(1).

Hemipene of *Epicrates*, **the slender boas.** Based on Dowling, 1975. *Yearbook of Herpetology,* 1974.

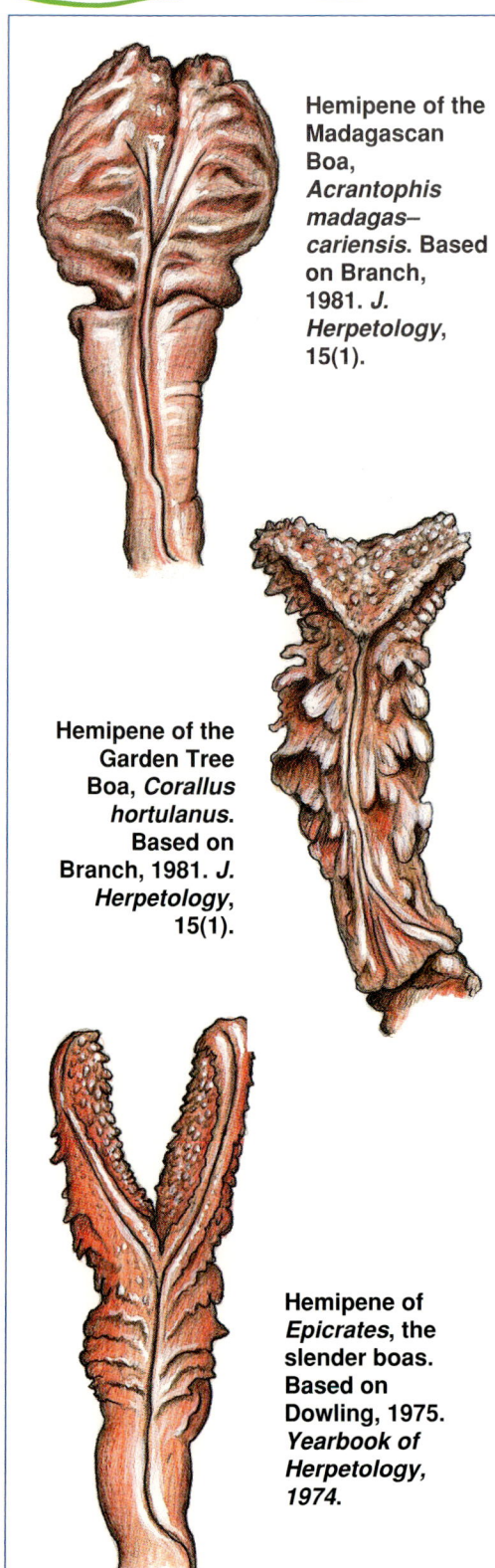

lack a seam dividing them into pairs and are entire. (Most true pythons, in contrast, have the subcaudals mostly divided.) It is not uncommon to have a few divided subcaudals in a series of otherwise entire subcaudals. The subcaudals are counted along one side of the tail and thus are presented as if they all were entire. The conical or oddly shaped scales or scale at the tip of the tail is not included in the subcaudal count.

Hemipenes

The copulatory or intromittent organ of a snake always is deeply forked and forms two symmetrical halves that can be erected independently during mating. Each half is a hemipenis, the entire organ the hemipenes. Erected hemipenes in boas lack spines and are relatively unornamented compared to those of many colubrid snakes. Each hemipenis can, in a very simplified way, be said to consist of a stalk that usually is forked at or beyond the center of the organ. The surface of the hemipenis bears a groove that during mating transmits sperm. This is the **sulcus spermaticus**. In most boas the sulcus is bifurcated, forming a Y with one arm passing over each fork of the hemipenis. The back (and sometimes front, the surface with the sulcus crossing it) of the hemipenis has chevron-like fleshy ridges called **flounces**.

The muscles that allow the hemipenes to be erected and withdrawn are rather complicated and are not discussed here. Suf-

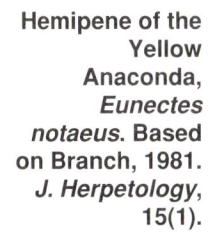

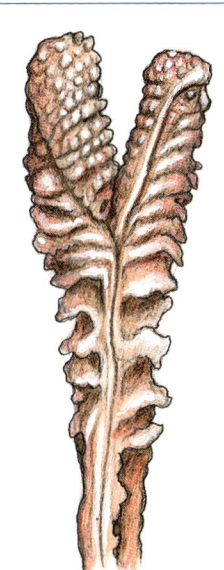

BOA STRUCTURE AND CHECKLIST

Hemipene of the Yellow Anaconda, *Eunectes notaeus*. Based on Branch, 1981. *J. Herpetology*, 15(1).

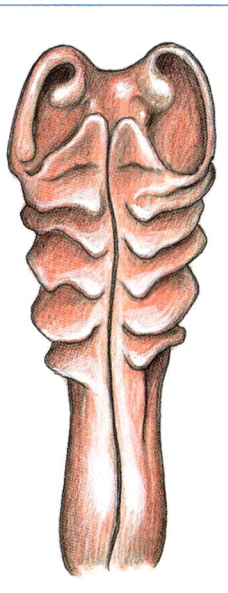

Hemipene of the Rubber Boa, *Charina bottae*. Based on Kluge, 1993. *Zool. J. Linnean. Soc.*, 107.

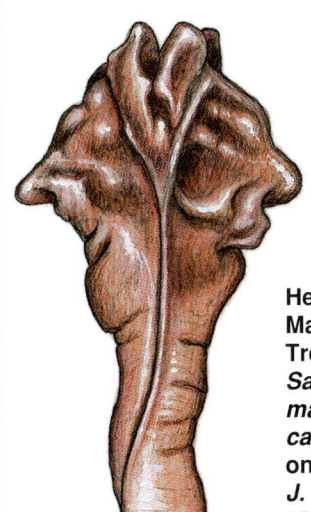

Hemipene of the Madagascan Tree Boa, *Sanzinia madagas-cariensis*. Based on Branch, 1981. *J. Herpetology*, 15(1).

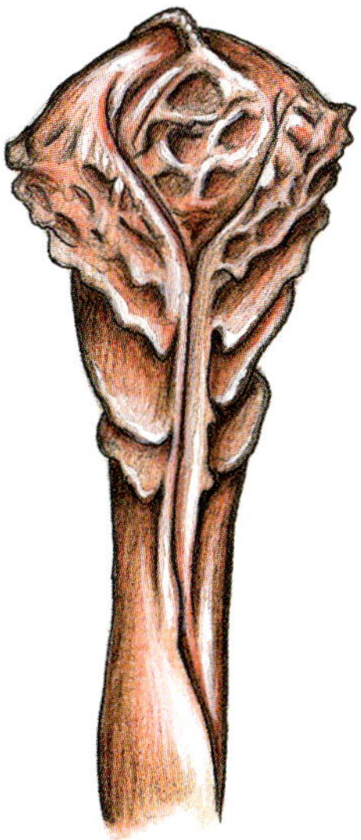

Hemipene of the Brown Sand Boa, *Eryx johni*. Based on Kluge, 1993. *Zool. J. Linnean. Soc.*, 107.

Hemipene of the Rosy Boa, *Lichanura trivirgata*. Based on Kluge, 1993. *Zool. J. Linnean. Soc.*, 107.

fice it to say that when withdrawn the hemipenes are like a pair of glove fingers. When you probe a snake using special equipment, you gently push the rod into an opening at the posterior edge of the cloaca and measure how far the rod enters in terms of number of subcaudal scales.

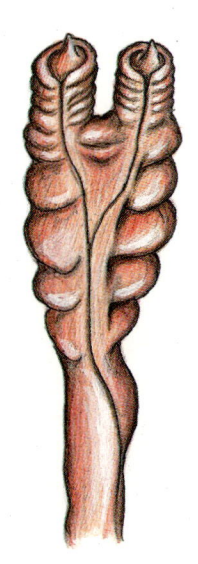

Hemipene of the Oaxacan Cloud Boa, *Exiliboa placata*. Based on Dowling, 1975. *Yearbook of Herpetology*, 1974.

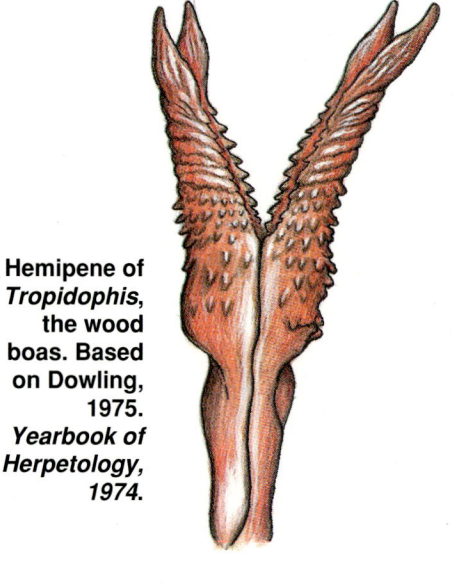

Hemipene of *Tropidophis*, the wood boas. Based on Dowling, 1975. *Yearbook of Herpetology*, 1974.

A CHECKLIST OF THE BOAS

As you know by now, the term boa is one of convenience and not really a scientific term. It represents part of a level of organization shared with the pythons and some other groups of snakes. For our purposes, I am recognizing three families of boas. They all give live birth and lack teeth on the premaxillary and have various combinations of primitive and specialized characters of the skeleton and soft anatomy. I've considered these groups to be full families because there is no overwhelming evidence that any of these groups are closely related to each other or to the various families of pythons other than by sharing a common ancestor (or several ancestors) at a very early level of their evolution.

I have taken a middle road on the genera recognized, with few deviations from tradition. A genus is an artificial grouping of species (only species exist in nature—all other categories are artificial assemblages put together by the minds of men) that must serve a practical purpose for identification. If a genus cannot be defined on the basis of external, visible characters, it probably serves no practical function and should not be recognized. This working definition applies well to all the genera recognized here, except that *Acrantophis*, which is quite distinct on the basis of internal characters, is for all practical purposes not distinguishable from *Boa*.

The number of species recognized here is a bit higher than usual because I define a species as a population of animals that is isolated from its closest relatives and has acquired a separate evolutionary history. This separate history may be indicated by either visible (morphological or behavioral) distinctions or invisible biochemical (genetic) deviations from related species. Isolation is assumed to be real unless there are indications in the litera-

BOA STRUCTURE AND CHECKLIST

Although hobbyists may consider the coloration of Dumeril's Boa, *Acrantophis dumerili*, and other boas to be flashy, in their natural habitat the pattern may provide some concealment. Photo by J. Merli.

ture that there has been an incomplete collecting effort in the apparent gap between species. Subspecies seldom are recognizable, and I have not listed them here even when I treat them in the text. As a rule, hobbyists should not place too much confidence in subspecies as identifiable forms.

FAMILY BOIDAE Gray, 1825
   ACRANTOPHIS Jan, 1860
   Acrantophis dumerili Jan, 1860
   Dumeril's Boa
   Acrantophis madagascariensis (Dumeril & Bibron, 1844)
   Madagascan Boa
   BOA Linnaeus, 1758
   Boa constrictor Linnaeus, 1758
   Red-tailed Boa
   Boa nebulosa (Lazell, 1964)
   Dominican Boa
   Boa orophias Linnaeus, 1768
   St. Lucian Boa
   CANDOIA Gray, 1842
   Candoia aspera (Guenther, 1877)
   Viper Boa
   Candoia bibroni (Dumeril & Bibron, 1839)
   Round-nosed Island Boa
   Candoia carinata (Schneider, 1801)
   Square-nosed Island Boa
   CORALLUS Daudin, 1803
   Corallus annulatus (Cope, 1876)
   Ringed Tree Boa
   Corallus caninus (Linnaeus, 1758)
   Emerald Tree Boa
   Corallus cropani (Hoge, 1953)
   Hoge's Boa
   Corallus hortulanus (Linnaeus, 1758)
   Garden Tree Boa
   EPICRATES Wagler, 1830
   Epicrates angulifer Bibron *in* Sagra, 1843
   Cuban Slender Boa
   Epicrates cenchria (Linnaeus, 1758)
   Rainbow Slender Boa
   Epicrates chrysogaster (Cope, 1871)
   Tan Slender Boa
   Epicrates exsul Netting & Goin, 1944
   Abaco Slender Boa
   Epicrates fordi (Guenther, 1861)
   Hispaniolan Slender Boa
   Epicrates gracilis (Fischer, 1888)
   Cryptic Slender Boa
   Epicrates granti Stull, 1933
   Tortola Slender Boa
   Epicrates inornatus (Reinhardt, 1843)
   Puerto Rican Slender Boa
   Epicrates monensis Zenneck, 1898
   Mona Slender Boa
   Epicrates striatus (Fischer, 1862)
   Fischer's Slender Boa
   Epicrates subflavus Stejneger, 1901
   Jamaican Slender Boa
   EUNECTES Wagler, 1830
   Eunectes deschaunenseei Dunn & Conant, 1936
   Conant's Anaconda
   Eunectes murinus (Linnaeus, 1758)
   Green Anaconda
   Eunectes notaeus Cope, 1862
   Yellow Anaconda

SANZINIA Gray, 1849
Sanzinia madagascariensis (Dumeril & Bibron, 1844)
Madagascan Tree Boa

FAMILY ERYCINIDAE Bonaparte, 1831

CHARINA Gray, 1849
Charina bottae (Blainville, 1835)
Rubber Boa

ERYX Daudin, 1803
Eryx colubrinus (Linnaeus, 1758)
Kenyan Sand Boa
Eryx conicus (Schneider, 1801)
Rough-scaled Sand Boa
Eryx elegans (Gray, 1849)
Elegant Sand Boa
Eryx jaculus (Linnaeus, 1758)
Javelin Sand Boa
Eryx jayakari Boulenger, 1888
Arabian Sand Boa
Eryx johni (Russell, 1801)
Brown Sand Boa
Eryx miliaris (Pallas, 1773)
Central Asian Sand Boa
Eryx muelleri (Boulenger, 1892)
West African Sand Boa
Eryx somalicus Scortecci, 1939
Somali Sand Boa
Eryx tataricus (Lichtenstein, 1823)
Tartar Sand Boa

LICHANURA Cope, 1861
Lichanura trivirgata Cope, 1861
Rosy Boa

FAMILY TROPIDOPHIIDAE Brongersma, 1951

EXILIBOA Bogert, 1968
Exiliboa placata Bogert, 1968
Oaxacan Cloud Boa

TRACHYBOA Peters, 1860
Trachyboa boulengeri Peracca, 1910
Horned Spiny Boa
Trachyboa gularis Peters, 1860
Keeled Spiny Boa

TROPIDOPHIS Bibron, 1840
Tropidophis battersbyi Laurent, 1949
Battersby's Dwarf Boa
Tropidophis canus (Cope, 1868)
Bahaman Dwarf Boa
Tropidophis caymanensis Battersby, 1938
Caymans Dwarf Boa
Tropidophis feicki Schwartz, 1957
Saddled Dwarf Boa
Tropidophis fuscus Hedges & Garrido, 1992
Brown Dwarf Boa
Tropidophis greenwayi Barbour & Shreve, 1936
Caicos Dwarf Boa
Tropidophis haetianus (Cope, 1879)
Haitian Dwarf Boa
Tropidophis jamaicensis Stull, 1938
Jamaican Dwarf Boa
Tropidophis maculatus (Bibron, 1843)

Green Anacondas, *Eunectes murinus*, are the longest and heaviest snakes in the New World. Photo by K. Switak.

Freckled Dwarf Boa
Tropidophis melanurus
(Schlegel, 1837)
Cuban Dwarf Boa
Tropidophis nigriventris
Bailey, 1937
Black-bellied Dwarf Boa
Tropidophis pardalis
(Gundlach, 1840)
Six-spot Dwarf Boa
Tropidophis paucisquamis
(Mueller *in* Schenkel, 1901)
Brazilian Dwarf Boa
Tropidophis pilsbryi Bailey, 1937
Pale-spot Dwarf-Boa
Tropidophis semicinctus
(Gundlach & Peters, 1864)
Two-spot Dwarf Boa
Tropidophis stejnegeri Grant, 1940
Grant's Dwarf Boa
Tropidophis taczanowskyi
(Steindachner, 1880)
Eastern Dwarf Boa
Tropidophis wrighti Stull, 1928
Wright's Dwarf Boa
UNGALIOPHIS Mueller, 1882
Ungaliophis continentalis
Mueller, 1882
Round-spot Banana Boa
Ungaliophis panamensis
Schmidt, 1933
Triangle Banana Boa

Most hobbyists will never see a Ringed Tree Boa, *Corallus annulatus*, in the flesh. Although not uncommon in the wild, they are seldom imported and have proven delicate in captivity. Photo by R. D. Bartlett.

THE TRUE BOAS: BOIDAE

The family Boidae is in many ways the American equivalent of the Pythonidae. All the species are large live-bearing constrictors, only a few Caribbean *Epicrates* not reaching a meter in length. They uniformly lack teeth on the premaxillary and lack the postfrontal bone that is typical of the Pythonidae. Almost all (except some *Candoia*) have spurs in both sexes, though usually they are smaller and hidden under scales in immatures and females. They are not especially adapted to burrowing, lacking the strong consolidation of the skull bones of the Erycinidae and their large and often sharp-edged rostral shield. The eyes, as typical of all the boas and pythons, have vertically elliptical pupils. The subcaudals are, with some exceptions, single, as is the anal; some species have a few divided subcaudals.

Unlike the Tropidophiidae, they have a strongly developed left lung that is about 50 to 60% of the length of the right lung (only about 33% in *Boa*) and there is no tracheal lung. It is likely that all the species can sense heat through the labial scales, but only a few genera have distinct labial pits. In the pythons the pits, when present, are developed *within* the body of the scale; in the true boas with labial pits they are developed *between* the scales and thus overlap onto two scales. The kidneys always are lobed (compact, without lobes in some Tropidophiidae). The number of teeth throughout the family is quite constant, perhaps an indication of the close relationships of the species in the family as restricted here. There are, in general, 16 to 20 maxillary teeth, 5 or 6 palatine teeth, 9 to 18 pterygoid teeth, and 16 to 22 dentary teeth. In almost all forms the anterior teeth are long and curved, gradually becoming shorter posteriorly; the anterior teeth are especially long in the arboreal species. The coronoid bone is large.

Once the burrowing boas and dwarf-boas are removed, the Boidae is a very uniform group with some 27 species recognized here in seven genera. Like other snake families where the species all are very similar, it is difficult to distinguish genera. The family was broken into two tribes by McDowell (1979) based on the presence or absence of an expansion of the intestine before (at the level of the kidneys) its entry into the cloaca, the rectal caecum, but this character of course is of no use to hobbyists and also appears to be difficult to distinguish in preserved specimens. Kluge (1993) has questioned the validity of the tribes, proposing a tighter classification that I feel probably is more realistic. In the McDowell classification the tribe Boini (which would be elevated to subfamily rank with the restriction of the Boidae as treated here) contains *Boa, Acrantophis, Sanzinia,* and *Xenoboa*; the Corallini contains *Corallus, Candoia, Eunectes,* and *Epicrates*. McDowell considered these tribes to be distinct at the same level as his tribe Erycini, which here is considered a full family, but I feel that the erycinids and boids are narrowly defined groups of closely related species and worth recognizing at the familial level. Additionally, I don't see any reason to separate the genera of Boidae (restricted sense) into smaller groups because once again they present a basically primitive structural level on which are superimposed a number of specializations; in fact, I think one could make a good argument for recognizing only five genera in the Boidae, which was the conclusion reached by Kluge in 1993.

One of the major problems in recognizing genera in the Boidae is the fact that six species of the 27 are isolated in two groups in the Old World, three in Madagascar and three in the New Guinea—Solomons area. In each area the species consist of two modified for one habitat and a third strongly specialized for a different habitat. In Madagascar the two species of *Acrantophis* are basically terrestrial, while the single *Sanzinia* is arboreal; in the New Guinea area *Candoia aspera* is strongly modified for a terrestrial existence, while the other two species are largely arboreal. It has been said that the three species of *Candoia* are more distinct from each other than are the other genera of boas, but this is an exaggeration, at least in my opinion, as the differences between *Sanzinia* and *Acrantophis* are much greater than those among the three *Candoia*. The Madagascan species are closely related to a form similar to *Boa* (which may be the most primitive genus of the family, so the statement may just mean that the Madagascan forms retain characters primitive for the family), while on very weak evidence *Candoia* is though to be related to a *Corallus*-like ancestor that

Viper Boas, *Candoia aspera*, **occur in Indonesia; presumably their ancestors originated in South America. Photo by R. D. Bartlett.**

THE TRUE BOAS: BOIDAE

may have rafted over from South America. All hypotheses of relationships of the Madagascan and New Guinea—Solomons forms are simple guesses with little science to back them up and at the moment are not worth further discussion.

Kluge (1993) synonymized *Xenoboa* with *Corallus*, a move with which I am in full agreement. He also synonymized *Acrantophis* and *Sanzinia* with *Boa*, a step with which I strongly disagree.

development of some minor scalation characters and body form for a similar type of existence. That *Sanzinia* and *Acrantophis* are closely related on the basis on non-superficial characters seems obvious, yet they have been evolving toward different specializations for so long that they have attained very different body forms.

The following key to the genera of Boidae is based on external characters and is not intended to

The tremendous range of Red-tailed Boas, *B. constrictor*, and occurrence in many habitats has led to many local variations in color and pattern. This specimen is from Amazonian Peru. Photo by R. D. Bartlett.

Sanzinia is one of the most distinct genera of the family, differing not only in external characters but in many features of the osteology, hemipenes, and musculature from *Acrantophis, Boa*, and other Boidae. *Acrantophis*, though resembling *Boa* in external characters, differs in hemipenes, musculature, osteology, and chromosomes, and I interpret the resemblance to *Boa* as parallel

imply any sense of relationships. I don't believe that subfamilies can be recognized in this family, but there are two groups of genera that could be recognized as tribes much as in the sense of McDowell with little problem. (I do not agree with the cladistic philosophy expressed by some workers that every level in a classification must be occupied; thus I see nothing wrong in recognizing tribes in a family lacking subfamilies if the morphological differences are not great enough to call subfamilies.) These are the Boa group and the Corallus group, which can be used without any formal groupings. The Boa group contains *Boa, Acrantophis*, and *Sanzinia*; the Corallus group has *Corallus, Candoia, Epicrates*, and *Eunectes*.

A KEY TO THE GENERA OF BOIDAE

A. Labial pits strongly developed, deep; arboreal species ..... B

AA. Labials without pits or with just shallow pits on a few scales C

  B. Madagascan; 48 or fewer subcaudals .... *Sanzinia*

  BB. American; 48 or more subcaudals .... *Corallus*

    C. Scales keeled .... *Candoia*

    CC. Scales smooth .... D

D. Nostrils dorsal in position, the nasals in contact behind the rostral shield; head not very distinct from neck .... *Eunectes*

DD. Nasals lateral in position; nasals separated; head distinct from neck .... E

  E. Many small scales in the loreal area, these the same size as the small scales covering the top of head; 45 or more subcaudals .... *Boa*

  EE. Two to about four enlarged loreal scales present; large scales often present on top of head, but if only small scales present, then 41 or fewer subcaudals .... F

    F. Madagascar; few or no head shields distinct; subcaudals 30 to 41 .... *Acrantophis*

    FF. America; several head shields (usually internasals and prefrontals, plus supraoculars) distinct; subcaudals usually 45 or more .... *Epicrates*

Genus Acrantophis Jan, 1860 (*Icon. gen. Ophid.*, 1: pl. 2). Type species by monotypy *A. dumerili*.

Synonyms: *Pelophilus* Dumeril & Bibron, 1844 [*madagascariensis*], preoccupied.

Large, terrestrial boas with the head distinct from the neck, the body cylindrical, and the tail short. The loreal region may have two to four enlarged scales between the nasal and the preorbital, sometimes with a few smaller scales above the major row and almost always separated from the supralabials by a row of small scales. There are 6 to 15 scales around the eye, which is not in contact with the supralabials. There is a large preorbital and sometimes one or more enlarged supraorbitals. The frontal scale may be represented by a group of large and small scales but is never a distinct shield. There are several small scales between the nasal shields. The labials are not separated by furrows. The mental groove is distinct.

The hemipenis probes 10 to 12 subcaudals. Unlike the hemipenes of other boas, that of *Acrantophis* is oval to weakly heart-shaped, with a shallow notch at the tip. The shaft is smooth, with the distal half of the organ broadened and covered with flounces often connected by vertical ridges. The sulcus spermaticus is forked at about two-thirds the length of the organ, but (uniquely) the forks fade before reaching the edges of the

THE TRUE BOAS: BOIDAE

hemipenis. There are 17 pairs of chromosomes (2N=34) as in *Sanzinia* but not in *Boa* (where 2N=36).

Though *Acrantophis* superficially resembles *Boa* in shape and head scalation (of at least *A. dumerili*, the head scales of *A. madagascariensis* being quite large and regular), the major differences in hemipenis structure (the organ is strongly bilobed in *Boa* and the forks of the sulcus reach the tips of the arms), chromosomes, and several aspects of scalation indicate that they are distinct genera though probably derived from a common ancestor that may have been the primitive form of the family. Both *Acrantophis* and *Boa*, however, are greatly specialized in scalation and their adaptation as large, heavy-bodied terrestrial boas may simply be the result of parallel evolution from a remote ancestor. I am not willing to speculate on how *Acrantophis* reached Madagascar, but the differences in scalation between *Acrantophis* and *Sanzinia*, while retaining similarities in hemipenes and chromosomes, indicate they have been isolated from the other boas for many years. Putting the Madagascan boas into *Boa* serves only to hide the distinctness of the Madagascan lineages and assert a relationship that cannot be proved.

The head scalation of *Epicrates cenchria* may bear an amazing resemblance to that of *A. madagascariensis*, as do several scale counts. In *E. cenchria*, however, there is a single large horizontal loreal that is not separated from the supralabials.

Two species of *Acrantophis* are recognized, and both are in the hobby. Though the two species have allopatric distributions, they differ greatly in many characters of scalation and color and must be considered full species.

Key to the Species of Acrantophis

A. Scales on top of head all small and irregular; about four enlarged loreals; 30 to 35 subcaudals; sides with horizontal H, the lower arm bearing a white spot .... *dumerili*

AA. Scales of top of head between eyes large; usually two enlarged loreals; 34 to 41 subcaudals; sides with groups of a dark horizontal lozenge and a separate ocellated spot below .... *madagascariensis*

ACRANTOPHIS DUMERILI

Dumeril's Boa

Recently this species has been bred in large numbers, and it has become quite affordable. The distinctive head pattern and the horizontal H-shaped blotches on the side, the lower arm of the H with a large white spot, are characteristic and allow immediate recognition from *Boa*, with which it shares a very similar overall appearance.

The top of the head is covered with small scales that may vary greatly in size and shape. There are 11 to 16 scales in a circle around the eye, including a large preorbital. The loreal area has

THE LIVING BOAS

Head and midbody views of A. dumerili.

about four enlarged scales in a row, separated from the supralabials by a row of small scales, and is quite distinct from the small scales of the top of the snout. There are 17 to 19 supralabials and 22 to 24 infralabials. The dorsal scales are smooth and in 59 to 68 rows at midbody. There are 225 to 236 ventrals and 30 to 35 subcaudals (a few may be divided).

A. dumerili tends to be a pale brown in overall coloration, often with a delicate pinkish tinge. The belly is white and either plain or with small brown spots. The head bears a distinct and constant pattern in the form of a bridle of narrow dark brown stripes. One stripe runs from the nostril through the eye to behind the corner of the mouth. A second shorter stripe starts behind the eye (usually not in contact with the eye) and runs to over the corner of the mouth. A third dark stripe runs from the upper edge of the eye and then back toward the nape. The third stripe is connected to its partner of the opposite side by one or more dark stripes running from eye to eye; the nape is not striped. Additionally, there are many small brown specks over the head and labials. The body pattern varies considerably, but the sides are marked with many dark brown horizontal H-shaped blotches. The upper arm usually is a solid horizontal lozenge, while the lower arm usually encloses a large white spot or stripe. There may be a second spot below the lower arm, and the upper arm may be connected to the blotch on the other side by a narrow brown band across the middle of the back. There may be shadowy brown patterning over the mid-back as

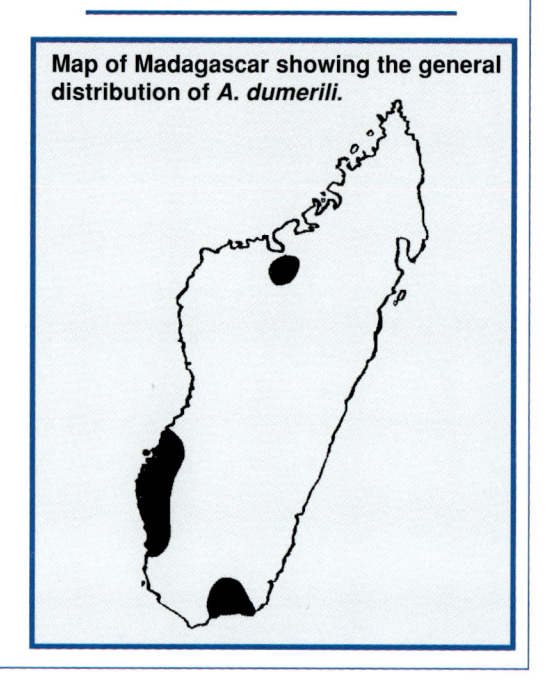

Map of Madagascar showing the general distribution of A. dumerili.

THE TRUE BOAS: BOIDAE

well, and there may be a large white spot between the arms of the H. Juveniles are more brightly and distinctly patterned than adults.

Most adult *A. dumerili* are 1.5 to 2 meters in total length. It has been repeatedly said that this species does not get as long as *A. madagascariensis*, perhaps with a total maximum length of under 3 meters. The tail is about 6 to 8% of the total length.

Dumeril's Boa is a species of Madagascar, where it is found in the southern, southwestern, and north-central areas, usually near the coast. All its known localities are to the south of those of *A. madagascariensis*, and the two species do not appear to hybridize or occur together. The species first was described by Jan in his *Iconographie generale des Ophidiens* (1: pl. 2) in 1860.

Little is reported about the natural history of Dumeril's Boa. It is an inhabitant of relatively dry savannas and open woods and often is found in villages. It is active mostly at night and is typically terrestrial. It feeds on small rodents and other small mammals, including introduced species of rats and mice. Commonly it occupies vacant mammal burrows in the tangled roots of trees, perhaps having first eaten the original inhabitants.

In captivity the boa is kept much like a Red-tailed Boa, being given a large terrarium with a disposable substrate such as newspaper or carpet or one of the wood shaving litters. The daytime temperature should be about 28°C (82°F) or so, dropping at night. The boas feed readily on rodents of all types of appropriate

Dumeril's Boa bears a striking resemblance to *B. constrictor*. The head patterns are very similar. However, genetic and internal differences, along with geographic isolation, argue for their placement in separate genera. Photo by G. and C. Merker, courtesy C. Reinman.

Some specimens of *A. dumerili* are more brightly colored than others. This one has an attractive peachy cast to the brown areas of the pattern. Photo by I. Francais.

Within its natural range, Dumeril's Boa is a rather common snake that is frequently seen by the local people. It is part of the local diet, and the skins are made into leather. Photo by R. D. Bartlett.

THE TRUE BOAS: BOIDAE

Dumeril's Boa are frequently docile animals that make fine pets as long as one is ready to care for a snake that can reach a bit over 2 meters / 6.5 feet in length. Photo by I. Francais.

size. Breeding is more likely to occur after a two-month brumation at about 22°C (72°F) or a bit less with short days and reduced or no food. A water bowl should always be available. This species breeds well in groups with two males to one female, and the males often fight, even to the point of inflicting vicious bites on each other. Pregnancy lasts some five to seven months, and the female often basks under a heat lamp. Spring breedings result in young in August or September. The litters are rather small, only six or seven young, each baby some 42 to 48 cm in total length. The young usually feed well after their first shed.

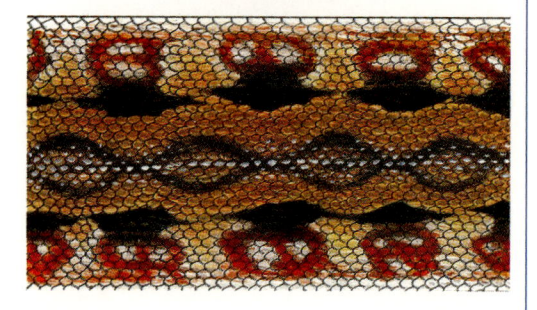

Head and midbody views of *A. madagas-cariensis.*

ACRANTOPHIS MADAGASCARIENSIS

Madagascan Boa

The Madagascan Boa is similar at first glance to both Dumeril's Boa and the species of *Boa*, but it is easily distinguished by a glance at the top of the head. This species has at least a few enlarged plates while the others lack them. The color pattern is much like that of *A. dumerili* but somewhat reduced and not as attractive.

The top of the head is covered with large to fairly large scales, sometimes just about five scales across the snout and only five scales between the eyes, including three large plates between the smaller supraoculars. There are just 6 to 10 scales in a circle around the eye, including a large preocular. There are two large and rather squarish loreals separated by a row of small scales from the supralabials. There are 16 to 18 supralabials and 22 or 23 infralabials. The dorsal scales are smooth and in 61 to 77 rows at midbody. There are 221 to 238 ventrals and 34 to 41 subcaudals, a few usually divided.

The Madagascan Boa is brownish above and pale dirty white below with many brown spots and smudges on the belly. The head has a heavy blackish brown stripe running from the nostril through the eye to beyond the corner of the mouth. There is a large black blotch below the eye on the supralabials and many black spots on the lower jaw as well. The top of the head is brown like the rest of the body but there usually are two curved darker

THE TRUE BOAS: BOIDAE

brown blotches or lines on the nape and often several small brown flecks as well. The body pattern varies quite a bit, but generally the sides have a row of elongated dark brown lozenges that often fuse into a broken stripe. These lozenges may have hazy white edgings. Below them are indistinct rounded brown spots with white centers, these spots often badly broken and irregular. Narrow and indistinct brown bars may cross the back to connect the pattern of the sides, and there may be hazy brown clouds over the back as well. Young specimens may have more distinctive dark brown lozenges on either side of the back, these connected into broken stripes.

Adults commonly are 1.8 to 2 meters in length; the maximum size remains unclear, but it per-

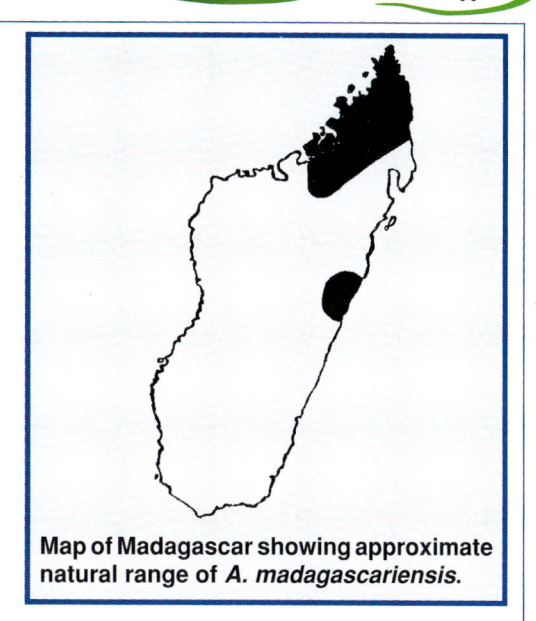

Map of Madagascar showing approximate natural range of *A. madagascariensis*.

haps reaches 4 meters. The tail is about 5 to 10% of the total length, longer in males than females.

Acrantophis madagascariensis seems to be restricted to the northern third of Madagascar. It

The head pattern of *A. madagascariensis* is similar to *dumerili* and to *Boa*, but is more reduced. This is true of the overall pattern of this snake as well, but some can be rather reddish. Photo by R. D. Bartlett.

Like most members of the family, *A. madagascariensis* is a powerful constrictor. It feeds mainly on mammals, which, in Madagascar, means mongooses, tenrecs, and rodents. Photo by K. H. Switak.

first was described by Dumeril & Bibron in 1844 as *Pelophilus madagascariensis* (*Erpetol. gen.*, 6: 524). The generic name *Pelophilus* is preoccupied for a frog.

As far as known, the natural history of this species is much like that of Dumeril's Boa. It is a mammal-eater active mostly at night. In captivity it is kept much like Dumeril's or Red-tailed Boas. The major difference between the two species of *Acrantophis* in captivity is their young. The Madagascan Boa is unusual in producing only a few very large young. Litters commonly consist of two to six young born after a pregnancy of as much as nine months. While the young of *A. dumerili* are under 50 cm in length, those of *A. madagascariensis* are 60 to 65 cm long. Though the young are large enough to eat quite large rodents from the beginning, the small size of the litters (and the relatively dull coloration) has not made them popular with breeders.

Genus Boa Linnaeus, 1758 (*Systema Naturae*, Ed. 10, 1: 214). Type species by subsequent designation *Boa constrictor* Linnaeus.

Synonyms: *Constrictor* Laurenti, 1768.

Large boas with cylindrical bodies, heads distinct from the neck, and a relatively long tail. The genus is easily recognized by the presence of uniformly small scales covering the entire top of the head from tip of snout to nape and from supralabials to supralabials. Only the nasal shields and sometimes a few scales below the eye are distinctly

THE TRUE BOAS: BOIDAE

A common view of *B. c. occidentalis*. This subspecies, occurring from Bolivia and Paraguay south to central Argentina, has a (deserved) reputation among hobbyists for aggressiveness. Photo by R. D. Bartlett.

enlarged. There are 14 to 20 scales around the eye and many small scales, none enlarged, in the loreal region (the loreal scales are the same size as those between the eyes). Typically the snout is high and rather squarish in profile rather than depressed as in most other boas. There usually are well over 45 subcaudal scales.

The hemipenes are deeply bilobed, the lobes occupying about a third the length of the organ. The shaft is about half the length of the hemipenis and is naked, while the rest of the organ is covered with flounces (about five on the upper shaft and another five to seven on each lobe), plus short connecting transverse ridges on the lobes. The sulcus spermaticus divides just below the forking of the lobes at a bit over half the length of the organ. The forks of the sulcus run to the tips of the lobes. Males probe 14 to 27 subcaudals, rarely to 38 subcaudals in the Peruvian long-tailed form described as *longicauda*. There are 18 pairs of chromosomes (2N=36).

Boa is quite distinct from *Acrantophis* in hemipene structure and chromosome number as well as many details of scalation (uniform loreal and head scale size, more subcaudals, etc.). I can see no reason to include the Madagascan species in the same genus as the American species and retain the two as full genera that might not even be closely related beyond sharing primitive characters and parallel adaptations to a mostly terrestrial existence.

Red-tailed Boas are opportunistic feeders, eating practically any bird, mammal, or reptile they can catch. This one is eating a Mexican Free-tailed Bat. Photo by P. Freed.

Though the Red-tailed Boa, *B. constrictor*, is one of the most common snakes in captivity, only recently has it been bred in quantity. It remains perhaps the most confused of the boas when it comes to taxonomy, with a multitude of described subspecies that are impossible to distinguish with certainty. At the moment I believe that is it dangerous to recognize most of the subspecies from Central and South America because the genus has not been reviewed in detail in modern times and most of the subspecies seem to be based on very local variations of scalation and color pattern. Thus I consider almost all described taxa of *Boa* as synonyms of *Boa constrictor*. However, I tentatively recognize the isolated and weakly distinguished boas on the Caribbean islands of St. Lucia and Dominica as full species because it is doubtful that they have been able to exchange genes with mainland boas for many years and are distinguishable with some certainty from mainland boas.

Key to the Species of Boa
  A. Ventral scales usually fewer than 260; Central America and South America .... *constrictor*
  AA. Ventral scales usually more than 260; St. Lucia and Dominica .... B
  B. Dominica; ventrals 258 to 273; dorsal blotches 32 to 35 on the trunk, often forming complete rings outlined with pale .... *nebulosa*
  BB. St. Lucia; ventrals 270 to 288; dorsal blotches 27 to 32 on the trunk, dark on pale brown. .... *orophias*

B. c. ortoni is a subspecies that hails from the desert and semi-desert region of northwestern Peru. It is a hard to distinguish form noted for a pale and reduced pattern. Photo by J. Balzarini.

BOA CONSTRICTOR

Red-tailed Boa

This is the only species of *Boa* seen in the terrarium hobby under normal circumstances. Though extremely variable in coloration, pattern, and counts, recognition should present few problems. The dark brown stripe down the center of the head, sometimes broken between the eyes, is a mark of the genus and not the species.

THE TRUE BOAS: BOIDAE

A boa with a high rostral area (squarish in profile). The nostril is within two or three slightly enlarged nasal shields. There typically are about 20 scales between the eyes and 14 to 20 scales around the eye, some of those below the eye enlarged. There are 17 to 25 supralabials and 20 to 28 infralabials. The dorsal scales are smooth and in 55 to 91 rows at midbody. There are 225 to 288 ventrals and 45 to 69 subcaudals. The exact limits of most of these counts are uncertain and in some cases the extremes are based on old literature records.

In typical specimens, the back is a pale grayish to sandy brown, becoming whiter on the tail. The belly is whitish and often has blackish spots and blotches, in some localities becoming largely dark posteriorly. The top of the head is pale tan except for a well-defined darker brown stripe running from the tip of the snout to the nape and sometimes the neck, widening behind the level of the eyes. This stripe may be broken above the eyes or may put out small lateral spurs over the eyes. The side of the snout in front of

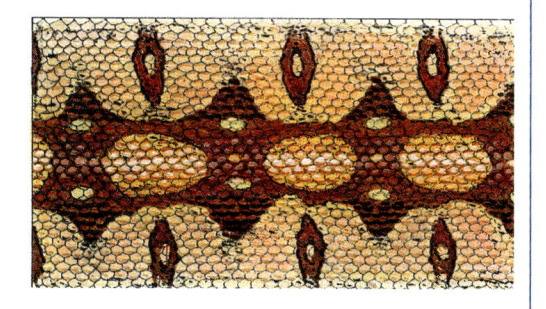

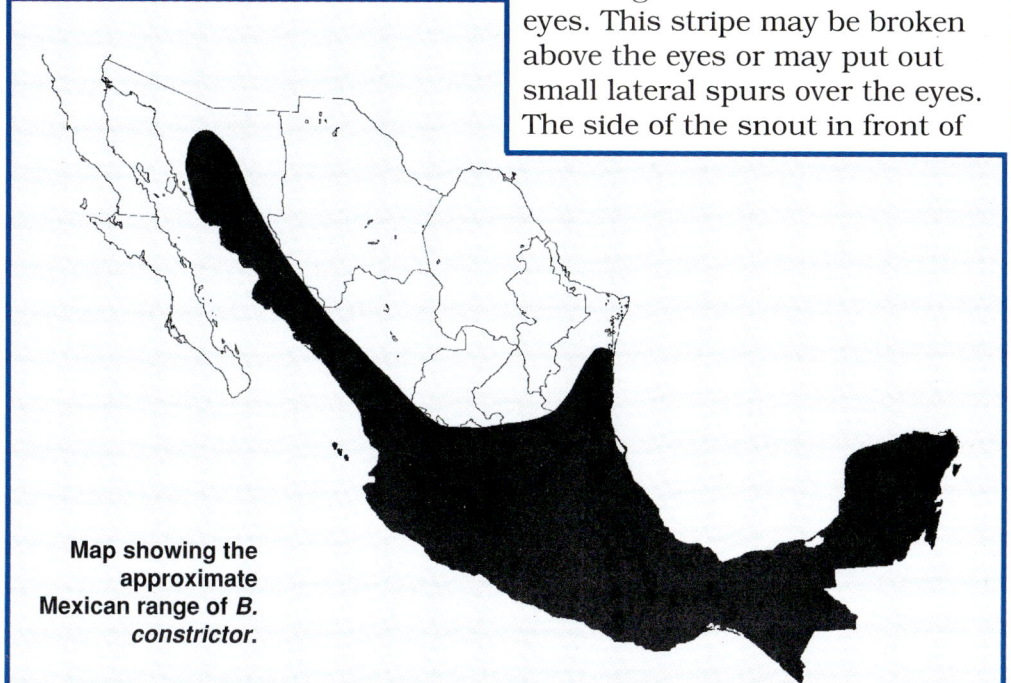

Head and midbody views of *B. constrictor*.

Map showing the approximate Mexican range of *B. constrictor*.

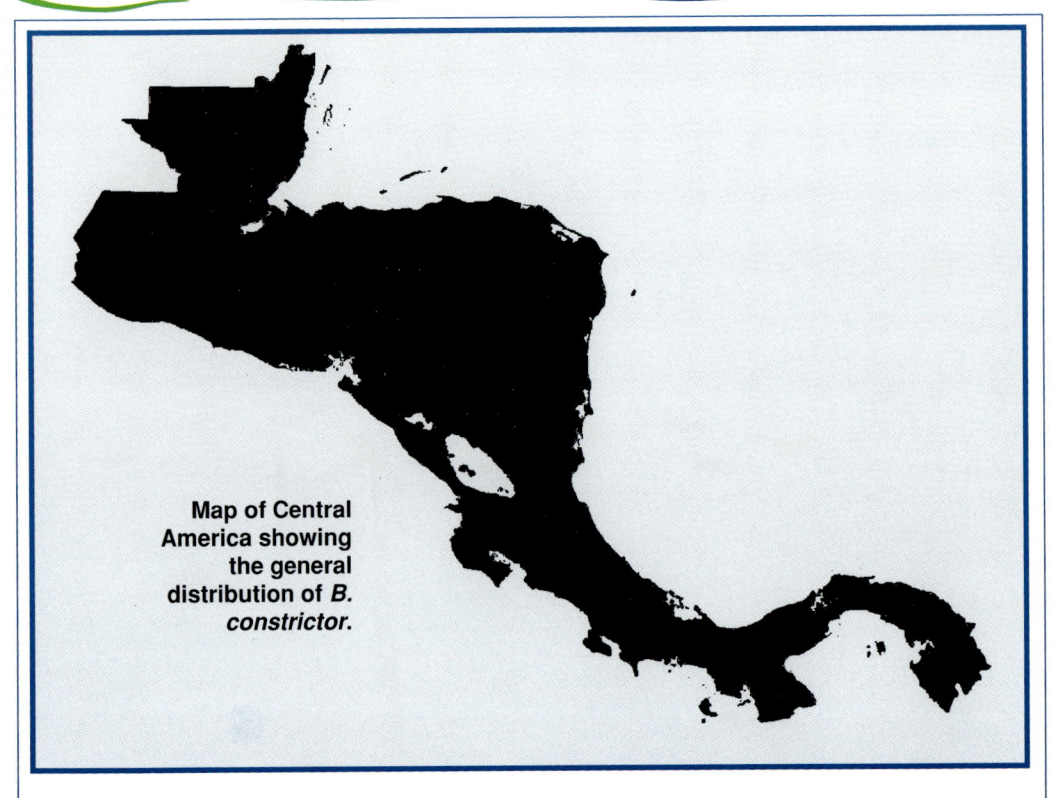

Map of Central America showing the general distribution of *B. constrictor*.

Map of South America illustrating the approximate range of *B. constrictor*.

the eye is occupied by a large dark brown rectangle, the lips are heavily spotted with dark, and there is a wide dark brown stripe running from the eye back to beyond the corner of the mouth and edged below by a white stripe. There also is a slightly oblique stripe running down from the eye over the upper lip. On the back are many (about 15 to 28) dark brown hourglass-shaped bands, widened into diamonds on the upper sides and there often containing a whitish to yellowish lozenge or oval. The cross-bands may be widened or narrowed in the center of the back and may be connected along the side of the back. On the lower side are smaller alternating dark brown diamonds or lozenges usually with pale centers. In many specimens from almost any part of its

THE TRUE BOAS: BOIDAE

Red-tailed Boas from northern South America generally have crisp markings and deep red tails. This example is from Guyana. Photo by R. D. Bartlett.

range, the species has the crossbands on the tail greatly widened and darker brown to bright mahogany red in color, outlined at times with black.

Average adults are about 2 to 3 meters in length. The tail is about 10 to 14% of the total length, longer and more tapered in males than females. The maximum size of this species is in question, the former record-holder at 5.6 meters from Trinidad having being reidentified as a young Green Anaconda (Joy, 1992). The next largest specimen is an unverified record of a specimen 4.5 meters long (15 feet). The actual maximum size of Red-tailed Boas today probably is only some 3.5 to perhaps 4 meters.

The Red-tailed Boa ranges over a tremendous area of tropical America from northwestern Mexico (Sonora just a few dozen kilometers below the United States border) to northern Argentina to south of Buenos Aires. It also occupies the near-mainland islands of Trinidad and Tobago. The range is not continuous, and there are many gaps where the species is uncommon, rare, or evidently absent. It also has been moved around by man over the years. The species was described by Linnaeus in 1758 in his *Systema Naturae*, Ed. 10, 1: 215. The type specimen was said to come from India, obviously in error, and today the name is used in the restricted sense for the

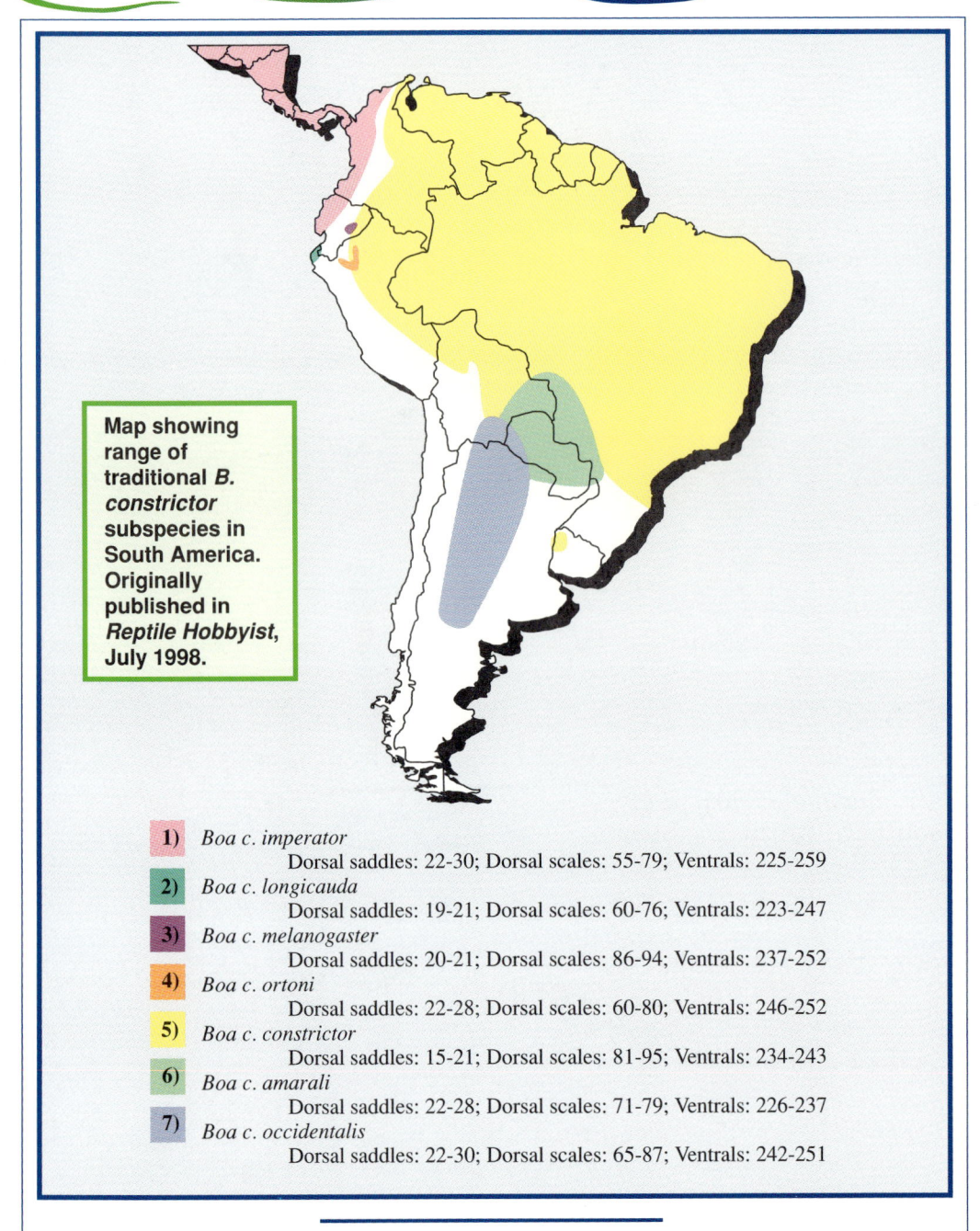

Map showing range of traditional *B. constrictor* subspecies in South America. Originally published in *Reptile Hobbyist*, July 1998.

1) *Boa c. imperator*
   Dorsal saddles: 22-30; Dorsal scales: 55-79; Ventrals: 225-259
2) *Boa c. longicauda*
   Dorsal saddles: 19-21; Dorsal scales: 60-76; Ventrals: 223-247
3) *Boa c. melanogaster*
   Dorsal saddles: 20-21; Dorsal scales: 86-94; Ventrals: 237-252
4) *Boa c. ortoni*
   Dorsal saddles: 22-28; Dorsal scales: 60-80; Ventrals: 246-252
5) *Boa c. constrictor*
   Dorsal saddles: 15-21; Dorsal scales: 81-95; Ventrals: 234-243
6) *Boa c. amarali*
   Dorsal saddles: 22-28; Dorsal scales: 71-79; Ventrals: 226-237
7) *Boa c. occidentalis*
   Dorsal saddles: 22-30; Dorsal scales: 65-87; Ventrals: 242-251

form found over most of northern South America.

I am going to side-step the problem of subspeciation in this species by not recognizing any subspecies. I feel, as do many herpetologists working with the American snake fauna, that this variable species simply is too poorly known to assign names to geographical variations. Variation is displayed in dorsal scale rows, ventral and subcaudal scales, and number of dorsal cross-bands, as well as details of coloration. As a general rule, specimens from

THE TRUE BOAS: BOIDAE

Mexico and Central America are rather dull in color, vicious in temperament (many exceptions), have fewer than 80 midbody scale rows, often have faint short spurs from the head stripe over the eyes, and have fewer than 252 ventrals. Within this area there are many local variants, especially the small specimens from the Cayos Cochinos (Hog Islands) off Honduras that have a very weakly developed dorsal pattern and colors tending toward a pale orange on the tail and a faint pinkish blush over the generally tan body. The Mexican form extends southward into South America west of the Andes as far as Peru. In most of South America east of the Andes and north of Bolivia and southern Brazil, the boas

Holotype of *B. c. melanogaster*. This subspecies is of very questionable validity. Photo by J. K. Langhammer

Ventral view of *B. c. melanogaster* holotype showing the dark belly from which the subspecific name is derived. Photo by J. K. Langhammer.

This Paraguan boa has a pale color, high number of saddles, and blackish tail, all of which are typical of *B. c. amarali*. Photo by P. Freed.

Argentine boas, *B. c. occidentalis*, are widely bred by hobbyists. However, they remain expensive and rarely show up in pet stores. Photo by I. Francais.

have 81 to 95 middorsal scale rows, about 230 to 250 ventrals, and no spurs on the head stripe. Specimens from many populations in this vast range may have varying degrees of red tints to the cross-bands on the posterior body and tail. South of this range the boas become more variable and several forms have been named. In the broad sense, the Mexican to Peruvian form could be called *B. c. imperator*, while that of northern South America would be *B. c. constrictor*, if subspecies were to be recognized, but there are so many distinctive populations within each "subspecies" that the names are practically meaningless.

This species has a formidable synonymy, including the following: *amarali* Stull, 1932 [southern Brazil]; *auspex* Laurenti, 1768 [northern South America]; *diviniloquus* Laurenti, 1768 [Mexico and Peru]; *eques* Eydoux & Souleyet, 1842 [Peru]; *formosissimus* Laurenti, 1768 [northern South America]; *imperator* Daudin, 1803 [Mexico]; *isthmica* Garman, 1883 [Panama and Colombia]; *longicauda* Price and Russo, 1991 [Peru]; *melanogaster* Langhammer, 1983 [Ecuador]; *mexicana* Jan, 1863 [Mexico]; *occidentalis* Philippi, 1873 [Bolivia, Paraguay and Argentina]; *ortoni* Cope, 1878 [Peru]; *rex-serpentum* Laurenti [northern South America]; *sabogae* (Barbour, 1906) [Saboga I., western Panama]; *sigma* Smith, 1943 [Tres Marias, Mexico];

Red-tailed Boas (also called Common Boa or simply Boa Constrictor) occur near water in

THE TRUE BOAS: BOIDAE

Hog Island boas are a local variant of *B. c. imperator*. Supposedly found on a few islands off the coast of Honduras, there is some speculation that they can be found on the mainland as well. Currently, it is considered a localized form and not given subspecific or specific status. They have been frequently bred by hobbyists of late. *above*: Photo by R. D. Bartlett. *below*: Photo by W. P. Mara.

Red-tailed boas appreciate having some form of climbing apparatus in their enclosures. The young are more arboreal than the adults, but even adults will climb occasionally if given the opportunity. Photo by J. Balzarini.

most of their range and in conditions ranging from rather dry savannas to deep rain forests. Adults are mostly terrestrial and nocturnal, feeding on a variety of mammals and birds and the occasional large lizard (and supposedly caimans as well). The young are more arboreal and likely to be found in the trees near water. In nature the young often are born during the summer months, but there is a great deal of variation, as might be expected, over the range.

Though small Red-tailed Boas are widely imported for the terrarium hobby, they usually are heavily parasitized and may have respiratory diseases, as well as being stressed. Most imports survive only a few months unless given extensive veterinary care. Increasing numbers of Red-tailed Boas of several color patterns and geographic ranges are being bred in captivity, and these make much better buys though often more expensive to purchase. If kept in a large, warm (27 to 32°C, 81 to 90°F), terrarium with an under-tank heater, a basking light, full-spectrum fluorescents, a large water bowl, and many hiding and climbing areas, Red-tails do well in captivity and may live 20 or even 30 years. The substrate should be newspaper or carpeting or a mixture of sand and peat; do not use cedar shavings (aspen is OK) or pebbles. The temperature should drop a bit at night, but many keepers let the lights stay on for

THE TRUE BOAS: BOIDAE

Amelanistic (albino) boas are still something of a rarity commanding high prices. So far, all of these individuals come from *B. c. imperator* stock. Photo by A. Both.

16 or more hours most of the year. These boas feed on a variety of mammals and birds of appropriate size, with the largest specimens able to take rabbits. Remember that living rodents may severely damage a boa, so if possible feed only freshly killed or frozen and thawed prey.

Breeding may take place any time of the year, possibly depending on the geographic variant being bred, but many keepers prefer to brumate their animals for six to eight weeks during the winter, allowing the temperature to drop slowly to about 22°C (72°F) while withdrawing food and reducing the daylength; water should always be available. When the snakes are brought back to normal temperature and lighting in the spring, they should breed readily. Males may fight over females, and they use their spurs to "tickle" the female during adjustment of their bodies before mating. Pregnant females often spend much of their time basking. Pregnancy may last six to eight months in average females, perhaps depending on temperature and size of the litter. The young are about 35 to 50 cm in length and often number 25 to 50 in a litter, with 60 and more reported. There often are several infertile eggs (slugs) and still-born embryos in various stages of development present in the litter. The young feed after their first shed in one to three weeks. They may reach sexual maturity in just three years.

Hobbyists differ greatly in just what type of Red-tailed Boa they prefer. Some prefer the brightly colored forms of northern South America (*constrictor*), the true red-

Hobbyists typically regard the dark boas of Mexico as dull, aggressive animals. However, they can show some fetching iridescence, as this one does. Photo by R. D. Bartlett.

tails that probably represent many different populations and local variants. A true red-tail with a very contrasting dorsal pattern is a striking snake whose aesthetic equal is hard to find. The grayish boas from southern Brazil and adjacent Argentina and Paraguay (*amarali*) and many parts of Mexico and Central America (*imperator*) may be quite unattractive and have a reputation as vicious snakes that strike repeatedly and never calm down. An exception is the somewhat smaller Hog Island form from Honduras, which when small is relatively gentle; the story (perhaps a legend) that this form is extinct in the wild and will eventually be described as a new species perhaps has increased its popularity; personally, I find it to be a dull and unattractive boa that in captivity is not especially smaller than normal Mexican boas and may be just as vicious; additionally, similar forms are supposed to be found on the Honduran and perhaps Belize mainland. The Argentine form (*occidentalis*) is very dark in color with no reddish on the tail. Although this variant has a reputation for being aggressive, it recently has been produced in fair numbers by breeders. It remains rather expensive.

Recently albino Red-tails have been bred in small numbers and are available at very high prices as investments; they may eventually come down in price. Personally, I find them to be dull and unattractive compared to the natural forms. Striped variants also are available, but it still has not been determined if these are genetic (and thus true-breeding) or the result of manipulation of temperature and humidity during certain stages of pregnancy.

If you want one of the larger boas, a nicely patterned captive-bred Red-tail from one of the colorful forms such as found in the Guianas may be your best buy. Remember that these snakes commonly will grow to over 3 meters and thus need a large terrarium from the start. Also don't forget to factor in the cost of guinea pigs, rats, and rabbits over the 20 years you might have the specimen.

When breeding Red-tails, be sure to try not to interbreed

THE TRUE BOAS: BOIDAE

specimens from different localities and color patterns or you will get mongrels (most of the Red-tails being bred today are such mongrels). Perhaps it would be best to specialize in specimens from parents from known localities and collect by locality.

BOA NEBULOSA

Dominican Boa

The Dominican Boa was described in 1964 by Lazell (*Bull. Mus. Comp. Zool.*, 132(3): 264) to formally recognize the dark boa constrictors found only on the lower Caribbean island of Dominica. This isolated form is basically similar to the Red-tailed Boa of the mainland but differs in scale counts and details of the color pattern.

The snout is lower than in *B. constrictor*, the profile depressed to slightly swollen, never squarish. The dorsal scales are in 59 to 69 rows at midbody and there are 258 to 273 ventrals.

The boa always appears dark compared to *B. constrictor*, being a dark grayish brown above with indistinct wide darker brown bands across the back. These bands number 32 to 35, a very high count for the genus *Boa*. The belly is grayish, heavily blotched and spotted with blackish brown. The head is dark but the pattern is reduced; the stripe on top of the head is short, weak, or broken, the squarish blotch in front of the eye is absent or barely indicated, and the stripe below the eye is weak or absent. Often the stripe back from the eye is indistinct at its upper edge from the generally dark smoky brown side of the head.

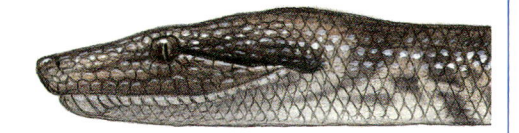

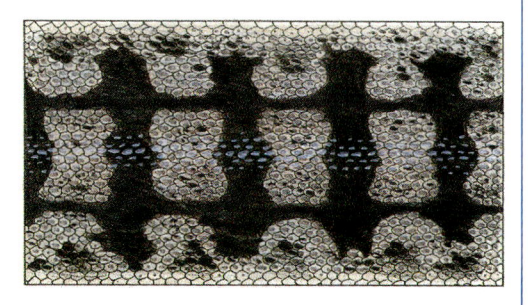

Head and midbody views of *B. nebulosa*.

Adult females reach almost 2 meters in total length, males being somewhat smaller.

Endemic to Dominica, this species is found over all the island where trees and moisture are present; they may be present in large numbers along the edges of banana plantations. Adults are largely terrestrial, and young are more arboreal. They feed on introduced rats and perhaps native agoutis. Adults seem to occupy the same area for long periods of time and are inactive during the day. They may den in small numbers in a suitable hollow log or tree stump.

This form is recognized as a full species because it is isolated, unable to share genes with any other form of the genus, and has several distinctive features of scalation and color pattern. Several other authors have considered elevating this form to specific status, but none seem to have actually done it before. The low dorsal scale count is very different from the closest South American form (which commonly has 81 or more scale rows) and closest to the Central American forms, but there can be little doubt that the ancestor of the Dominican Boa reached the island by rafting from South America. Few specimens are kept in captivity.

Map of the eastern Caribbean showing the general distribution of *B. nebulosa*. The southernmost island is Trinidad, and the large island in the northwest is Puerto Rico.

BOA OROPHIAS

St. Lucian Boa

Linnaeus described the St. Lucian Boa in 1758 (*Systema Naturae*, Ed. 10, 1: 215) from a specimen from unknown locality. It was resurrected by Lazell (1964) and here is formally elevated to specific rank because it is both isolated and thus unable to share

While completely absent from the U.S. hobby, *B. nebulosa* is kept and bred in Europe. Eventually, it could make its way into American collections. Photo by R. D. Bartlett.

THE TRUE BOAS: BOIDAE

genes with its neighbors and has distinctive characters of scalation and coloration.

The snout of the St. Lucian Boa is somewhat less square than in *Boa constrictor* but not as depressed as in *B. nebulosa*. The dorsal scales are in 65 to 75 rows at midbody, and there are 270 to 288 ventrals.

The coloration is not greatly different from mainland *Boa constrictor*, being brown above and whitish below with many blackish spots and clouds. There are 27 to 31 rectangular dark brown crossbands on the back, these often completely broken from the blotches on the side of the back and with large pale spots within them. The bands are less regular than in most *Boa constrictor* and higher in number. The head pattern is similar to mainland *B. constrictor*, but the dark rectangle in the loreal region often is absent.

Large females exceed 2 meters in total length, and the species probably reaches 3 meters.

This species is endemic to the lower Caribbean island of St. Lucia, where it is found in forested areas and the edges of fields and plantations along the eastern and western coasts; it is absent from the center and the southern coast, as well as the northern tip of the island. Young specimens are more arboreal than the adults, which are sedentary, sometimes occupying the same log or burrow for years at a time. They are nocturnal and feed on the available mammals.

In many respects this species is intermediate between its ancestor,

Head and midbody views of *B. orophias*.

Map of the eastern Caribbean showing the general distribution of *B. orophias*. The southernmost island is Trinidad, and the large island in the northwest is Puerto Rico.

the mainland *Boa constrictor* (form or subspecies *constrictor*), and the Dominican Boa. There thus is a sequence in numbers as follows:

Dorsal scales: Mainland: 81 to

95; St. Lucia: 65 to 75; Dominica: 59 to 69; **Ventrals**: Mainland: 234 to 243; St. Lucia: 270 to 288; Dominica: 258 to 273; **Dorsal cross-bands**: Mainland: 15 to 22; St. Lucia: 27 to 31; Dominica: 32 to 35. There are no indications that the island forms have been in contact and able to share genes for many thousands of years, and thus they are considered species. It should be noted that the scale row and ventral counts will not distinguish the island species from the Red-tailed Boas from other than northern South America. The St. Lucian Boa is not common in captivity.

Genus Candoia Gray, 1842 (*Zool. Misc.*: 43). Type species by monotypy *Boa carinata* Schneider.

Synonyms: *Erebophis* Guenther, 1877 [*aspera*].

The tail may be short or long and prehensile, the body slender or very stout, and the head is very distinct from the neck. The scales of the head and body are keeled, except for the lower rows on the sides. The rostral shield is wide, flat, and often square-edged, and there may be a sharply defined ridge from the snout to the eye, the canthus rostralis. The scales on top of the head are small and irregular, there being no normal shields. Three or more small scales contact the upper edge of the rostral. The loreal region is covered with one or two rows of scales that are larger than those on top of the head. The eye is encircled by small scales and separate or not from the supralabials. Labial pits are absent. The mental groove is distinct. Spurs are present in males but may be greatly reduced or absent in females.

The hemipenes of males probe about 9 to 14 subcaudals. The hemipenis is deeply forked. The sulcus spermaticus is deeply forked as well, each branch in a distinct fold, the sulcus fading out just before the end of the arm of the hemipene. There are flounces over most of the shaft of the hemipenis and papillae on the back of the arms.

Candoia is a genus that has been revised recently (McDowell, 1979) and is fairly well understood. Its range in the New Guinea and Solomons area is unique for a boa, and it is assumed to have evolved from some South American *Epicrates* or perhaps *Corallus* that drifted to the Pacific islands on a mass of floating vegetation. This seems so unlikely to me that it seems more scientific to just say that the ancestor of *Candoia* is not known. The squarish (usually) snout and strongly marked canthus rostralis, in combination with the presence of keels on the scales and the absence of labial pits, make the genus easy to recognize. The three species accepted by McDowell's revision also are easy to separate.

Key to the Species of Candoia

A. Tail short, less than twice length of head, and incapable of forming a complete coil; body very stout; eye separated from supralabials by small scales; ventrals 127 to 153 .... *aspera*

THE TRUE BOAS: BOIDAE

AA. Tail longer, more than twice length of head, capable of forming a complete coil; body not stout; eye separated from supralabials or not; ventrals more than 159......................... B

B. Eye separated from supralabials by small scales; canthus rostralis rounded, the rostral shield rather convex; ventrals 203 to 266 .... *bibroni*

BB. Eye in contact with supralabials; canthus rostralis sharp, the rostral shield flat and square; ventrals 160 to 202 .... *carinata*

All three species of *Candoia* are present in the hobby, though only *C. carinata* is common as a captive-bred species.

CANDOIA ASPERA

Viper Boa

This very stout, flat-headed and short-tailed terrestrial boa is easily told from the other species of its genus by the short tail and few ventrals.

The rostral shield is flattened and sharp-edged, the canthus rostralis strongly angled. The eye is surrounded by 10 to 18 small scales and is not in contact with the supralabials. There are 9 to 14 supralabials and 12 to 17 infralabials. The dorsal scales are heavily keeled, as are the head scales, and are in 30 to 45 rows at midbody (typical formula 26/36-30/45-20/30). There are 127 to 153 ventrals and 11 to 22 subcaudals (rarely some divided).

These mud-dwelling boas are brownish (varying from distinctly yellowish to distinctly reddish)

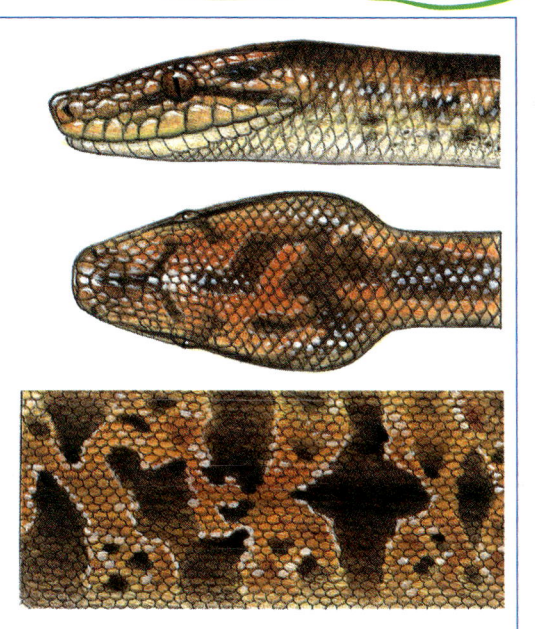

Head and midbody views of *C. aspera*.

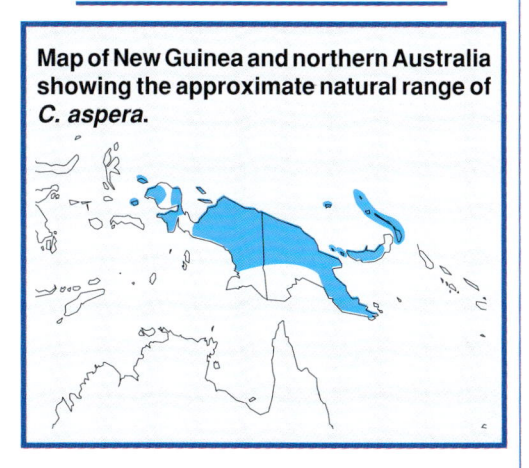

Map of New Guinea and northern Australia showing the approximate natural range of *C. aspera*.

above with large squarish darker brown to grayish brown saddles down the middle of the back and large vertical blotches on the sides. The side blotches may be connected to the dorsal saddles or alternate with them, and the dorsal saddles may be partially fused into long or short zigzag stripes down the center of the back. The short tail usually has about three pale bands against a dark brown background. A dark brown stripe may be present from the nostril through the eye to the corner of the mouth. The belly is yellowish with dark checking or bands and may be uniformly dark.

Adults typically are 60 to 80 cm in total length, but the species probably reaches a meter. The tail is about 7 or 8% of the total length.

The Viper Boa is found over most of New Guinea, including the Manus Islands and Bismarck Archipelago to the northeast. It is absent from the south-central area opposite Queensland, however. The species was described by Guenther in 1877 as *Erebophis asper* (*Proc. Zool. Soc. London*, 1877: 132), a new genus and species from Duke of York Island in the Bismarcks. Like the other species of the genus, it long was referred to *Enygrus*. The subspecies *schmidti* Stull, 1932 , is considered a synonym.

Viper Boas inhabit lowlands near the coast and the floodplains of rivers. They seldom climb, and their shape and color pattern allow them to disappear from sight in the mud and debris, such as dead leaves. However, a few specimens have been found in low trees, and they are recorded from relatively dry areas as well. They are secretive and nocturnal but appear to be mimics of the Death Adder, *Acanthophis antarctica* (or the local representative of this group), where the species occur together, as near Lae. Such specimens may be completely ringed in reddish brown like the Death Adder and hard to tell apart at a quick glance. When disturbed they coil into a tight ball with the head at the center and may erect the tail in place of the head.

Frogs and skinks appear to be the preferred foods of *Candoia*

Viper Boas spend much of their time buried in leaves or mud. Despite their stoutness and sluggish demeanor, prey walking over them is quickly and violently seized. Photo by K. H. Switak.

THE TRUE BOAS: BOIDAE 67

All the *Candoia* have keeled scales as evident on this Viper Boa. This species also has subocular scales separating the eye from the labial scales. Photo by R. D. Bartlett.

Banded specimens of Viper Boas resemble some of the local adders and vipers. This may provide them with some protection from predators. Photo by P. Freed.

aspera, in keeping with the habitat of the species in very moist situations. Larger specimens also take small mammals on occasion.

This species is not especially common in the terrarium, but imports are seen occasionally. They can be kept much like *C. carinata* in a warm, moist terrarium with a soft substrate and a large water bowl. Some specimens adapt to mice, but many do not. Captive breedings are not common. Females usually lack spurs, which are always present and large in males. The litters typically number about 15 to 20 very slender young only 20 cm in length. Larger females give birth to more and possibly larger young. The young may have to be individually fed on small pieces of frogs and seldom do well. Attempts to convert them to pinkie mice or bits of mice may not work.

Though not colorful and certainly a challenge to the most dedicated keeper, these are among the most unusual of the boas and may be worth your attention if available at a reasonable price.

It is not always easy to tell *C. bibroni* from *C. carinata*. This snake has the eye separated from the suboculars and a rounded snout identifying it as *C. bibroni*. Photo by R. D. Bartlett.

CANDOIA BIBRONI

Round-nosed Island Boa

The largest and most arboreal species of the genus, the Round-nose also is quite uncommon in captivity. It may be recognized by the combination of long tail, eye surrounded by small scales (and thus not touching the supralabials), and the rounded canthus rostralis and slightly convex rostral shield.

The rostral shield is wide but slightly convex rather than strongly flattened. The canthus rostralis is rounded and not very distinct. There are 13 to 18 scales around the eye, including one enlarged preocular. The supralabials number 10 to 17, the infralabials 13 to 21. The dorsal scales are keeled and in 29 to 43 rows at midbody (typical formula 25/35-29/43-19/24). There are 203 to 266 ventrals and 44 to 64 subcaudals.

Like the Square-nosed Island Boa, this species shows many different color patterns. Typically it is brown above, sometimes with a reddish tinge, and white to yellow on the belly with few dark markings. The middle of the back has rounded blackish blotches or saddles that alternate with smaller blotches on the sides. The top of the head is dark brown with fine white specks, and there may be a dark line back from the

THE TRUE BOAS: BOIDAE

C. bibroni are extremely variable in color and pattern. This one has an unusual greenish coloration. Photo by I. Francais.

Head and midbody views of *C. bibroni*.

eye. Any of the blotches and stripes may be edged with white or gold. McDowell (1979) recognized six different pattern variants in this species: a) striped, pale brown with a pair of whitish stripes edged with darker brown running from the neck to the tail, the belly white to yellow and sometimes with spots; b) blotched with neck stripes; c) blotched with two dark stripes running along the edge of the lateral edges of the ventrals from under the throat sometimes to under the tail, sometimes with a median row of dark spots down the belly; d) blotched with a median dark stripe on the throat; e) blotched with no fusion of the blotches into stripes; f) solid pale brown or reddish brown without a dorsal

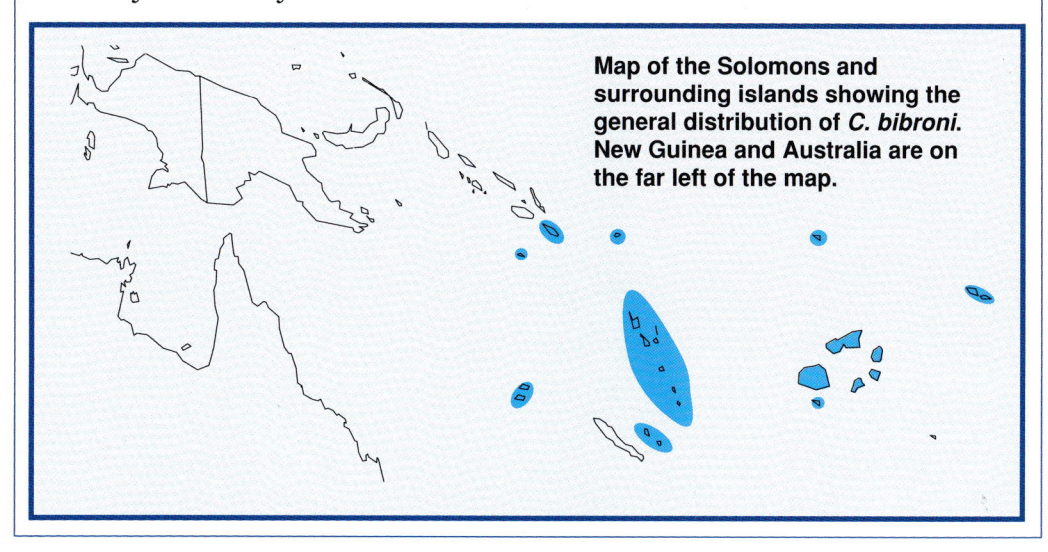

Map of the Solomons and surrounding islands showing the general distribution of *C. bibroni*. New Guinea and Australia are on the far left of the map.

More arboreal than other members of the genus, *C. bibroni* prefer to have climbing branches in the terrarium. Photo by K. H. Switak.

pattern. Additionally, hobbyists record specimens with the dorsal blotches partially fused into long or short zigzag stripes down the center of the back. The unicolored pattern may represent a xanthic form.

Adults are about 1 to 1.5 meters in length, perhaps reaching 2 meters in very large females. The tail is about 10 to 14% of the total length.

The yellow or gold morph of *C. bibroni* is in the hands of only a few breeders and hobbyists. It is an uncommon morph in captivity and probably the wild as well. Photo by I. Francais.

Round-nosed Island Boas are found in the eastern Solomon Islands, Vanua Lava Island, the New Hebrides, the Loyalty Islands, the Fiji Islands, and Western and American Samoa. Records from other South Pacific islands have not been confirmed. As might be expected of a snake found on small, isolated islands yet still probably subject to occasional exchange of genes through movement of individuals in floating rafts of vegetation, it shows a great amount of variation from one island to the next, especially in ventral counts. The species was first described by Dumeril & Bibron in 1844 (*Erpetol. gen.*, 6: 483) as *Enygrus bibroni*. The type locality is Viti Levu in the Fiji Islands. Presently no subspecies are recognized, as McDowell showed that variation was not geographic in nature but apparently at random from one population to the next. The name *australis* (Montrouzier) has been used for the populations of this species with higher ventral and middorsal scale counts. However, the type locality of this name is New Caledonia, where there are no terrestrial snakes, and McDowell considered the name to be unrecognizable. When the name *australis* is used as a subspecies, it is applied to specimens from the western part of the range (Solomons to Samoa) and the nominate form is considered to range through the Fiji Islands. However, this assignment of the names appears to be purely speculative and not based on information in the description,

THE TRUE BOAS: BOIDAE

Among hobbyists, *C. bibroni* has a reputation for being delicate and aggressive. Since most are wild-caught, consider having a new specimen examined by a vet and keep it away from other reptiles for at least 3 months. Photo by R. D. Bartlett.

such as it is, of *australis*. Low and high scale count specimens occur in different populations throughout the range, and there is no correlation between scale counts and color pattern or any other variable. I agree with McDowell that there is no reason to recognize subspecies in *C. bibroni*, and hobbyists should cease using the name *australis*.

This large species is found both on the ground and in trees, but it is a bit more arboreal than *C. carinata*, a species with which it often is found. It is more slender than the other island boas. Young feed largely on skinks and geckos, taken both on the ground and in trees, while adults take more rats and mice, with one record of a fruit bat. Litters average about 15 young (commonly 6 to 20), which are relatively large for the genus at about 30 to 35 cm in total length. An individual female may breed only every second year. This usually is an aggressive species that may be hard to tame and adjust to captivity.

It should be kept in a large vertical terrarium maintained at 28°C (82°F) or warmer, dropping a bit at night. If given climbing branches, it will spend most of the day relaxing above the ground. A large water bowl can be used to help maintain a high humidity at all times. Hiding boxes must be provided, including one well above the ground. About half the females lack spurs, and in those that have them the spurs are slender and small compared to the male spurs. The male uses the spurs to help maneuver the female's vent into position for mating. Males may fight viciously before mating. There are few captive-breeding records so far. The young, though larger than those of other *Candoia*, are difficult to feed and may demand lizards and frogs.

CANDOIA CARINATA

Square-nosed Island Boa

This is the most common island boa and the only one with the supralabials touching the bottom of the eye. In combination with the keeled dorsal and head scales and the extremely angular snout and canthus rostralis, it is easy to recognize.

The wide, sharp-edged rostral shield combined with the very sharp, angular canthus rostralis give the head a very wide, leaf-like appearance. There are 7 to 13 small scales around the eye plus one to three supralabials (usually two) contacting the orbit. There are 10 to 15 supralabials and 10 to 18 infralabials. The dorsal scale rows are strongly keeled and in 31 to 46 rows at midbody (a typical formula being 26/40-31/46-22/33). The ventrals number 165 to 202, with 35 to 60 subcaudals.

Head and midbody views of *C. carinata*.

Typical adults are a pale sandy tan, often rather reddish in overall tone, with a zigzag dark brown or grayish brown stripe down the middle of the back. There are smaller blotches on the sides. The belly usually is yellowish with or without dark spots and smudges.

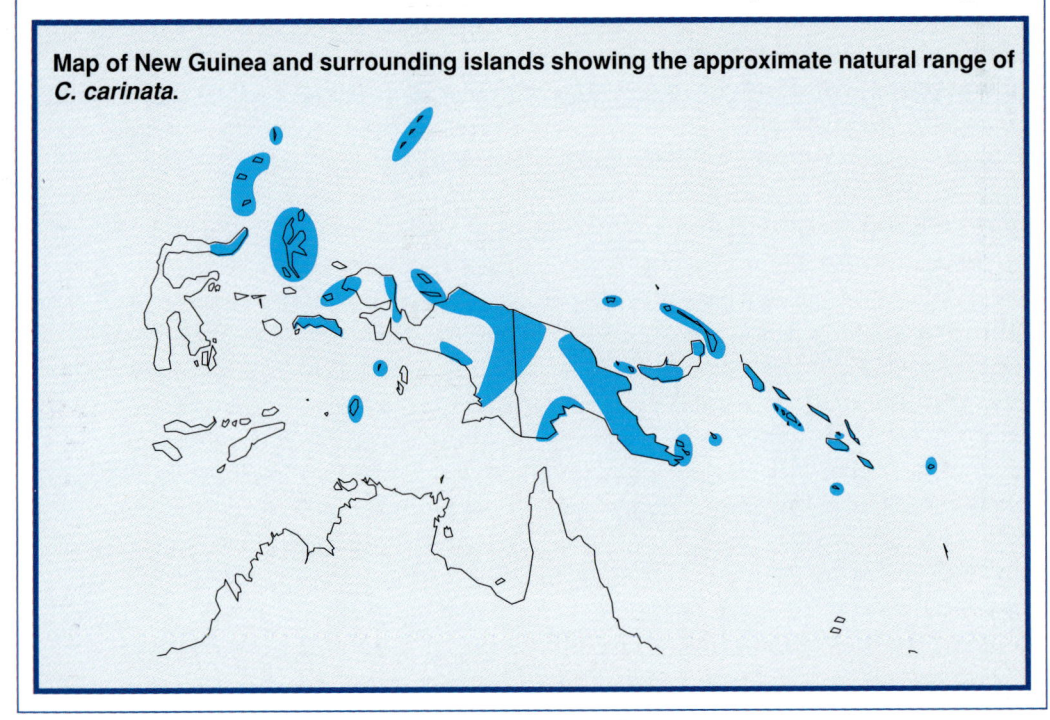

Map of New Guinea and surrounding islands showing the approximate natural range of *C. carinata*.

THE TRUE BOAS: BOIDAE

When threatened, *C. carinata* may coil into a loose ball. Waving the tail around will trick the predator into thinking the tail is the head. Alternately, sometimes this species will spread its neck and act like a cobra. Photo by K. H. Switak.

In many specimens the dark blotches down the center of the back are separate, not fused into a stripe, and may be outlined with white to gold. Still other specimens lack dorsal spotting in part or entirely. Usually the head has a dark stripe from the nostril through the eye to the corner of the mouth and speckles and blotches scattered about, including on the lips. Some specimens are very attractive, others very dull. A xanthic (yellow) mutation is being bred but is quite variable in intensity of the yellow.

Typical adults are about 50 to 60 cm in total length, with some specimens reaching a meter or a bit more. The tail is some 10 to 14% of the total length.

Candoia carinata has a wide range in the Pacific, including the Solomon Islands, New Guinea and adjacent islands, the eastern Indonesian islands, the Celebes (Sulawesi) and north to the Palau Group. The species was described as *Boa carinata* by Schneider in 1801 (*Hist. Amph.*, 2: 261) from an unknown locality. *Enygrus*

The sharp snout of *C. carinata* is clearly visible on this neonate. Also apparent is the small size of the newborns of this species. Photo by G. Moore.

This specimen of C. carinata has the pattern and coloration typical of those in the hobby, but remember that this is a very variable snake. Photo by I. Francais.

superciliosus Guenther, 1863, from Palau is a synonym. In 1956, Stull described the Solomons form as a new subspecies that she called *Enygrus carinatus paulsoni*, a name widely used in the hobby literature. McDowell (1979) believes that, much as in *C. bibroni*, variation in this species is not especially correlated with geography, populations showing almost random variation in most features of scalation and color pattern. There are, however, long-tailed and short-tailed forms of this species that may be correlated with geography, long-tailed forms coming mostly from the center of the range (New Guinea) and short-tailed forms mostly from the outlying islands. The Solomons are inhabited by the short-tailed form, but so are the Celebes and some parts of New Guinea. The two forms cannot be subspecies in the usual sense because they do not occupy geographically exclusive ranges. They also cannot be species because both forms occur in some areas, intermediates may be found in a few populations, and it might be that tail length represents a simple genetic dimorphism that is incomplete. The possibility that specimens of *carinata* are introduced in plants to new areas, thus confusing the distribution of the forms, has been suggested. McDowell does not recognize *paulsoni* as a distinct subspecies, which seems well in keeping with the available data, and hobbyists should stop using the name for specimens from the Solomons.

Over its range it may be terrestrial or arboreal but usually is found in low-lying areas. It adapts well to human presence and often is found in villages, feeding on lizards and rodents. It usually is a gentle snake, though it may either spread the neck when cornered or coil into a loose ball with the head in the center.

If it can be made to feed regularly, *C. carinata* is hardy and easy to care for. Keep it in a tall terrarium (it likes to climb on occasion) with many branches and hide boxes both on the ground and in the branches. Keeping the terrarium warm (over 28°C, 82°F) and humid is necessary. Specimens may insist on lizards as food, but many can be adapted to taking small rodents or pieces of mice instead.

Though males have large spurs, females of some populations lack spurs entirely, while they may occur in occasional females of other populations. Males may fight before mating. Litters are born after a five- or six-month pregnancy. The young, which may number from 10 to 60, usually about a dozen, are tiny, only 16 to 20 cm long and very slender. When touched they exhibit tetany, stretching out the body and going stiff. Their small size makes young very difficult to feed, and most die without eating.

Though this species has been bred by many hobbyists, most specimens seen still are wild-caught imports, and most young seen are the offspring of gravid imports. The small size of the young, as well as the dull colors of many adults, may be the main reason this species is not more popular.

Like the other members of the genus, *C. carinata* needs a warm, humid terrarium with a soft substrate. Cork bark or some other hiding area will be used extensively. Photo by W. P. Mara.

Genus Corallus Daudin, 1803 (*Revue encycl.*, [8] 5: 434). Type species by monotypy *Corallus obtusirostris* Daudin = *C. hortulanus*.

Synonyms: *Chrysenis* Gray, 1860 [*caninus*]; *Xenoboa* Hoge, 1953 [*cropani*]; *Xiphosoma* Wagler in Spix, 1824 [*caninus*].

Large, mostly arboreal boas with the head very distinct from the neck, the tail moderately long (more than 45 subcaudals) and prehensile. The body is oval to distinctly compressed and ridge-backed. The anterior teeth are long and curved, with heavy bases. The labials are deeply pitted, the body scales smooth (but sometimes wrinkled). The top of the head is covered with irregular but often large scales, the frontal not visible; often there are larger scales on the snout. Typically there are several enlarged scales in the loreal region, with a row of somewhat smaller scales separating them from the supralabials and continuing under the eye.

The hemipenis is weakly bilobed. The organ is naked or nearly so for only its proximal third, then it is covered with thick flounces and transverse ridges as well as large and small papillae. The sulcus forks in the distal third of the organ, the forks ending near the edges of the shallow arms. The chromosome number is derived in the two tested species, 2N=40 in *Corallus hortulanus* and 2N=44 in *Corallus caninus* (the basal number for the family is 2N=36).

Corallus is a quite distinct and specialized genus as shown by the deep labial pits and modified chromosome numbers. It might be confused with *Sanzinia*, which also is an arboreal green boa, but that species (in addition to exhibiting many differences in hemipenes, skeleton, and chromosome number) has small scales in the loreal area and a shorter tail, as well as having relatively more and smaller scales on top of the head. *Corallus* appears to be related to *Epicrates*, which has shallow labial pits, but that genus typically has a distinct frontal scale, other large scales on top of the head, and a long, horizontal loreal. *Xenoboa* was synonymized with *Corallus* by Kluge (1993), a move with which I definitely concur. For many years this genus was called *Boa*, while the real *Boa* was called *Constrictor*.

Key to the species of Corallus
 A. Tail long, with more than 100 subcaudals .... *hortulanus*
 AA. Tail shorter, with fewer than 85 subcaudals .... B
 B. Fewer than 55 subcaudals; middorsal scales in 30 rows .... *cropani*
 BB. More than 60 subcaudals; middorsal scales in more than 50 rows C
 C. Dorsal scales in more than 60 rows at midbody; adults bright green .... *caninus*
 CC. Dorsal scales in fewer than 60 rows at midbody; adults patterned .... *annulatus*

THE TRUE BOAS: BOIDAE

When keeping any of the *Corallus*, remember that these are snakes specialized for an arboreal lifestyle. Tall terraria with plenty of climbing branches are a must. This is the Garden Tree Boa, *C. hortulanus.* Photo by R. D. Bartlett

The common and scientific names for the Ringed Tree Boa, *C. annulatus*, come from the occellated pattern on the sides. However, in many specimens, the circles are broken or indistinct. Photo by P. Freed.

CORALLUS ANNULATUS

Ringed Tree Boa

Though it is widely distributed, the Ringed Tree Boa appears to be an uncommonly collected species that seldom enters the hobby and is poorly known even in collections. Its colors are dull and probably of little interest except to specialists.

The snout is deep, with a squarish profile. The rostral shield is visible from above and separates the nasal shields in front, while the nasals are in contact with two or three rather large internasals posteriorly. The scales on top of the head are large but irregular, with about 10 to 12 between the eyes and no distinct supraoculars. The eye is encircled by 12 or 13 small scales, including a rather large vertical preocular, and is not in contact with the supralabials. The nostril is situated among a nearly complete circle of three to five scales. Three or four enlarged loreal scales occupy the space between the posterior nasal and the preocular; beneath them is a row of three to five smaller scales separating the loreals from the supralabials. There are some 13 to 17 supralabials, though some may be variably fused, with deep pits between the scales. The dorsal scales are in 50 to 55 rows at midbody. There are 252 to 273 ventrals and 76 to 86 subcaudals.

Most specimens are gray to brown above, dirty yellow below. Over the sides are about 40 to 45 pairs of pale brick red ovals outlined with dark gray. They may be indistinct and almost disappear into the background, with only

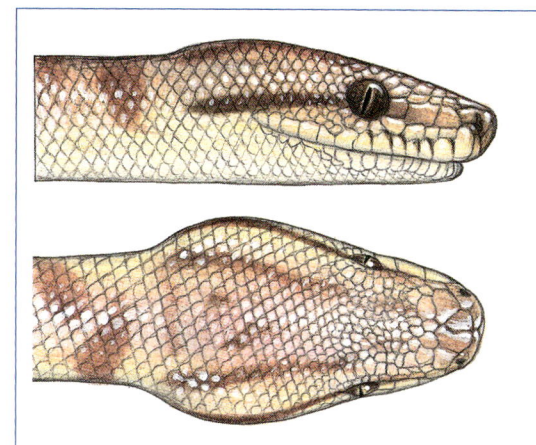

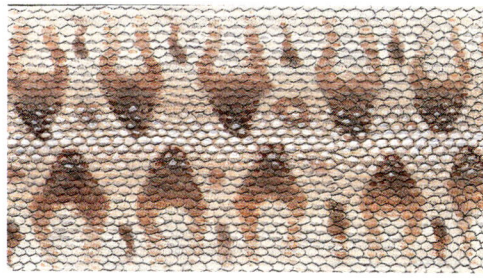

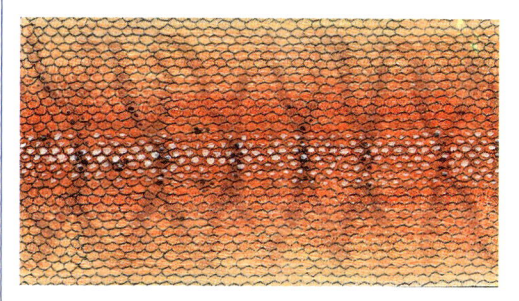

THE TRUE BOAS: BOIDAE

slightly paler centers, or in strong contrast with bright reddish centers containing a small white spot toward the tail. Commonly the ovals meet at the middle of the back. The belly and the head may be heavily marked with brown specks and blotches. Young may be bright red or almost black, assuming adult colors in about one to two years.

This is a fairly large species, with adults averaging about a meter in total length; the record may be 2 meters. The tail is about 18% of the total length.

The Ringed Tree Boa occurs from Nicaragua and Costa Rica in Central America (and perhaps north into Honduras and Guatemala) to Colombia and Ecuador in South America. It was first described by Cope in 1876 as *Xiphosoma annulatum* (*J. Acad. Nat. Sci. Philadelphia*, (2) 8: 129) from Costa Rica. Few specimens have accumulated in collections since then, and there has been no recent revision. Though three subspecies have been described,

Head and midbody views of *C. annulatus*.

A small percentage of Ringed Tree Boas are bright orange or orange-red, and the young can be very red. Most adults are much more gray or brown in color. Photo by R. D. Bartlett.

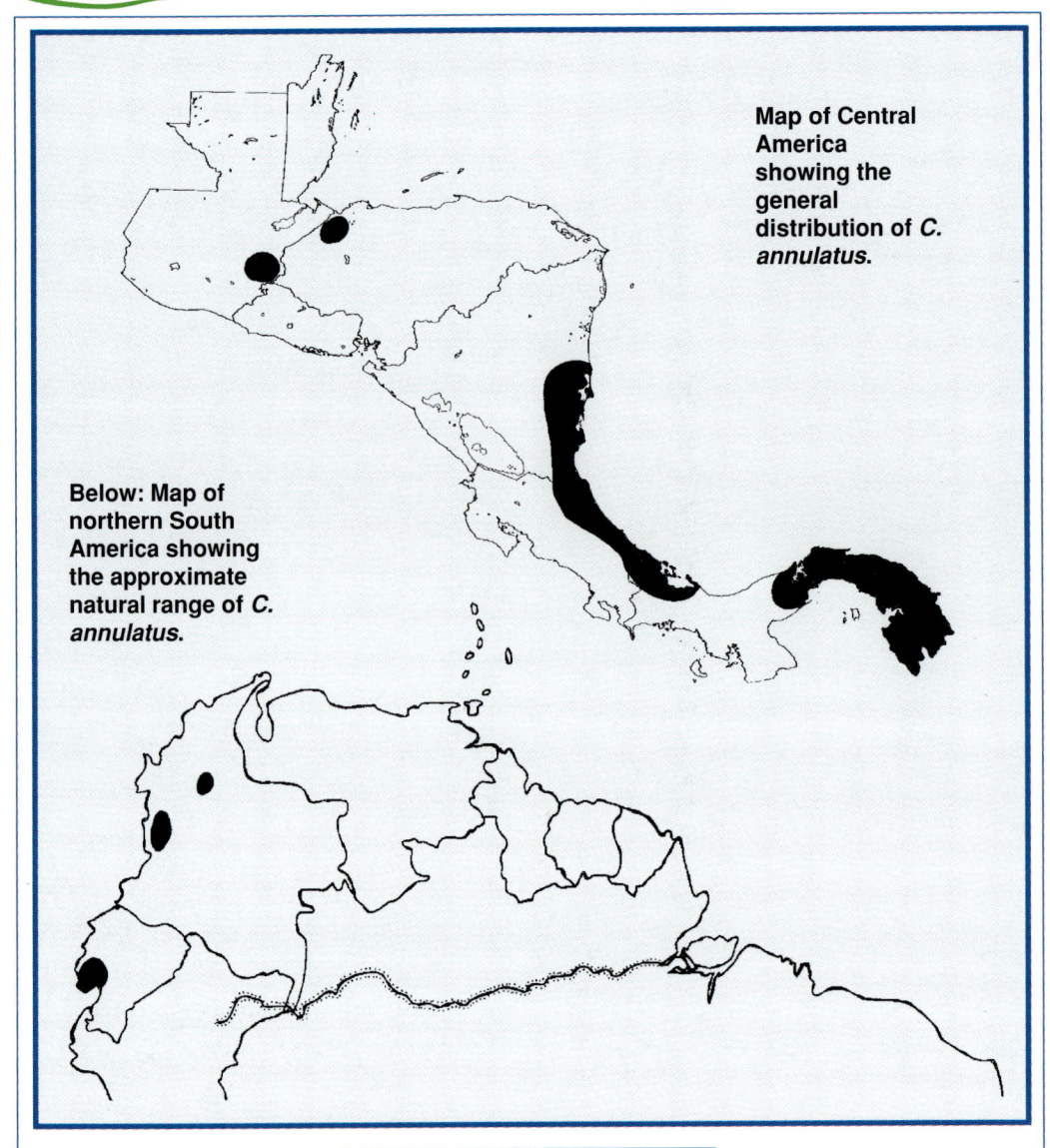

Map of Central America showing the general distribution of *C. annulatus*.

Below: Map of northern South America showing the approximate natural range of *C. annulatus*.

the two from South America (*blombergi* Rendahl and Vestergren, 1941, and *colombianus* Rendahl and Vestergren, 1940, both in the genus *Boa*) are based on very few specimens and were distinguished by subtle details of rostral scalation that do not appear to hold. Peters (1957) did point out a tentative difference between Central American and South American specimens that might be used as a subspecific character: in Central American specimens the scales below the loreals (the infraloreals) run from the nasal to the preocular; in South American specimens the infraloreals are blocked from the nasal by contact between the third upper labial and the anterior loreal. This might indicate that two subspecies could be recognized: *C. a. annulatus* from Central America into northern Colom-

THE TRUE BOAS: BOIDAE

bia, and *C. a. colombianus* from the rest of the South American range. More specimens are needed to understand the situation, and it has been stated that more than one species is hiding under this name.

Little is reported on the natural history of this species, and it seldom has been maintained by private hobbyists. It is arboreal, secretive, and occurs in both dense and open forests. It probably comes to the ground at night to search for the mammals and birds that comprise the diet. It has managed to survive in Central American banana plantations and has lived for over 12 years in captivity. Though it has been bred by a few zoos, it is almost unavailable to the average hobbyist. Litters contain 8 to 13 young mostly born from August to October after a winter mating.

C. annulatus, like other members of the genus, have relatively large eyes, a definite benefit to a nocturnal, arboreal hunter. Photo by W. Wüster.

CORALLUS CANINUS

Emerald Tree Boa

Every hobbyist knows the Emerald Tree Boa, though they may on occasion confuse it with the superficially similar Green

The fragmented distribution of *C. annulatus* could be the result of inadequate collecting. At this time it is impossible to reliably say if there are valid subspecies or even if all the known specimens belong to one species. Photo by W. Wüster.

Although Emerald Tree Boas are beautiful, they are also delicate, expensive, and often aggressive. Consider these factors carefully before purchasing one. Photo by R. D. Bartlett.

Tree Python, *Python viridis*, from New Guinea. (Look at the snout; in *viridis* it is covered with tiny scales and one pair of internasals, while in *caninus* there are several larger scales on the snout; the pits of *viridis* are very deep and distort the anterior profile, raising the nasal area well above the level of the snout.)

The body is compressed, with a ridge-backed shape. The rostral shield is barely visible from above and is followed by the nasals, which are nearly in contact but separated by a pair of small internasals. Behind these there may be a pair of prefrontals or just a mixture of large irregular scales. There may be a large supraocular or it may be split into smaller scales. Commonly there are 9 to 15 scales between the eyes and 10 to 14 around the eye, the eye not in contact with the supralabials. Usually there are three or four squarish loreals between the nasal and the large preocular, with a row of smaller scales separating the posterior loreals from the supralabials. There are 12 to 14 supralabials with deep pits between the scales and about 14 infralabials, most with deep pits on the sutures. The dorsal scales are in 61 to 74 rows at midbody. There are 188 to 219 ventrals and 64 to 79 subcaudals.

THE TRUE BOAS: BOIDAE

Adults are bright green above and yellow below, but they vary greatly in details of coloration. Usually there are narrow white lines a scale or so wide and only 5 to 12 scales long over the center of the back, but these may be absent or widened into small diamonds and even connected by a narrow white middorsal stripe; they may be outlined with black head may be the last part to change.

This is a large tree-boa, with adults commonly 1.5 to 2 meters in length. The record appears to be about 3 meters. The tail is about 15% of the total length.

Though it seldom is locally common, the Emerald Tree Boa is one of the most widely distributed South American snakes, ranging

Despite their usual sluggishness, Emerald Tree Boas are watchful and alert, striking at any nearby movement. Their enlarged and recurved anterior teeth can produce bad bites. Photo by K. H. Switak.

or not. There may be large round white spots on the lower side, these often outlined with black or dark green. The newborns are very different in color, being bright reddish brown or orange with distinct white cross-bands over the back. Over their first 18 months or so they gradually get spots of green on the back, often one scale at a time, until the body turns more green than red. The through rainforest situations of the Amazon and related basins from Colombia and Ecuador to the Guianas and south to northern Bolivia. First described by Linnaeus in 1758 (*Systema Naturae*, Ed. 10, 1: 215) as *Boa canina*, it accumulated many synonyms before the change in colors was understood. These include: *hipnale* Linnaeus, 1758; *thalassina* Laurenti, 1768;

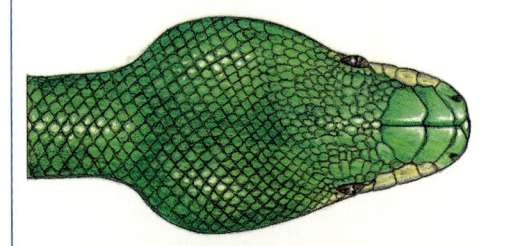

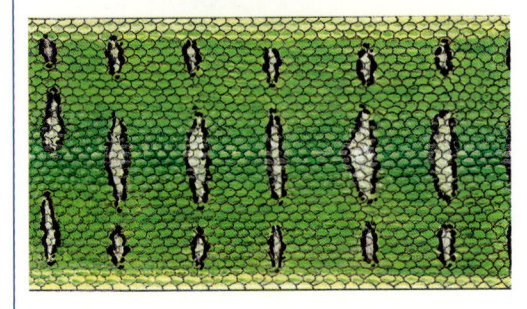

Head and midbody views of C. caninus.

aurantiaca Laurenti, 1768; *exigua* Laurenti, 1768; *araramboya* Wagler in Spix, 1824; and *batesi* Gray, 1860. No subspecies are recognized.

Emerald Tree Boas have become rather common in the terrarium hobby and now are bred in decent numbers. In nature they are arboreal as adults, though the young may stay nearer the ground, moving higher into the trees as they become greener. The snakes spend most of the day resting in a flat coil with the head in the center, almost invisible against the leaves of the trees. They feed on mammals and birds that are grabbed with the large front teeth (which can penetrate feathers with ease) and then constricted. Feeding occurs mostly at night, when the snake may come to the ground to look

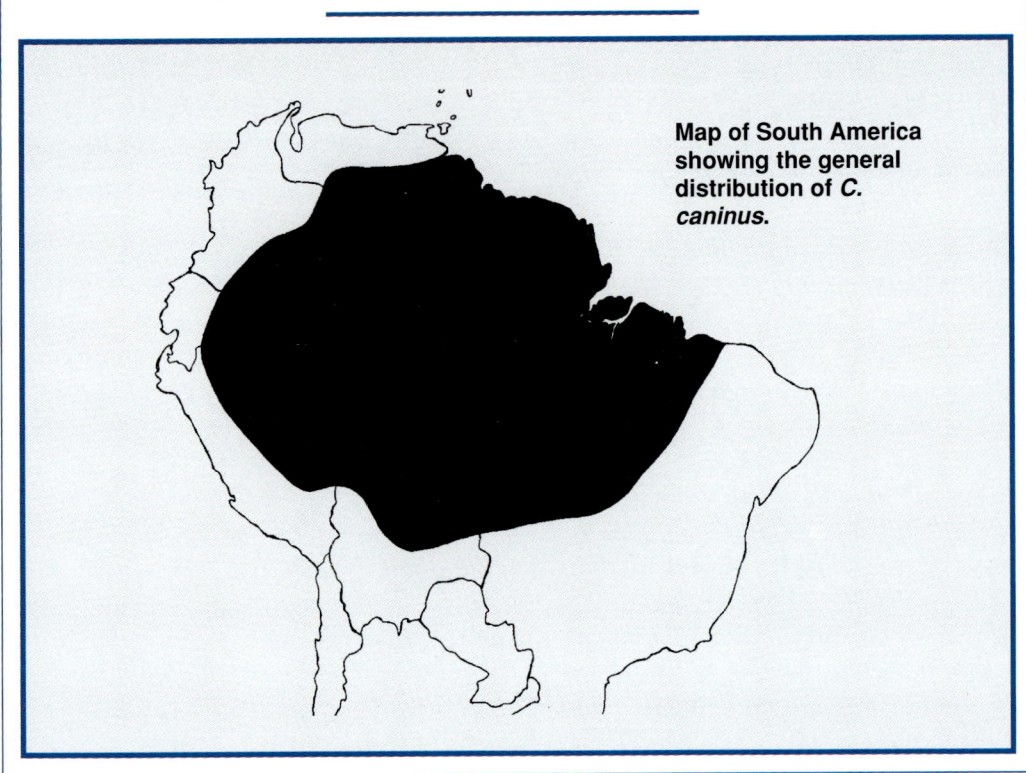

Map of South America showing the general distribution of *C. caninus*.

THE TRUE BOAS: BOIDAE

Neonatal Emerald Tree Boas can be red, yellow, or green, with two or three colors sometimes occurring in the same litter. Breeders are now selecting for individuals that retain the juvenile colors. Photo by R. B. Bartlett.

for prey. They also swim well. Though relatively complacent, they may be quick to strike and can produce deep lacerations with much blood and pain.

These tree boas, like other arboreal boas and pythons, are best kept in a tall terrarium heavily planted or with many climbing branches. The humidity should be kept high, over 70%, and the daytime temperature may vary between about 26°C (79°F) and 32°C (90°F), dropping a bit at night. A basking light will be used, especially by pregnant females. Spray or mist the tank each day both to help maintain humidity and also so the snake can drink; few Emeralds recognize a water bowl. The terrarium should be well ventilated and not allowed to become stagnant. Wild-caught specimens may be heavily parasitized and stressed, and they may refuse to eat. Captive-breds generally eat most rodents and birds offered by the keeper. Because they are inactive snakes, do not over-feed; a good meal every

Occasionally odd variants of snakes turn up. This Emerald Tree Boa has a very odd pale coloration, although the mother appeared normal. Photo by K. H. Switak.

other week is sufficient, and specimens often fast for a month or more without bad effects.

Breeding may be induced at any time of the year, though most keepers tend to keep the snakes a bit drier and cooler during the winter and then put the sexes together to mate in the spring. Males tend to be smaller than females and have larger spurs.

Emerald Tree Boas require very high levels of humidity. Frequent misting and a moisture-retaining substrate are necessary for successful keeping. Photo by I. Francais.

Pregnancy lasts about seven months, with an autumn delivery of litters of some 8 to 15 young each about 45 cm long. The young commonly will take pinkies after their first shed, but some may prefer lizards for a few weeks. As mentioned, most newborns are red or orange, but some may be green, yellow, or combinations of all these colors. Sexual maturity is reached in about three to four years, with specimens commonly living 10 to 15 years.

Because captive-bred young now are widely available, it is best to start with a reddish specimen that is known to be feeding. Keeping these snakes may require quite a bit of hardware, including misting systems and specially built terraria, and you would be well off having a long talk with breeders before trying this species. Many people have excellent luck with Emerald Tree Boas, but others probably just do not have the time or patience to successfully maintain the species.

CORALLUS CROPANI

Hoge's Boa

For many years a mystery snake, Hoge's Boa was described as a distinct genus, *Xenoboa*, and at various times postulated to be

THE TRUE BOAS: BOIDAE

The most obvious detail on heads of Emerald Tree Boas are the grossly enlarged pits. This feature is found in the other members of the genus and the arboreally specialized Green Tree Python, *P. viridis*, as well. The pits contain heat-sensitive tissue enabling them to locate warm-blooded prey with great accuracy even in total darkness. *above:* Lateral view of head. Photo by W. Wüster. *below:* Ventrolateral view of head. Photo by R. D. Bartlett.

Head and midbody views of *C. cropani*

related to *Epicrates* and *Corallus*, but today it seems pretty certain that is a *Corallus* perhaps related to the Emerald Tree-Boa.

A stout-bodied snake with a short but prehensile tail and a wide head distinct from the neck. The internasals and anterior prefrontals are relatively large and distinct. There are about nine scales across the head between the eyes, including moderately enlarged supraoculars. There is a large preocular and a single squarish loreal separated from the supralabials by a row of smaller scales. A circle of about nine scales rings the eye, which is not in contact with the supralabials. There are 13 or 14 supralabials with deep pits between them and about 14 infralabials, the posterior one irregularly fused, with shallow pits between the infralabials. The scales are in about 30 rows at midbody, the lowest count for the genus. There are 179 ventrals and 52 subcaudals.

Adults are dull olive-green with about 40 distinctly diamond-shaped dark brown spots over the midline of the back and smaller spots alternating on the lower sides. The diamonds may be very indistinct and fused into an irregular zigzag stripe over part of the back. There are pale scales outlining most of the diamonds and dark scales speckling the interspaces and also the top of the head. The large scales of the back appear to be outlined with dark brown, and the lip scales are outlined with dark brown also. The belly is dirty yellowish white with faint brown smudges anteriorly, becoming darker posteriorly and mostly dark brown with pale

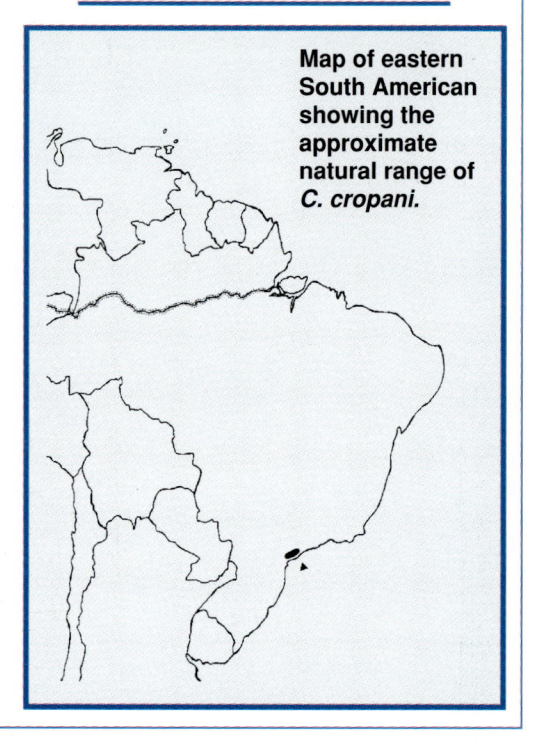

Map of eastern South American showing the approximate natural range of *C. cropani.*

THE TRUE BOAS: BOIDAE

Views of a preserved specimen of Hoge's Boa. The coloration is somewhat faded from life. *top*: Dorsolateral view of the head. As with the other members of the genus, Hoge's Boa has greatly enlarged labial pits. *center*: Ventral view of head. Note the deep and darkly pigmented mental groove. *bottom*: Lateral view of the body. Hoge's Boa has rather enlarged scales, resembling those of a fish. This is a feature not otherwise found in the genus. All photos by M. Walls, courtesy of the American Museum of Natural History.

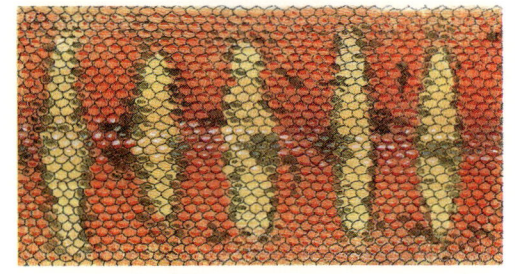

It is unfortunate that Hoge's Boa occurred in so small an area, as its habitat has succumbed to development. This species is in all likelihood extinct. Photo by M. Walls, courtesy of the American Museum of Natural History.

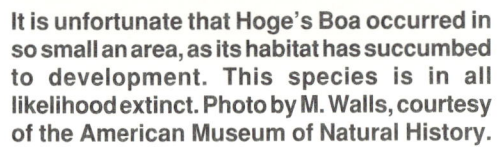

Head and midbody views of *C. hortulanus*.

smudges on the back half and under the tail.

The type was almost 1.3 meters long. The tail is 13% of the total length.

Possibly extinct, this very distinctive species is known from only a few specimens collected near Miracatu and Pedro de Toledo in Sao Paulo State, southern Brazil. It occupies (or occupied, as the case may be) the smallest range of any South American boid, only some 600 square kilometers. Virtually nothing is known of its natural history, but it probably is not dissimilar to the other treeboas.

CORALLUS HORTULANUS

Garden Tree Boa

I realize that the use of the name *hortulanus* for this species, more familiarly known as *enydris* for the last 60 years, is unusual. When the species was described by Linnaeus in 1758 (*Systema Naturae*, Ed. 10, 1: 215), on the same page he described both *Boa hortulana* and *Boa enydris*. Both names represent the same species, which was realized at an early date. The classic catalogs of the last century used *hortulanus* in preference to *enydris*. The name was changed to *enydris* by Stull in her 1935 checklist of the boids, apparently on the basis of what used to be called line priority; i.e., *enydris* was described on line 32 of page 215 in Linnaeus, while *hortulanus* was described on line 36. At the time this step was approved by the rules, though rather stupid and anal retentive it seems to me, but today situations such as this must be judged on the basis of first reviser; i.e., who first selected one name over the other (also rather stupid in my

THE TRUE BOAS: BOIDAE

Coloration and pattern vary widely in the Garden Tree Boa. Virtually no two are identical, and this species occurs in a large range of colors. Some are very bright and vivid like the specimen above. This individual was collected in the Amazon Basin. Others are brown with or without a contrasting pattern. The genetics of color and pattern inheritance in this species are poorly understood. Top photo by K. H. Switak. Bottom photo by R. D. Bartlett.

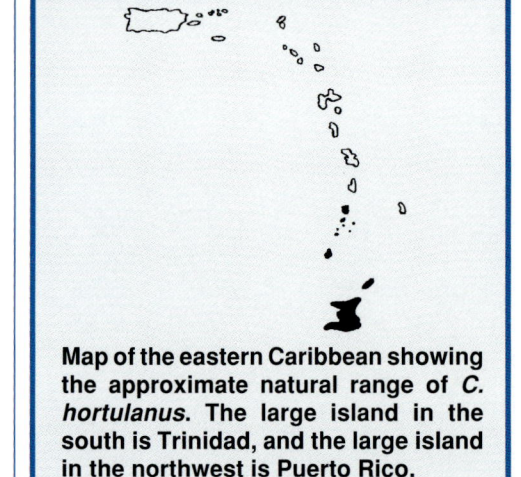

Map of the eastern Caribbean showing the approximate natural range of *C. hortulanus*. The large island in the south is Trinidad, and the large island in the northwest is Puerto Rico.

opinion). For a full discussion of this problem, see McDiarmid, Toure, & Savage, 1996, *J. Herpetology*, 30 (3): 320-326. It would appear that Stull should never have changed the name to begin with and that the correct solution is to return to the once-familiar name *hortulanus* for the Garden Tree Boa.

Map of Central America showing the general distribution of *C. hortulanus*.

This is a slender, ridge-backed tree boa with a very wide head and slender neck. The nasals are in touch with each other behind the rostral, not separated by small scales. A pair of rather large internasals or prefrontals lies to the back of the nasals, and there usually is a small pair of posterior prefrontals behind these. There are some 12 to 15 scales between the eyes (sometimes with a slightly enlarged supraocular on each side) and 12 to 17 scales around the eye, which is separated from the supralabials. The large vertical preocular and two large rather oval loreals follow the nasal. There are 11 to 15 supralabials with deep pits between the scales from under the eye back. There are about 17 to 20 infralabials (the posterior one often small and crowded), the anterior ones weakly pitted, but those beneath the eye with fairly deep pits. The dorsal scales are in 38 to 59 rows at midbody. There are 253 to 299 ventrals and 103 to 130 subcaudals.

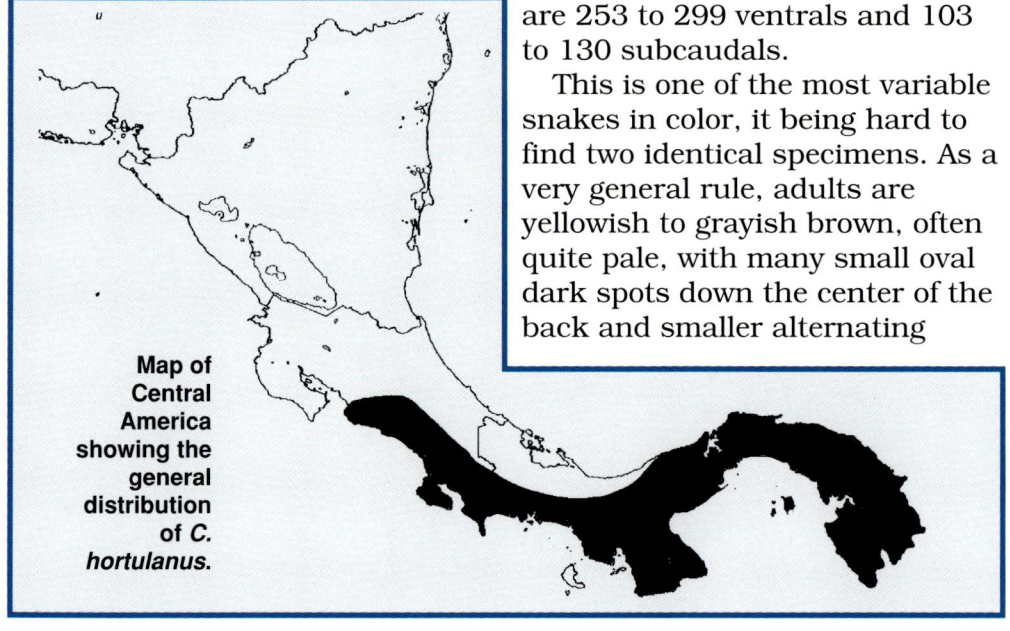

This is one of the most variable snakes in color, it being hard to find two identical specimens. As a very general rule, adults are yellowish to grayish brown, often quite pale, with many small oval dark spots down the center of the back and smaller alternating

THE TRUE BOAS: BOIDAE

Although they may rest motionless through the day, Garden Tree Boas actively patrol their habitat of branches at night searching for prey. They are generalist feeders eating mammals, birds, lizards, and frogs. Photo by P. Freed.

(often diamond-shaped) spots on the lower side. Commonly the dorsal spots (and lateral spots) have paler centers. Often the dark outlining is on a scale by scale basis, giving the appearance of individual brown scales arranged in a circle. The belly is grayish yellow to whitish, with few or many dark blotches. Occasionally there are bright red colors in the pattern, and the dorsal circles may be outlined with bright red or yellow. The top of the head is heavily marked with blackish irregular lines in most specimens, with distinct dark stripes running back from the eye to the corner of the mouth and outlined above with white and a second stripe or pair of stripes separated by white from the top of the eye to the bulge of the head. The lips are

Map of South America indicating the approximate range of *C. hortulanus*.

Some Garden Tree Boas are nearly solid in color with few or no spots or rings. Pale yellow to tan specimens appear rather commonly in the hobby. Photo by I. Francais.

The Garden Tree Boa ranges from Costa Rica (and Nicaragua?) in Central America over most of northern South America, south to Bolivia and southern Brazil. It also occurs in the Guianas and Venezuela and Colombia, plus Trinidad and Tobago. Additionally, it is common in the Windward Islands of the southern Caribbean, St. Vincent and Grenada and the Grenadines. Two subspecies are recognized by many workers though others feel that the species is too variable to allow recognition of subspecies. The distinctions are strictly those of scale counts, not coloration. *C. h. hortulanus* occurs over most of South America from southern Venezuela and the Guianas over the Amazon basin to Peru and Bolivia. It has more than 50 middorsal scale rows (fewer in *cooki*) and tends to have somewhat more ventrals than the other subspecies (about 270 to 299 in *hortulanus* versus 253 to about 285 in *cooki*). The northern subspecies, *C. h. cooki* Gray, 1842,

pale, whitish to reddish, with black spots and lines. The extremes of pattern in this species, however, may range from uniformly reddish above and below (the reddish belly in young) to deep blackish brown with black spots outlined with bright red or yellow. Any and all color patterns may occur in one litter.

Adults commonly are a meter in length. The maximum length is about 2.5 meters. The tail is 15 to 20% of the total length.

THE TRUE BOAS: BOIDAE

This specimen from Costa Rica shows just how drab Garden Tree Boas can be. However, note that the caudal end of this animal becomes black, which is unusual in the species. Photo by P. Freed.

ranges over Central America through northern Colombia and Venezuela into the Caribbean islands; it may also occur in the Guianas or this may represent an intergrade area with the nominate subspecies. The scale count differences are not separated by a gap in counts, and it is possible to find virtually identical specimens at one locality (as in the Guianas) with scale counts agreeing with both taxa. The scale counts seem to be lowest in the Windward Islands, where few specimens have more than 45 scale rows. Efforts to distinguish the subspecies on the basis of color or pat-

It is often said the elongated, recurved teeth of *C. hortulanus* are an adaptation for eating birds, but research suggests that this species preys more heavily on mammals than birds. Photo by R. D. Bartlett.

Neonatal Garden Tree Boas are often difficult to feed. Feeding frogs or small geckos may tempt them if they are not accepting rodents. Some may require force-feeding. Photo by R. D. Bartlett.

tern have failed. It probably would be best not to recognize subspecies in the Garden Tree-Boa, but the species presently is being revised. The prominent dark stripes back from the eye usually will identify most specimens of this boa.

As this book was being prepared for press, the revision by Henderson of this species was received (*Carib. J. sci.*, 33 [3/4]: 198-221, Dec. 1997). based on the study of 600 specimens from the entire range, and including an analysis of scalation, color, pattern, and gene sequencing, Henderson recognizes four species within *C. hortulanus* in the broad sense:

C. hortulanus (Linnaeus, 1758) in the restricted sense is found from southern Colombia to Brazil and Bolivia, plus the Guianas.

C. cooki Gray, 1842, restricted to St. Vincent, is always dull in color with an irregular hourglass pattern.

C. grenadensis (Barbour, 1914) occurs on the islands of the Grenada Bank.

C. ruschenburgeri (Cope, 1876) is the form of Central America and northwestern South America, from Costa Rica to the Orinoco delta, including Trinidad and Tobago.

THE TRUE BOAS: BOIDAE

Single specimens of all these species are difficult or impossible to distinguish visually without scale counts and a knowledge of locality. They probably have been hybridized in the terrarium hobby. Hobbyists perhaps are better off continuing to treat *C. hortulanus* as a single species, but be sure to interbreed only specimens from the same locality. All four species (except perhaps true *C. cooki* from St. Vincent) seem to be available in the hobby.

It should be noted that a major problem exists with Henderson's use of the name *cooki*, as the holotype, from an unknown locality, does not agree with specimens from St. Vincent, and Henderson's usage of the name is easily challenged. Additionally, some populations of Garden Tree Boas from tropical South America do not fit the diagnosis of *C. hortulanus* as restricted by Henderson. The separation of *C. ruschenbergeri* and *C. grenadensis* also is not as simple and clean as Henderson implies, being based on maximum size and relative rarity of certain dorsal patterns.

Hobbyists should read Heanderson's paper in detail before blindly accepting his conclusions.

Synonyms include: *enydris* (Linnaeus, 1758); *bitis* (Laurenti, 1768); *madarensis* (Laurenti, 1768); *merremi* (Sentzen in Meyer, 1796); *obtusirostris* Daudin, 1803; *ornatum* (Wagler in Spix, 1824); *dorsuale* (Wagler in Spix, 1824); *modesta* (Reuss, 1834); and

Preferring to stay high up at the top of a cage, Garden Tree Boas will come down to soak in the water bowl occasionally. They usually do this right before a shed. Photo by R. D. Bartlett.

maculatus Gray, 1842. Several of these names were based on specimens from unknown localities; they are not placed in the paper by Henderson.

This is a very adaptable boa that is found from deep moist rainforest to dry scrubby savanna with few trees. Usually it prefers drier conditions than Emerald Tree Boas, and it can adjust easily to disturbed conditions, including human gardens, fields, villages, and plantations and orchards.

a tall terrarium that is heavily planted or has many branches. Because this species is not really a rainforest species, it needs a bit less humidity than the Emerald and tolerates more variation in temperature. Small specimens can be kept in rather small terraria, but try to keep each specimen separately to prevent fights and to make the monitoring of feeding easier. Provide hide boxes both on the bottom of the terrarium and in the branches.

The Garden Tree Boa is less dependent on high humidity than the other *Corallus*. In the terrarium, the humidity can safely drop below 60% at times. Photo by R. D. Bartlett.

Like other boas, it is nocturnal and not likely to be seen during the day, when it rests in trees and shrubs. At night it feeds on birds (especially when young), mammals, and lizards, depending on what is available locally.

Specimens born in captivity are readily available, though the species does not seem to be that popular with hobbyists. Keep it in

Full-spectrum fluorescent lights and a small basking light complete the setup, except for a large water bowl and perhaps a misting system. The cage should be misted daily, especially if you realize that your specimen does not recognize water in a bowl. Young specimens may prefer to feed on lizards and frogs instead of small rodents, and it may take

THE TRUE BOAS: BOIDAE

some effort to get them to feed on pinkies. Breeding may occur at any time of the year, but most hobbyists try to condition the specimens for a spring mating. Brumation is not required, but usually the snakes breed better if the hours of light are shortened a bit and the cage is drier during the winter. In the spring increase the light and spray the specimens heavily as a breeding incentive. Males may fight, so the specimens are kept separately until ready for breeding, when usually the male is put in the female's cage after she sheds. Pregnant females bask often and feed heavily. Pregnancy lasts about seven months, with births commonly from October to December. Litters may include from four to 14 young (sometimes to 20) about 30 to 38 cm long. The colors and patterns of the young cannot be predicted and may not be related to the colors of the parents. Young may take pinkies after their first shed at two to three weeks of age, or they may need frogs or lizards as a first food. Sexual maturity is attained in about four years, specimens living for 10 to 15 years.

Though slender and not as heavy as many other boas, the Garden Tree Boa can be a very

Example of the great range of colors and patterns in *C. hortulanus*. Such extreme variations in individuals can occur in one litter. Photo by V. Jirousek.

nervous charge and may strike at slight movements. Its teeth are just as large and curved as in the other tree boas, and it can produce bad bites.

Genus Epicrates Wagler, 1830 (*Nat. Syst. Amph.*: 168). Type species by subsequent designation *Boa cenchria* Linnaeus.

Synonyms: *Boella* Smith & Chiszar, 1992 [*inornatus*]; *Chilabothrus* Dumeril & Bibron, 1844 [*inornatus*]; *Cliftia* Gray, 1849 [*cenchria maurus*]; *Epicarsius* Fischer, 1856 [*cenchria maurus*]; *Homalochilus* Fischer, 1856 [*striatus*]; *Piesigaster* Seoane, 1880 [*inornatus*].

The species of *Epicrates* are medium to large boas that may be terrestrial or arboreal. The head usually has distinct internasals and prefrontals, with the frontal and supraoculars distinct in most species. The loreal usually is a long, horizontal scale that contacts the supralabials anteriorly but is separated from them posteriorly by a row of small scales. The upper labials commonly bear shallow pits that may be difficult to see. The dorsal scales are smooth. The tail is moderately long, prehensile, with over 45 subcaudals.

The hemipenis is deeply bilobed, with the proximal third of the shaft naked, the next third with several thick flounces, and the arms with papillae. The sulcus spermaticus forks at about two-thirds the length of the organ, its forks extending to the tips of the arms. The sulcus may lie on a smooth fold for its entire length.

Epicrates is mostly a Caribbean genus, with 10 of the 11 species I recognize here being restricted to the islands. Only one species, *E. cenchria*, occurs on the American mainland, and it is distinctive in both coloration and scalation. If only *cenchria* were in *Epicrates* and the island species were referred to *Chilabothrus*, it would be much easier to define and recognize the genus. The long loreal usually allows the genus to be recognized, however. *Epicrates* appears to be closely related to *Corallus*, with more distinct head shields and less developed labial pits. Some of the arboreal species of *Epicrates* bear a striking resemblance to *Corallus hortulanus*.

For full keys and information on the Caribbean *Epicrates*, see the book by Tolson and Henderson (1993). The key that follows has been simplified and may not work in the absence of locality data and comparative specimens.

Key to the species of Epicrates

A. Dorsal scales in about 45 to 51 rows at midbody; ventrals fewer than 270; head shields broken, with several small scales between the supraoculars; head with a black middorsal stripe and two stripes behind the eye, at least in juveniles .... *cenchria*

AA. Dorsal scales in over 50 rows at midbody; ventrals more than 270; head shields varied, but typically with a frontal scale (may be split), large supraoculars, and distinct prefrontals; head seldom with a distinct black middorsal stripe .... B

THE TRUE BOAS: BOIDAE

The most common *Epicrates* in the hobby is also one of the most beautiful. The Rainbow Boa, *E. cenchria*, is bred in substantial numbers by hobbyists and commercial breeders. Photo by A. Both.

B. Eye separated from supralabials by small scales; subcaudals 45 to 55; typically more than 55 middorsal scale rows .... *angulifer*

BB. Eye in contact with at least one supraocular; scale counts higher C

C. Between the supraoculars there are 2 scales anteriorly, 1 scale at the middle, and 2 scales posteriorly (formula 2-1-2) .... D

CC. Formula not as above .... E

D. Usually 9 scales in a circle around the eye; over 350 scales under body plus tail; Jamaica .... *subflavus*

DD. Usually only 8 scales in a circle around the eye; fewer than 350 total scales under body and tail; Puerto Rico .... *inornatus*

E. Scale rows at neck usually more than 40 (34 to 49); ventrals plus subcaudals about 345 to 390; Hispaniola .... *striatus*

EE. Scale rows at neck usually fewer than 40 (28 to 42); ventrals plus subcaudals about 305 to 400 .... F

F. Supraocular formula 4-1-2; ventrals plus subcaudals more than 350 .... *gracilis*

FF. Supraocular formula seldom 4-1-2; ventrals plus subcaudals fewer than 350 ...... G

G. Dorsal scale rows usually fewer than 40 at midbody .... H

GG. Dorsal scale rows usually more than 40 at midbody I

H. Hispaniola; supraocular formula 3-1-3 .... *fordi*

HH. Bahamas; supraocular formula 5-2-4 .... *exsul*

I. Ventrals plus subcaudals fewer than 340 (to over 360 in one subspecies); supraocular formula 3-2-3 .... *chrysogaster*

II. Ventrals plus subcaudals about 340 to 350; supraocular formula 3-1-X........................... J

J. Mona Island; supraocular formula 3-1-3; dorsal scale rows at midbody 39 to 42; fewer than 60 dark blotches on body .... *monensis*

JJ. Tortola and Virgin Islands; supraocular formula 3-1-5; dorsal scale rows at midbody 41 to 47; over 60 dark blotches on body................................. *granti*

EPICRATES ANGULIFER

Cuban Slender Boa

The only Cuban slender boa, this is a large species in which the supralabials are separated from the eye by suboculars, a unique character in the genus.

Dorsal scales 44 to 55 on neck, 53 to 69 at midbody. Supraocular formula 3-3-4. Usually 14 supralabials. Ventrals 268 to 292, subcaudals 45 to 55.

Head and midbody views of *E. angulifer*.

THE TRUE BOAS: BOIDAE

Young specimens of the Cuban Slender Boa have a more contrasting pattern than the adults, but the adults are still very pretty animals with intricate markings. Photo by W. P. Mara.

Usually some 42 to 65 brown blotches on the body, with vertically elongated alternating blotches on the sides. The blotches typically are outlined with white, but often the entire pattern is faded and not distinguishable from the background color. The head is brown and usually unmarked (sometimes with a dark blotch posteriorly).

The belly is yellowish, strongly clouded with gray posteriorly.

A large species, *Epicrates angulifer* reaches at least 5 meters in length but always remains relatively slender.

This species is found through most of Cuba and the outlying islands. It was described by Bibron in Sagra in 1843 (*Hist. Phys. Polit. Nat., Cuba, Rept.*:

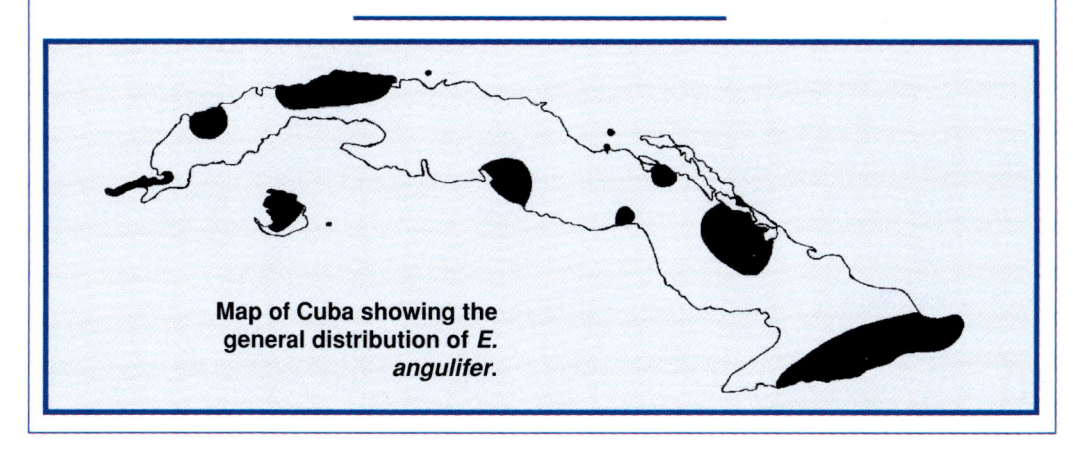

Map of Cuba showing the general distribution of *E. angulifer*.

THE LIVING BOAS

Because of import restrictions, Cuban Slender Boas have never become common in the American hobby. They are bred in small numbers which represent the only legal new specimens entering the hobby. Photo by R. D. Bartlett.

dents, while young prefer lizards. Males fight before mating, which occurs in the spring. Young are born in the autumn. Newborns are 65 to 72 cm long.

Though it may be locally common where protected in Cuba, it has lost much of its range to agriculture and random killing by residents. It usually is not available to hobbyists.

215). It inhabits open, rather dry wooded situations and often is found in caves and in rocky areas as well as in palm stumps. Adults feed on bats, chickens, and ro-

EPICRATES CENCHRIA

Rainbow Slender Boa

The Rainbow Slender Boa, more familiarly just called the Rainbow

Like the Rainbow Boa, Cuban Slender Boas can have a splendid iridescent sheen to their scales. This is a half-grown animal, approximately 2.2 meters / 7 feet long. Photo by K. H. Switak.

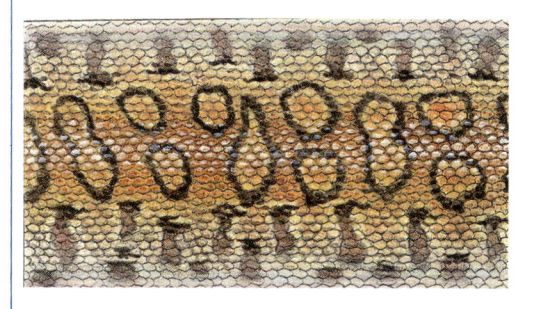

THE TRUE BOAS: BOIDAE

105

Head and midbody views of *E. cenchria*. This one fits the description of *E. c. cenchria*.

Head and midbody views of the Argentine subspecies, *E. c. alvarezi*.

Head and midbody views of *E. c. assisi*.

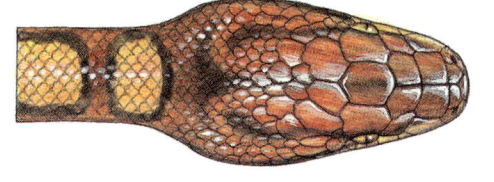

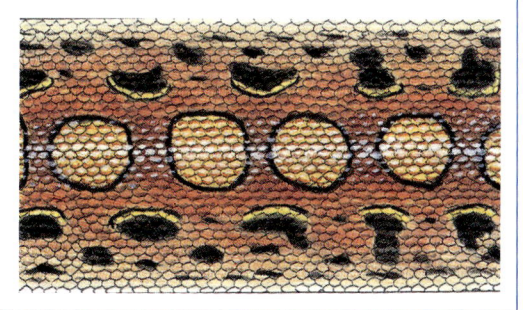

Midbody pattern of the Paraguayan Rainbow Boa, *E. c. crassus*.

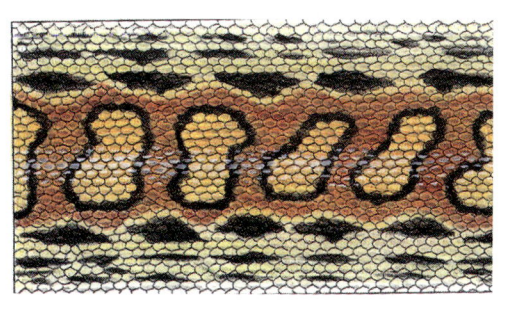

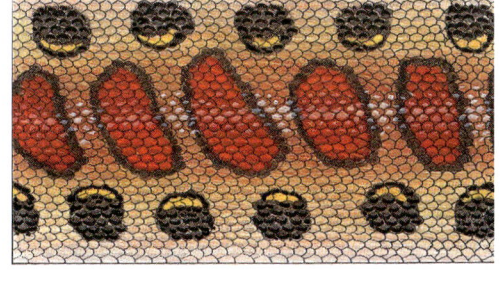

Above: Because Brazil does not export its fauna, *E. c. assisi*, **coming from the northeastern section of the country, is a true rarity in the herp hobby. The legality of specimens offered for sale is questionable. Photo by W. Wüster.**

Map of Central America showing the approximate natural range of *E. cenchria.*

Boa, is one of the more familiar American boas and one of the most beautiful. The only mainland species of *Epicrates*, it also is the type species of the genus and quite different from the other species put here (though many Caribbean species still retain the distinctive head pattern of, in part, two black stripes back from the eye). It can be distinguished from other boas by the head pattern of five black stripes, the weakly pitted labials, the open and often ocellated spots on the side, and the iridescent color.

The rostral shield is just visible from above and is followed by a pair of nasals that meet at the midline. Behind them is a pair of large internasals and usually a large median scale that commonly is called an azygous prefrontal.

THE TRUE BOAS: BOIDAE

There may be small scales between the prefrontal and the internasals. The remaining scales on top of the head are very variable, but there is no recognizable frontal; a supraocular may be present, but more typically it is broken into two or three smaller scales. The loreal usually is a single elongated, rather rectangular scale between the posterior nasal and a large prefrontal; it may be broken into two scales. Below the loreal is a series of smaller infraloreals separating the loreal from the supralabials. There are 11 to 15 supralabials

The Paraguayan subspecies, *E. c. crassus*, is in the hands of few hobbyists. Although it lacks the brilliant colors of some of the subspecies, it has an attractive pattern. Photo by P. Freed.

Map of South America showing the general range of *E. cenchria*.

and 14 or 15 infralabials. Two supralabials enter the bottom of the eye. The labials have shallow pits in the sutures between them. The midbody scales are in 43 to 51 rows, are smooth, and are highly iridescent. There are 223 to 275 ventrals and 50 to 66 subcaudals.

Details of the color and pattern vary with geography and often with age, but in the most fully developed patterns the boa is an iridescent pale brown

Perhaps the most distinct form of Rainbow Boa is the Colombian subspecies, *E. c. maurus*. This form may represent a full species, as it is known to occur with *E. c. cenchria* but does not appear to intergrade. Photo by W. Wüster.

above and white below. The head is marked with five black stripes, including a median stripe and two stripes back from the eye (much as in some *Eunectes*); the lips are whitish, sometimes with weak brown stripes. Down the center of the back runs a row of large pale orange ocelli bordered by narrow black rings. On the side are black spots or lozenges bordered by pale orange and then by black; when fully developed these spots are orange with black centers and outer rings. Often the lateral spots are incomplete and they may be fused into long or short black and orange stripes on the neck and anterior sides. The pattern may be clearest in juveniles, fading or becoming irregular in adults.

Adults commonly are 1 to 1.5 meters long, with a record length of about 2 meters. The tail is about 12 to 15% of the total length.

Rainbow Slender Boas have a gigantic range, extending from Costa Rica and Panama south over much of northern South America to northern Argentina. The range has many discontinuities, and there are many gaps where Rainbows are not found. Though some nine subspecies are recognized, some are doubtfully distinct and others probably are full species as they seem to be isolated and not sharing genes with other forms. However, because so much of South America is poorly collected, it is difficult to determine where Rainbows don't occur and where they haven't been collected. Because hobbyists recognize the nine subspecies and most of them are

THE TRUE BOAS: BOIDAE

109

Rainbow Boas need very high humidity in order to thrive in captivity. A substrate such as sphagnum moss will help raise the relative humidity, and using a large water bowl in the cage is wise. Photo by I. Francais.

distinguishable, the separatory characters (to be used with caution) are given here. The species was described by Linnaeus in 1758 as *Boa cenchris* (*Systema Naturae*, Ed. 10, 1: 215) from Surinam. The following older names certainly should replace the names of some of the recognized subspecies but have never been placed by workers: *tamachiai* Scopoli, 1877; *ternatea* Daudin, 1803; *aboma* Daudin, 1803; *annulifer* Daudin, 1803; *liberiensis* Hallowell, 1854. The names *fusca* Gray, 1849, and *cupreus* Fischer, 1856, seem to apply to the subspecies *maurus*. The specific name often is spelled *cenchris* in older literature.

Subspecies of the Rainbow Slender Boa

cenchria: Southern Venezuela and the Guianas through the Amazon basin; lateral ocelli with no outer ring of orange and without paler center, the ventrals with dark spotting on the lateral margins.

alvarezi Abalos, Baez & Nader, 1964: Santiago del Estero, Argentina. Some lateral ocelli bordered by orange; median brown area bordered on sides by black stripes; more than 47 middorsal scale rows and 47 to 55 subcaudals.

assisi Machado, 1944: Caatinga of northeastern Brazil (includes *xerophilus* Amaral, 1954). Some lateral ocelli bordered by orange;

Young Argentine Rainbow Boas, *E. c. alvarezi*, do not feed well. Some success has been had using lizards and frogs as first foods. The animal pictured is an adult. Photo by K. H. Switak.

THE TRUE BOAS: BOIDAE

no black stripes outlining median brown area; median dorsal spots round; median head stripe broken by stripe on nape; over 245 ventrals.

barbouri Stull, 1938: Ilha Marajo, mouth of Amazon, Brazil. Some lateral ocelli bordered by orange; no black stripes outlining median brown area; median dorsal spots saddle-shaped.

crassus (Cope, 1862): Southern Brazil and Paraguay into northern Argentina. Some lateral ocelli bordered by orange; median brown area bordered on sides by black stripes; fewer than 47 middorsal scale rows and 34 to 45 subcaudals.

gaigei Stull, 1938: Bolivia and southern Peru. Lateral ocelli without outer ring of orange but with a pale central spot

hygrophilus Amaral, 1954: Espiritu Santo State, eastern coastal Brazil. Like *cenchria* but the ventrals without lateral spots.

Cenchria is the only *Epicrates* to have obvious labial pits. Although present, the pits of the Rainbow Boa are rather shallow when compared to those of the closely related *Corallus*. Photo by R. D. Bartlett.

Ranging through Bolivia and Peru, *E. c. gaigei* is extremely similar to *c. cenchria* in color, pattern, and iridescence. It is uncommon in the hobby, but appears occasionally. Photo by R. D. Bartlett.

maurus Gray, 1849: Costa Rica across northern Colombia and Venezuela to coastal French Guiana and offshore islands. Adults uniformly tan above with just traces of pattern. May occur sympatrically with *cenchria* and may be a full species.

polylepis Amaral, 1935: Junction of Goias, Bahia, and Minas Gerais States, eastern Brazil. Some lateral ocelli bordered by

112   **THE LIVING BOAS**

If kept warm and humid, the Rainbow Boa is a hardy captive that will not grow to a problematic size. *E. c. assisi* pictured here. Photo by W. Wüster.

orange; no black stripes outlining median brown area; median dorsal spots round; median head stripe fused with nuchal stripes; ventrals fewer than 240.

Rainbows are very adaptable terrestrial boas that also climb well. They are found from relatively dry savannas to within and on the edges of rain forests and also along the coast. Active at night, they feed on mammals and birds that they often catch in the trees. They are strong constrictors with long anterior teeth and very adept hunters. They often are found near villages and plantations.

These can be relatively active boas, so they need a large terrarium with lots of hiding places and climbing branches as well as a large water bowl. The temperature and other circumstances of captivity can be much as for the Red-tailed Boa, though Rainbows require high humidity. Both imports and captive-bred specimens feed well on rodents and other small mammals as well as chicks. Many specimens are relatively gentle, but they excite easily and can produce vicious bites; care is advised. They respond well to a short winter brumation at somewhat lower temperatures than normal (21°C brumation, 29 to 32°C normal). Males have larger spurs than females and a more slender tail. Females carry their litters

Generally speaking, young Brazilian Rainbow Boas, *E. c. cenchria*, are more brightly colored than the adults. Breeders are selecting for very orange adults. Photo by K. H. Switak.

THE TRUE BOAS: BOIDAE 113

E. c. polylepis is a poorly differentiated subspecies. Although identified as *polylepis*, this individual would be very hard to tell from *cenchria* or *gaigei*. *E. c. polylepis* is not present in the hobby. Photo by V. Jirousek.

for about five to six months. A litter consists of 10 to 30 young some 50 to 65 cm long.

Several subspecies are being captive-bred and are available at relatively low cost. Unfortunately several different color forms or subspecies often have been interbred, producing mongrels. The subspecies *maurus* is especially interesting in that the young are virtually identical to *cenchria cenchria* but the ocelli begin fade by the age of two years until older adults are uniformly pale iridescent tan. This supposed subspecies may occur alongside *cenchria cenchria* and differs in having fewer ventrals (227-237 vs. 260-275), fewer supralabials (11-12 vs. 14-15), and a smaller maximum size seldom exceeding 1.2 meters (vs. to 2 meters).

EPICRATES CHRYSOGASTER

Tan Slender Boa

This slender boa is found in the Turks and Caicos Islands and the adjacent southern Bahamas. It exhibits two distinct color patterns (spotted and striped), making it unique in the genus.

Dorsal scales in 33 to 37 rows on the neck and 39 to 47 rows at midbody. The supraocular formula is 3-2-3. There usually are 14 or 15 supralabials. The ventrals number 245 to 277, and there are 74 to 95 subcaudals.

These are pale brown to grayish boas with two distinct black stripes back from the eye in most specimens. Typically there are 30 to 70 irregular spots down the back, these often fused or broken into pairs, the blotches weakly outlined with gold. On the Caicos Bank a striped phase occurs; these unique snakes carry four

Approximate distribution of *E. chrysogaster* in the Bahamas

Head and midbody views of *E. chrysogaster*. The head views are of the striped phase and the midbody view is of the spotted phase.

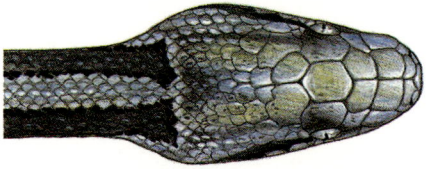

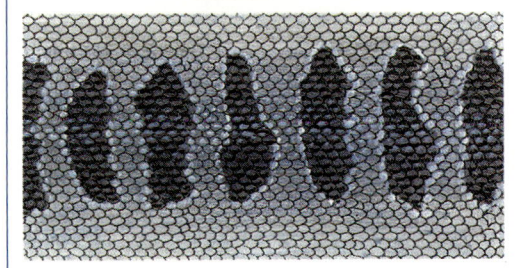

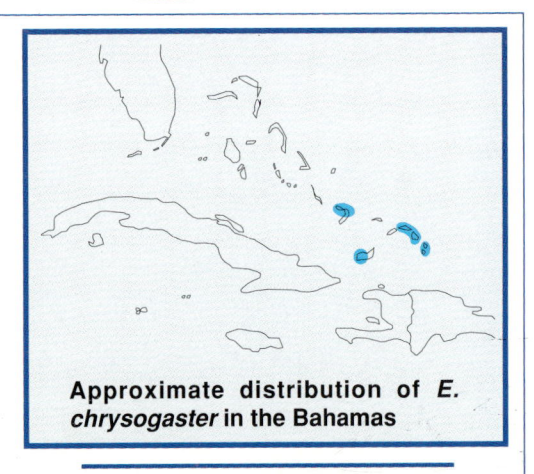

dark brown stripes, one on each side of the midline and one low on each side at the back of the body. The lateral stripes often are discontinuous. The belly usually is pale, becoming darker posteriorly.

The maximum known length is 1.3 meters.

Three subspecies are recognized from several neighboring banks and islets in the southern Bahamas area: *E. c. chrysogaster* is from the Turks and Caicos islands; *E. c. relicquus* Barbour & Shreve, 1935, is from Great Inagua Island and adjacent Sheep Cay; and *E. c. schwartzi* Buden, 1975, comes from Acklins and Crooked Islands in the Bahamas. The species was described by Cope in 1871 as *Homalochilus chrysogaster* (*Proc. Amer. Philos. Soc.*, 11 557). For many years it was considered a subspecies of *E. striatus*.

The Tan Slender Boa occurs in the usual dry woodlands and open areas of these low islands. It sometimes is found near houses and gardens At night it feeds on rodents and birds, the juveniles probably feeding on frogs and lizards. A litter may contain some

THE TRUE BOAS: BOIDAE

E. chrysogaster is unique in the genus in that it occurs in two phases, spotted and striped. The striped phase only occurs on the Caicos Bank and is placed in the nominate subspecies. The spotted snake pictured is *E. c. relicquus*, coming from the southern end of the range. Photos by R. D. Bartlett.

nine young born after a pregnancy of almost eight months. A few specimens occasionally appear in the hobby.

EPICRATES EXSUL

Abaco Slender Boa

One of the more attractive island slender boas, *E. exsul* has a pattern of widely spaced narrow black blotches down the back and is found in the northern Bahamas.

There are 28 to 33 rows of scales on the neck and 35 to 40 at midbody. Typically there are 13 supralabials. The supraocular formula is 5-2-4. There are 236 to 251 ventrals and 69 to 75 subcaudals.

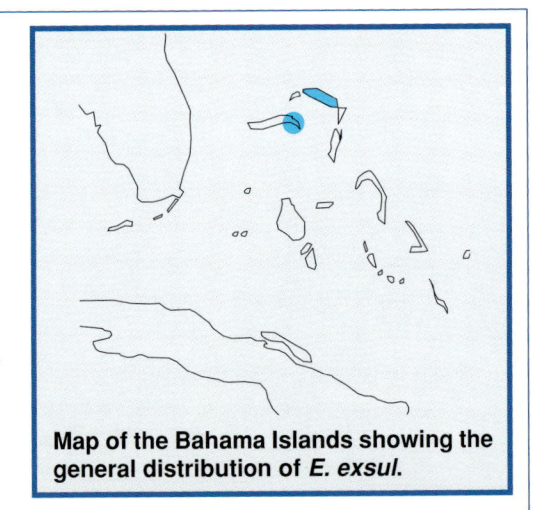

Map of the Bahama Islands showing the general distribution of *E. exsul*.

The snakes are tan to pale gray. There are 41 to 57 narrow oval blackish blotches down the back, these widely spaced and continuing on the lower side as isolated small and indistinct spots. The

The Abaco Slender Boa is one of the prettiest of the Caribbean boas. It is a rather small species that unfortunately has not made its way in to the hobby. It is present in the collections of some U.S. zoos. Photo by R. D. Bartlett.

THE TRUE BOAS: BOIDAE

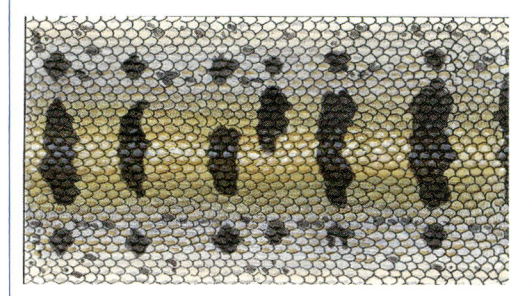

Head and midbody views of *E. exsul*.

head is without pattern. Young specimens may be distinctly reddish in tone.

The maximum length is under a meter.

This poorly known but sometimes common species is found on Grand Bahama and the cays of Great Abaco and Little Abaco Islands, Bahamas. It is found in pine forests and under trash in rather dry situations. It has been bred in zoos but is not available to the general hobbyist. Young are some 23 to 28 cm long, and there may be nine babies in a litter.

EPICRATES FORDI

Hispaniolan Slender Boa

This is one of three species of slender boas found on the large island of Hispaniola. Of the three, it resembles *E. gracilis* in having fewer than 48 middorsal scale rows but has fewer ventrals and subcaudals than that species.

The dorsal scales are in 28 to 35 rows at the neck and 31 to 39 at midbody. There usually are 13 supralabials. The supraocular formula is 3-1-3. There are 231 to 261 ventrals and 69 to 89 subcaudals.

Typical specimens are grayish to pale brown with about 60 to 90 oval to squarish chocolate brown to reddish dorsal blotches out-

***E. fordi* is one of the few Caribbean *Epicrates* that shows a lot of iridescence. Otherwise, it is a rather plain animal. Photo by M. Walls, courtesy Gary Lorio.**

lined with black and narrowly spaced. The blotches may be narrowly fused into broken chains. Young are redder than average adults. The head is grayish with some brown blotches and a blackish stripe back from the eye. The belly varies from whitish to clouded with dark gray or brownish.

The maximum length is about 90 cm.

The numbers of *E. fordi* in the hobby are on the rise, it being a smallish and docile boa. They are rather hardy if kept warm and are not overly sensitive to humidity levels. Photo by V. Jirousek.

The species is confined to Hispaniola and adjacent islands, and three subspecies are recognized. Their distribution is poorly known and appears rather spotty, with many gaps. *E. f. fordi* is found in the southern part of the island; *E. f. agametus* Sheplan & Schwartz, 1974, is definitely known from the northwestern part of Haiti; and *E. f. manototus* Schwartz, 1979, is known only from Ile a Cabrit off central western Haiti (within the range of *E. f. fordi*). The species was described by Guenther in 1861 as *Pelophilus fordi* (*Proc. Zool. Soc. London*, 1861: 142). For many years it was considered a subspecies of *E. ornatus*.

This is a species of dry habitats such as cactus scrub and rocky hillsides. It is nocturnal, mostly terrestrial, and feeds on small

Map of Hispaniola showing the approximate natural range of *E. fordi*.

THE TRUE BOAS: BOIDAE

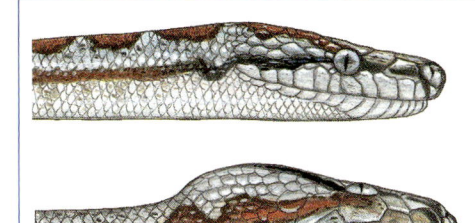

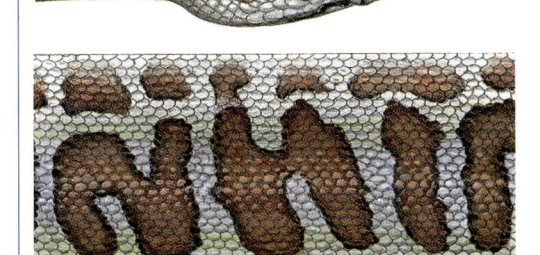

Head and midbody views of *E. fordi*.

rodents and lizards. Litters of 3 to 7 young are born in the summer months. This has proved to be a long-lived species in zoo collections, with specimens living more than 15 years. Though colorful for an island slender-boa, it seldom is available to the average hobbyist and when it is, it is confused with the more commonly seen *E. striatus*.

EPICRATES GRACILIS

Cryptic Slender Boa

The Cryptic Slender Boa is a species with a very slender neck, relatively wide head, a large eye, and many small oval dark blotches on the back. See *E. fordi* for how to distinguish it from other Hispaniolan species.

The dorsal scales are in 27 to 42 rows at the neck and 33 to 47 rows at midbody. There typically are 13 supralabials. The

The Cryptic Slender Boa (also called the Haitian Vine Boa) is an extremely slender, arboreal species. Photo by R. D. Bartlett.

supraocular formula is 4-1-2. There are 271 to 304 ventrals and 90 to 111 subcaudals.

This is a brownish boa with many (about 60 to 100) rather circular to oval darker brown spots along the middle of the back. Often the blotches are split into staggered pairs. Smaller spots or dashes are present on the lower sides. The head is well-marked, with two dark brown lines behind the eye and usually a dark line down the center of the

Head and midbody views of *E. gracilis*.

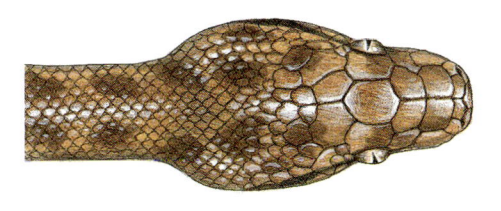

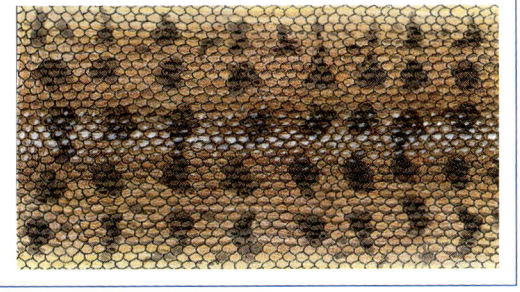

Feeding *E. gracilis* in captivity is often a challenge; they often reject rodents and are so slender as to have difficulty with prey of any significant size. Photo by R. D. Bartlett.

Map of Hispaniola showing the general distribution of *E. gracilis*.

intergrades are known from the Barahona Peninsula of the central southern coast. The species was first described by Fischer in 1888 as *Chilabothrus gracilis* (*Jb. Hamburg wiss. Aust.*, 5: 35) from Cap Haitien.

Unlike many other island boas, *E. gracilis* is arboreal and feeds almost exclusively on anoles. It is nocturnal, likely to be found near water in deciduous forests, and adapts well to disturbed habitats. Females have given birth to litters of three young in October. Though it may be locally common, it seldom enters the hobby market. Captive specimens have been able to adjust to a diet of mice.

head as well, plus other lines and blotches; large adults may lose the head pattern, however. The belly is white with little or no pattern. Young specimens may have strong orange tones dorsally and ventrally.

The maximum length is almost one meter.

Epicrates gracilis contains two subspecies that may be isolated, but there are unidentified populations known. *E. g. gracilis* is found along the northern slope of Hispaniola, while *E. g. hapalus* Sheplan and Schwartz, 1974, comes from the Tiburon Peninsula of southwestern Haiti. Possible

EPICRATES GRANTI

Tortola Slender Boa

Though this form usually is considered a subspecies of *Epicrates monensis*, the distribution of these snakes makes no sense as subspecies. *E. monensis* is found on an island to the west of Puerto Rico, while *E. granti* is found on islands to the east of Puerto Rico. Neither form occurs on Puerto Rico, and there is no chance that they can exchange genes. In addition, the two show many differences in scalation and color pattern, and for the life of me I cannot understand why they

THE TRUE BOAS: BOIDAE

E. granti is normally considered a subspecies of *E. monensis*. The author here elevates it to a full species based on the probable isolation of the two. Photo by R. Kayne.

have been considered subspecies. *Epicrates granti* is here elevated to specific status as an evolutionary species.

The dorsal scales are in 34 to 39 rows at the neck and 41 to 47 rows at midbody. There usually are 13 supralabials. The supraocular formula is 3-1-5. The ventrals number some 161 to 271, with 80 to 84 subcaudals.

These slender, big-headed and big-eyed boas are grayish to brownish with 61 to 73 dark brown or reddish brown dorsal blotches that may be outlined with black. The blotches are variable in shape, often broken or partially fused and may extend low on the sides to fuse with dark lateral spots. The head is unmarked in adults but may have a U-shaped dark bar across the back of the head in young. The belly is yellowish with a variable amount of black or dark brown spotting and may be clean.

Midbody view of *E. granti*.

The higher number of middorsal scale rows, 3-1-5 supraocular formula, and greater number of dorsal blotches distinguish *E. granti* from *E. monensis*.

The maximum length is about a meter.

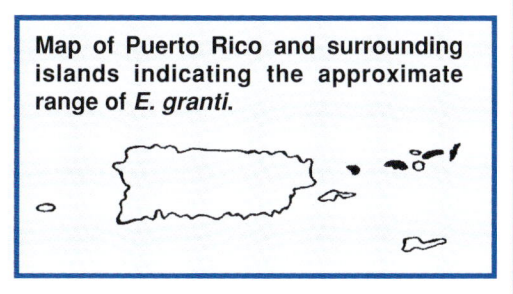

Map of Puerto Rico and surrounding islands indicating the approximate range of *E. granti*.

Epicrates granti was first described by Stull in 1933 (*Occas. Papers Mus. Zool., Univ. Michigan*, No. 267: 1) as *E. inornatus granti* from Tortola Island off eastern Puerto Rico. It now also is known from various islands in the U.S. and British Virgin Islands to the east of Puerto Rico, including St. Thomas, Virgin Gorda, Culebra (off Puerto Rico), and various smaller islands.

A nocturnal, arboreal species that feeds mostly on lizards and small birds, the Tortola Slender Boa occupies rather dry habitats. An endangered species, it has been bred by various zoos but is unavailable to hobbyists. Females give birth to three to seven young that are 20 to 28 cm in length.

Head and midbody views of *E. inornatus*.

EPICRATES INORNATUS

Puerto Rican Slender Boa

The Puerto Rican Slender Boa probably is related to the Mona and Tortola species but differs in counts and supraocular formula as well as being almost twice as long.

The dorsal scales are in 31 to 34 rows at the neck and 38 to 42 rows at midbody. There usually are 11 supralabials and just 8 scales around the eye. The supraocular formula is 2-1-2. There are 258 to 273 ventrals and 66 to 74 subcaudals.

Well-patterned adults are brownish to grayish brown with 66 to 73 darker brown narrow blotches down the back, these often outlined with blackish. Smaller blotches on the lower sides may fuse with the dorsal blotches. Many adults are very dark with no visible pattern. There is virtually no head pattern. The belly is dark brown with darker specks.

Adults commonly exceed a meter in total length, with the maximum length over 1.9 meters.

Reinhardt first described this species as *Boa inornata* in 1843 (*K. danske Vidensk. Selsk. Skr., Kjobenhavn*, (4) 10: 253). *Piesigaster boettgeri* Seoane, 1880, is the same species although described as from the Philippines. The species as today understood is restricted to Puerto

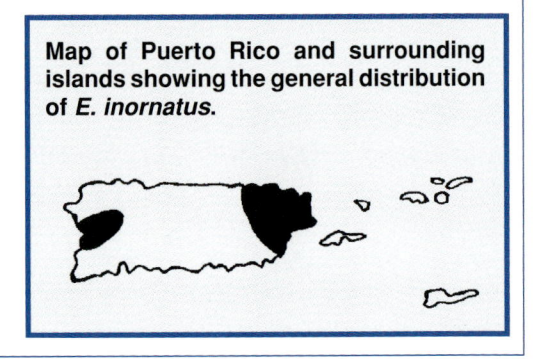

Map of Puerto Rico and surrounding islands showing the general distribution of *E. inornatus*.

THE TRUE BOAS: BOIDAE

Adult Puerto Rican Slender Boas are generalist feeders, but they are known to prey heavily on bats. They hang on branches, vines, and other perches and snap bats from the air as they emerge from the caves at dusk. Photo by V. Jirousek.

Rico, where it is recorded from both the east and the west of the island but not the center.

An adaptable species, the Puerto Rican Slender Boa is found from moist rainforests to dry plantation field edges and even enters towns. Usually it is found near water. It is nocturnal and feeds on chickens and other birds, bats, and rodents. It may congregate at the mouth of caves, feeding on the bats that emerge at night while hanging from vines and projections around the cave mouth. Babies feed mostly on anoles and small frogs. Mating occurs during the spring wet season, the young being born about six months later. As might be expected for such a large snake (by Caribbean standards), it has large litters of young, about 23 to 32, that are 33 to 37 cm long.

As the forests of Puerto Rico have vanished, the numbers of *E. inornatus* have fallen. Although it can be found in disturbed habitat, such areas cannot support large populations. Photo by R. D. Bartlett.

Males may be extremely aggressive during pre-mating rituals with both other males and females, and females have been noted to eat their mates. Obviously these snakes are best caged separately. Because it has lost most of its forest habitat, the Puerto Rican Slender-Boa has become rare and is protected by law. Thus it is unavailable to the average hobbyist, though it is bred in several zoos.

Map of Puerto Rico and Mona Island. *E. monensis* is restricted to Mona Island.

EPICRATES MONENSIS

Mona Slender Boa

See the discussion of *Epicrates granti* for an explanation of why I've separated these two forms. As treated here, *Epicrates monensis* is a monotypic species restricted to Mona Island west of Puerto Rico.

The dorsal scales are in 34 to 39 rows on the neck and 39 to 42 rows at midbody. There are 13 supralabials on average, and in some specimens none enter the eye (though usually a single scale enters the eye). The supraocular formula is 3-1-3. There are about 261 to 271 ventrals and 80 to 84 subcaudals.

Against a grayish or brownish background, there are 47 to 56 dark brown angulate blotches along the back, these sometimes fused with each other and to smaller blotches along the sides. The head is unmarked except for a U-shaped bar at the back of the head. The belly may be pale or

Because of their small range, *E. monensis* and other island species are especially vulnerable to extinction caused by introduced species, cultivation, and human population growth. Photo by R. Kayne.

THE TRUE BOAS: BOIDAE

Like many of the *Epicrates*, *E. monensis* is rather arboreal in habits. Presumably, it feeds mainly on lizards and some rodents. The young may take frogs as well. Photo by P. Freed.

heavily clouded with dark brown.

Adults reach almost a meter in length.

This species is restricted to the small, dry Mona Island some 65 kilometers west of Puerto Rico. It was first described as a full species by Zenneck in 1898 (*Z. wiss. Zool., Leipzig*, 64: 64). It probably feeds mostly on anoles taken while hunting at night among shrubs and vine tangles several meters above the ground. Litters are small, often four young some 28 to 30 cm long. Because it is protected by law, this species is unavailable to the average hobbyist though several zoos have breeding projects that are more or less successful.

EPICRATES STRIATUS

Fischer's Slender Boa

Fischer's Slender-Boa is a widely distributed and common snake found over much of Hispaniola and also on many islands in the Bahamas. It is a hard species to categorize because it is so variable over this large range, with eight subspecies of varying distinctiveness recognized. Three of these occur on Hispaniola, with the other five in the Bahamas. It might make sense to separate the Bahaman forms as a separate species (the oldest available name is *strigilatus* Cope, 1862), but it is difficult to

Head and midbody views of *E. striatus*.

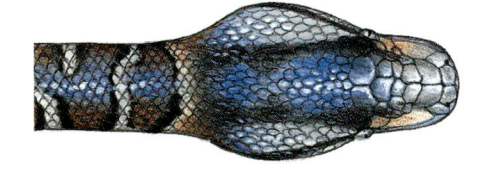

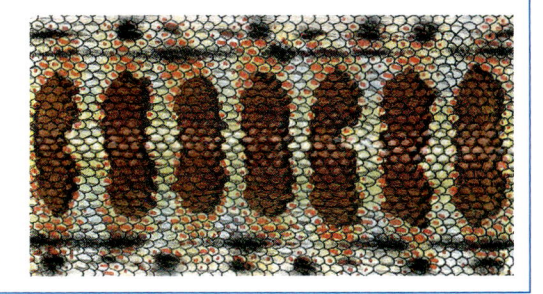

Because of its discontinuous distribution, Fischer's Slender Boa may be more than one species. Thus far, not enough differences have been found to support this conclusion. Photo by R. D. Bartlett.

find any characters that really separate the Bahaman snakes from those of Hispaniola as distinct groups. The species can be distinguished by a combination of scale counts, the rows of scales on the neck and the combined ventral plus subcaudal count, plus the usually quite strong and often colorful blotched pattern.

The scale counts will distinguish it from the often very similar *E. fordi*.

There are 34 to 49 rows of scales at the neck and 35 to 65 at midbody. There usually are 14 or 15 supralabials. The supraocular formula varies from 3-1-5 to 5-2-5. There are 266 to 299 ventrals and 76 to 102 subcaudals, for a combined total of 343 to 390 scales under the body.

Though many large adults may be so dark as to be almost patternless, well-marked adults are grayish to tan with brown or gray blotches of various shapes outlined with black. The blotches are closely spaced and may fuse to

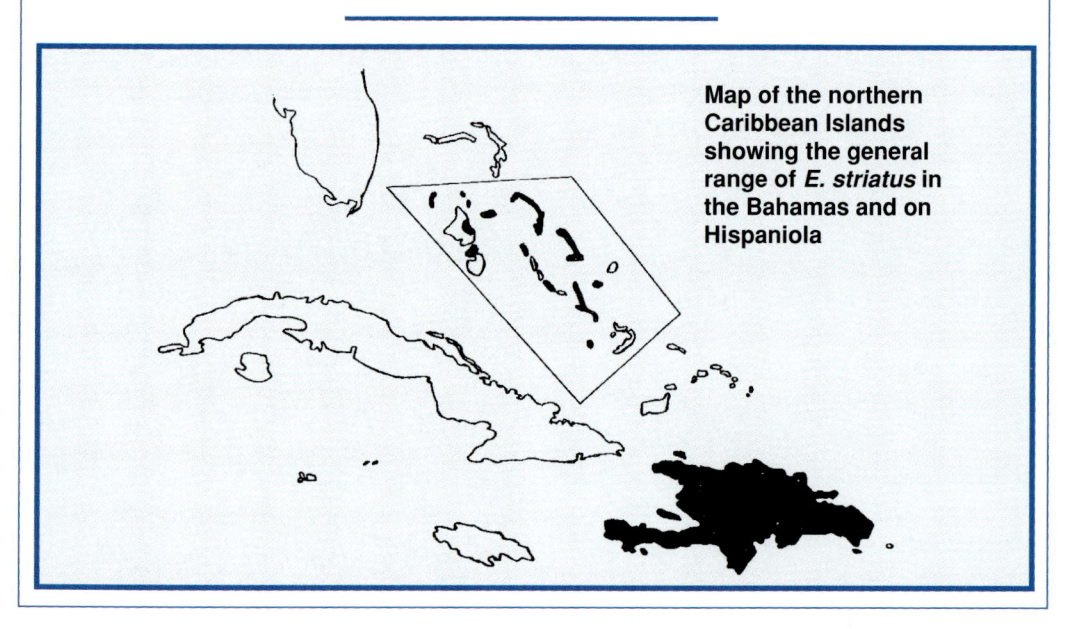

Map of the northern Caribbean Islands showing the general range of *E. striatus* in the Bahamas and on Hispaniola

THE TRUE BOAS: BOIDAE

On the islands on which they occur, Fischer's Slender Boa (also called the Haitian Boa in the hobby) is the largest predator, reaching lengths of up 2.5 meters/8 feet. They prey on rodents, lizards, and birds. Photo by R. D. Bartlett.

leave only rather small pale oval spots down the middle of the back. There may be from 60 to over 120 blotches on the back. The head often has five dark brown or blackish lines visible, two back from each eye and one down the center, much as in the Rainbow Slender Boa. The belly varies from clean white to heavily blotched with dark brown or gray.

This is a large island boa, with adults commonly 1 to 1.5 meters long. The maximum length is about 2.4 meters, perhaps as much as 3 meters.

First described in 1856 by Fischer (*Abh. Geb. naturwiss., Hamburg*, 3: 102) as *Homalochilus striatus* from a variety of Caribbean islands (including many where it does not occur), the typical subspecies has gathered two synonyms (*multisectus* Cope, 1862, and *versicolor* Steindachner, 1864) and has been joined by seven other subspecies. As currently understood, *E. striatus* includes the following subspecies. Hispaniola: *E. s. striatus*, virtually all of mainland

This captive-born Fischer's Slender Boa sports an interesting banded pattern. Some individuals have nice lavender highlights. Photo by I. Francais.

Hispaniola; *E. s. exagistus* Sheplan and Schwartz, 1974, the western Tiburon Peninsula; *E. s. warreni* Sheplan and Schwartz, 1974, Ile de la Tortue off northwestern Haiti. Bahamas: *E. s. ailurus* Sheplan and Schwartz, 1974, Alligator Cay and Cat Island; *E. s. fosteri* Barbour, 1941, Bimini Islands; *E. s. fowleri* Sheplan and Schwartz, 1974, Andros and Berry Islands; *E. s. mccraniei* Sheplan and Schwartz, 1974, Ragged Islands; *E. s. strigilatus* (Cope, 1862), New Providence Island and islets to Exuma Cays.

This is perhaps the only island slender boa that is moderately common in the terrarium. Like the other species, it is nocturnal and feeds on a variety of birds and small mammals when adult, while young specimens take mostly lizards. This species typically is found in moderately humid forests, but some forms are at home in dry pine forests and even cactus and thorn scrub. In captivity, it does well in a tall terrarium that is heavily planted or has many climbing branches. It spends much of the day sleeping in the branches. Keep the temperature about 24 to 30°C (75 to 86°F) during the day, dropping a bit at night. There should be a large water bowl to help increase the humidity, but the air in the terrarium must not become stagnant. The boas like light, so give them a bank of fluorescent lights and also a basking light. Many specimens bask for several hours each day, while others spend days at a time in the water bowl. Feed-

E. s. fosteri originates in the Bimini Islands. It is a dark form that has a very indistinct pattern as an adult. However, it is more iridescent than most of the Caribbean *Epicrates*. Photo by R. D. Bartlett.

THE TRUE BOAS: BOIDAE

ing activity is largely at night and on the ground. Adults usually will take mice and other rodents, but young specimens may require lizards or at least mice rubbed with lizards or soaked in a cocktail of homogenized lizard. Males may fight before mating, so keep specimens individually. Mating typically occurs in the spring, with birth in the autumn. Litters may include 10 to 20 young that are 40 to 50 cm long. The babies first want to feed after their first shed, but they will want lizards, which will cause problems and possibly lead to forced-feeding.

It might be noted here that most female island slender-boas do not breed each year in nature. Instead, females take two years to mature their eggs before fertilization, having litters only every

Although not readily available to the average hobbyist, some commercial breeders are propagating E. subflavus. Photo by I. Francais.

Several subspecies of Fischer's Slender Boa are imported for the hobby, and locality and identification are often lacking. One of the prettier forms is E. s. strigulatus from the central Bahamas. Photo by R. D. Bartlett.

other year. In captivity this cycle may be broken by regular feeding and more constant temperature and humidity conditions that allow a female to recover more quickly from the stress of pregnancy.

Good numbers of captive-bred *Epicrates striatus* are available if you look around, though the species is not very popular. Several subspecies and mixtures of subspecies are bred, so much of the terrarium material is mongrel stock. If you buy a young specimen, try to be sure that is it feeding on mice and not lizards.

EPICRATES SUBFLAVUS

Jamaican Slender Boa

The rare and generally unavailable Jamaican Slender Boa is one of the more distinctive species of island boas. The color pattern and large size allow easy recognition.

The dorsal scales are in 33 to 41 rows on the neck and 41 to 47 rows at midbody. The supraocular formula is 2-1-2. There are 277 to 283 ventrals and 78 or 79 subcaudals.

Adults are reddish tan or olive, the head especially being olive with one or two dark stripes back from the eye. The anterior body lacks a distinct pattern though there may be many dark brown scales scattered about. Before midbody a regular pattern of blackish bands develops, these separated by narrow tan interspaces. The bands begin to fuse by midbody, and in many specimens the back half of the body is almost solid black. The belly is tinged with orange anteriorly, with black spots becoming more abundant posteriorly until the back half of the belly and tail

Map of Jamaica showing the approximate distribution of *E. subflavus*.

Head and midbody views of *E. subflavus*.

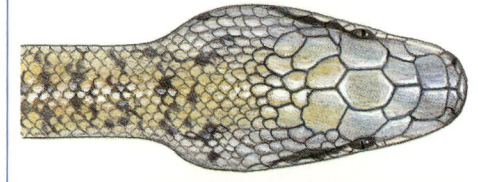

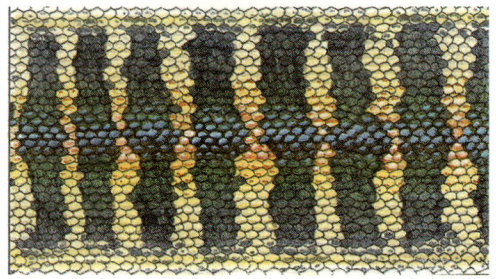

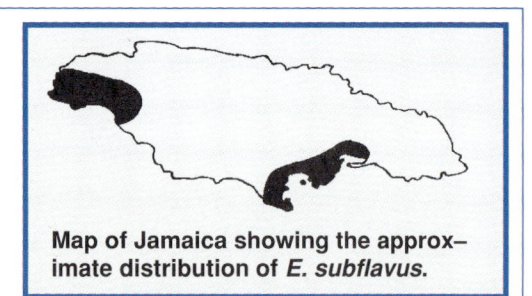

Like many of the boas, *E. subflavus* is fond of soaking in the water bowl. Keep the water clean at all times. Photo by I. Francais.

THE TRUE BOAS: BOIDAE

above: Although it is primarily terrestrial, the Jamaican Slender Boa will climb to bask and feed. In the terrarium it appreciates having a few climbing branches. Photo by V. Jirousek.

below: *E. subflavus* inhabits the forests of southern Jamaica, an area that is fast becoming agricultural land. The result is that this snake and other endemic animals are disappearing quickly. Photo by R. D. Bartlett.

This Jamaican Slender Boa has just been misted in order to raise the humidity in the terrarium. Although they live in dry forests, they lair in areas of moderate humidity. Photo by I. Francais.

are solid black. Young specimens are orange to tan above, unmarked pale below, with indistinct darker cross-bands on the back, these more obvious posteriorly.

Many adults are over 1.5 meters in total length, with the record a bit over 2 meters.

Epicrates subflavus is known only from a few localities in southern Jamaica, where it is becoming even more uncommon as forest habitat is converted to human usage. It was first distinguished from the similar *E. inornatus* of Puerto Rico by Stejneger in 1901 (*Proc. U. S. Natl. Mus.*, 23: 409).

This is a species of moist forests over limestone soils. It is active at night, feeding on rodents, bats, and birds, with young probably feeding on lizards. Though largely terrestrial and often seen basking during the day, it climbs well when searching for food. Males may fight viciously when put together before mating, and this is another species where a female has been noted to have eaten a potential mate. Like most *Epicrates*, they should be housed separately. In nature, mating takes place in the spring and birth occurs in autumn. Pregnancies last about six months, producing litters often containing 10 to almost 40 young. The babies are 36 to 53 cm long.

This species, like so many other Caribbean snakes, is suffering the results of growing human populations on its home island. Though it probably once was common over much of southern Jamaica, most of the forests have been cut and many snakes have been killed as a result of random contacts with farmers. Today the species is known to survive in only a few localities, mostly in the sparsely settled Cockpit Country of the central southern coast, and it continues to decline. Several zoos have breeding colonies, but the species is protected and not

THE TRUE BOAS: BOIDAE

available to the average hobbyist.

Genus Eunectes Wagler, 1830 (*Nat. Syst. Amph.*: 167). Type species by subsequent designation *Boa scytale* Linnaeus = *Eunectes murinus*.

Synonyms: None.

Very large, thick-bodied aquatic boas with depressed head barely distinct from the neck and very small eyes. The nostrils are dorsal in position at the tip of the snout and can be closed by valves. Each nostril is surrounded by three large nasal shields, the anterior shields meeting behind the rostral shield and thus separating the internasals from the rostral. The internasals are large and rather strap-like and look more like prefrontals (which they may well be if the internasals are considered to be absent). The eyes also are dorsal in position and there is a large supraocular on each side. A large squarish loreal separates the posterior nasal from a large preocular scale.

All the anacondas are large, heavy-bodied snakes that spend most of their time in the water. This is the Green Anaconda, *Eunectes murinus*. Photo by J. Merli.

There are one or two rows or suboculars. The mental groove is developed. The dorsal scales are smooth and in many rows. The tail is short and somewhat prehensile.

The hemipenes are long and are deeply bilobed. The shaft is about two-thirds the length of the organ and has many heavy flounces over its length. The arms are covered

The dorsally placed nostrils of anacondas give them a pug-like appearance. Pictured is a Yellow Anaconda, *E. notaeus*. Photo by I. Francais.

with finer flounces on the face with the sulcus and have a mixture of flounces, connecting ridges, and papillae on the back. The sulcus spermaticus forks at the point where the shaft forks, and its branches end below the tips of the arms. Males probe about 20 subcaudals.

Everyone can recognize an anaconda, but there remains some question as to just how many species are in the genus. Two species are commonly seen in nature and the terrarium, while one is apparently rare. The following key should separate the species.

Key to the species of Eunectes

A. Top of head with a median dark stripe; one row of small scales between the eye and the supralabials .... B

AA. Top of head without a median dark stripe; two rows of small scales between the eye and the supralabials .... *murinus*

B. Back with a single row of large blackish spots down the center; one row of large blackish spots along the side .... *deschauenseei*

BB. Back usually with a double row of large blackish spots that usually have pale centers and may be variably fused across the back; sides with two or three irregular rows of dark spots or crescents that may form jagged lines .... *notaeus*

EUNECTES DESCHAUENSEEI

Conant's Anaconda

This rare anaconda is the northern version of the Yellow Anaconda and like it has a blackish stripe down the center of the head. It differs mostly in having large non-ocellated spots in one row on the lower side.

There are 13 or 14 supralabials and 16 infralabials. One row of scales separates the eye from the supralabials. The maximum number of dorsal scale rows is 39 to 48. There are 222 to 234 ventrals and 52 to 60 subcaudals.

The background color is a rather bright yellowish brown. The head has five black stripes, two back from each eye and one down the center of the head. The middle of the back has a single row of about 40 large, uniform black spots that are much wider than long and narrowly spaced. They continue

Midbody view of *E. deschauenseei*.

THE TRUE BOAS: BOIDAE

onto the tail. On the side are two rows or a single staggered row of smaller solid black spots. The belly is yellow or olive-yellow with one or two rows of small black spots.

Adults appear to be 1.8 to 2.5 meters in total length.

So far Conant's Anaconda seems to be known only from Ilha Marajo, Brazil, and the coastal region of French Guiana. It appears to be quite rare and seldom is collected. It gives birth to small litters of only three to seven young 35 to 55 cm in length. As far as known, it is aquatic like the other anacondas. The species was described by Dunn and Conant (*Proc. Acad. Nat. Sci. Philadelphia*, 88: 505) in 1936 from a unique example. The black dorsal spots of the Yellow Anaconda often are evenly fused across the back and lack pale centers, but the pattern of the lower side never is as uniform as in Conant's Anaconda. Counts for the two species overlap broadly.

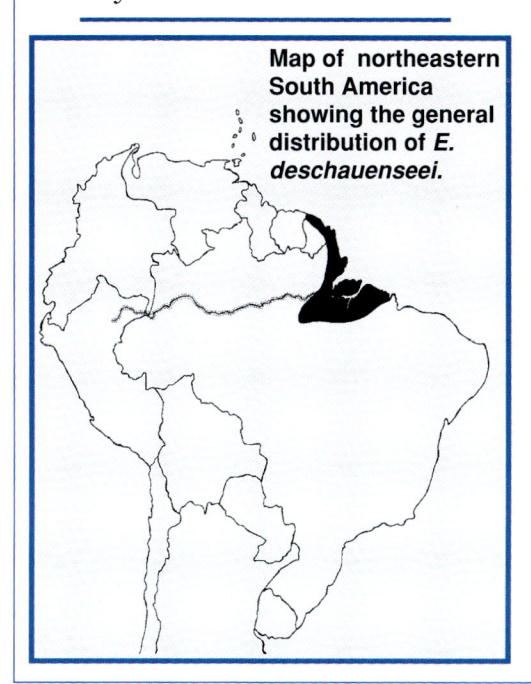

Map of northeastern South America showing the general distribution of *E. deschauenseei*.

EUNECTES MURINUS

Green Anaconda

The Green Anaconda is a beast of legend, one of those snakes about which there are continual arguments. What is the maximum size? Are any of them tamable? Why does an almost strictly aquatic snake feed mostly on mammals rather than fishes? The species is easily recognized by the greenish color and irregular, staggered black spots on the back.

There are two rows of scales between the eye and the supralabials. There are 14 to 18 supralabials and 20 to 22 infralabials. The maximum number of dorsal scale rows is 59 to 70. There are 230 to 262 ventrals and 62 to 75 subcaudals.

The overall color is distinctly greenish, varying from grayish green to bright olive or even a clean bright green. The belly is yellowish with many small black spots. There two black stripes back from each eye enclosing a greenish to yellowish area, and

The eyes of Green Anacondas are placed rather dorsally on the head, allowing them to see the shore when most of their body is submerged. Photo by G. Dingerkus.

136 THE LIVING BOAS

above: Dorsal and lateral head views of *E. murinus*.

right: Midbody views of *E. murinus*. The bottom drawing is of an aberrantly patterned snake formerly assigned to its own species, *E. barbouri*.

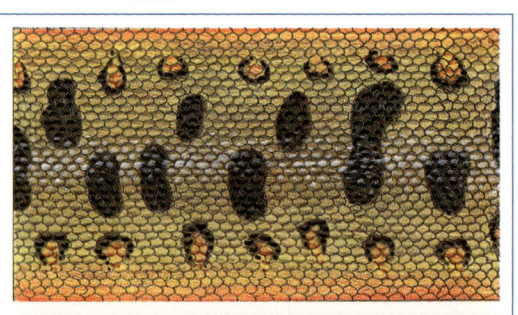

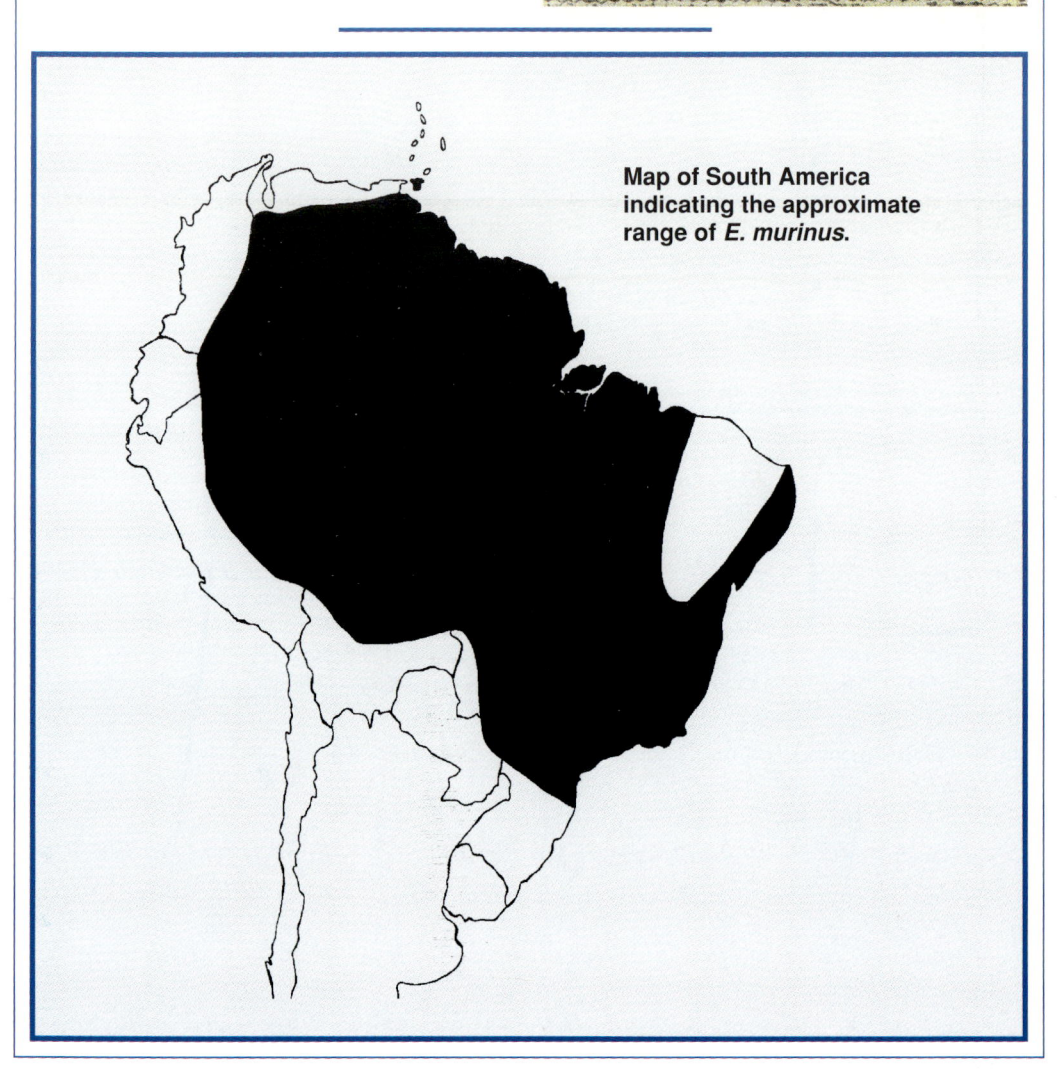

Map of South America indicating the approximate range of *E. murinus*.

there is no dark stripe down the center of the head. On the back is a double row of large round black spots (rarely pale-centered), these often partially fused across the back and appearing to be staggered or in alternating rows. The spots continue onto the tail. On the lower side are one or two irregular rows of small black ocelli with yellow centers.

Green Anacondas are widely distributed over northern and central South America, ranging from Colombia and Venezuela (including Trinidad) through the Guianas south over the Amazon basin to Bolivia. First described by Linnaeus in 1758 (*Systema Naturae*, Ed. 10, 1: 215) as *Boa murinus*, the species is thought to have two subspecies, though their

Adult Green Anacondas are large enough to prey upon almost any other animal in their habitat. Capybaras, deer, and even small crocodiles are eaten by these giant serpents. Photo by A. Norman.

Adults commonly are 4 to 5 meters in total length. The maximum length for the species is debatable, but probably 8 meters (28 feet) is close to maximum for modern specimens. The widely accepted record of 11.4 meters (37.5 feet) recently has been strongly questioned (Gilmore and Murphy, 1993). Specimens of 6 to almost 7 meters (21 to 25 feet) have been recorded with certainty.

validity has been questioned. In the northern form, *E. m. gigas* (Latreille, 1802), the area between the stripes back from the eye is pale, usually orange or yellow, while in the Amazonian form, *E. m. murinus*, the area between the stripes is greenish like the rest of the head. There are differences in scale counts recorded for specimens from different areas of South America (ventrals 230 to

245 in French Guiana, 242 to 262 in Venezuela, and 246 to 259 in Para State, Brazil), but these count differences do not correspond with coloration differences. The subspecies are probably not biologically significant.

A form known as *E. barbouri* Dunn and Conant, 1936 (*Proc. Acad. Nat. Sci. Philadelphia*, 88:504) was distinguished by having pairs of small black spots with pale greenish centers staggered on each side of the midline. Strimple, et al., 1997 (*J. Herpetology*, 31(4):607-609) presented evidence that *barbouri* is an individual pattern variant of *E. murinus*.

The large size and heavy body force this species to stay in or near the water as an adult, and even juveniles seldom venture far from water. All the snake's activities, including mating and birth, occur in the water, and it is not unusual for captives to spend days in their pond without coming up to bask or move around. The tropical waters it inhabits have even temperatures most of the year, though during the dry season the snake may be forced to brumate in the mud until water levels rise again. The food consists largely of mammals of appropriate size and occasionally small caimans, larger fishes, and smaller anacondas. The species can be quite cannibalistic, so specimens should always be kept separated except during breeding. Green Anacondas are active mostly at night, when they may venture onto land in search of prey, though they usually wait in

Though they may not be the longest snakes, Green Anacondas are definitely the heaviest. This captive specimen weighs over 136 kg / 300 lbs. Photo by P. Keeler.

THE TRUE BOAS: BOIDAE

If you decide to keep a Green Anaconda, house them in large quarters with a large water area. The humidity must be very high and the substrate soft. Photo by P. Freed

shallow water with the eyes and nostrils at the surface and the rest of the body submerged. They strike quickly but not too accurately at anything that moves, including the keeper, and many specimens never adapt to captivity.

Green Anacondas need very large terraria with large and deep ponds. Taking care of an adult Green Anaconda probably is beyond the ability of most hobbyists, but they are commonly maintained in zoos. It generally is suggested that there should be little difference between daytime high temperatures and nighttime lows. Males ready to mate may follow a female for days, rubbing against her and trying to coil so his tail is

Think carefully before purchasing a Green Anaconda. These are large, often irascible animals that can seriously, even fatally, harm a careless keeper. Photo by W. Wüster.

Green Anacondas are prone to skin infections if their enclosures are not kept very clean. Careful hygiene is a must in keeping this species. Photo by R. D. Bartlett.

under hers. Mating occurs in the water. Pregnancy lasts some eight or nine months, producing large litters of large young. Typical litters may include 50 to 80 young about 75 cm long. The young grow fast and are sexually mature in about four years. The young should be separated from the mother and from each other as soon as possible to prevent fatal culinary accidents.

Though interesting to look at in a zoo or on a vacation trip to Brazil or Ecuador, Green Anacondas simply are too large for almost any private keeper. Their reputation as vicious animals that never tame usually is deserved. Though newborns may be relatively gentle, specimens over a meter in length may require two or three people to handle safely, and many dealers selling this species simply refuse to try to take even a small specimen out of a cage to display it to a potential customer. The bite wounds are deep and easily become infected, requiring medical attention. My advice would be look but don't touch—or wear heavy gloves and a face mask. Somewhat to the contrary, however, large specimens in nature may be very docile—when removed from the water.

EUNECTES NOTAEUS

Yellow Anaconda

The Yellow Anaconda is a bit smaller than the Green Anaconda, more attractively marked, and more tolerant of cool keeping conditions. It also is somewhat more gentle, though still not to be trusted, and is a better choice as a pet for the keeper who just has to have an anaconda in the collection.

There is a single row of scales between the eye and the supralabials. The dorsal scales are in a maximum of 45 to 48 rows. There are some 218 to 237 ventrals and 50 to 60 subcaudals.

Most specimens are yellowish tan to mustard yellow, the belly bright yellow with small black spots. Some specimens have much more contrast and brightness of pattern than others. There are five black stripes on the head, two back from each eye and one down the center of the head. On the back are many (often 50 to 60) pairs of large black spots that may have indistinct paler centers (but not true ocelli). The spots

THE TRUE BOAS: BOIDAE

The lateral markings of Yellow Anacondas are fragmented and irregular compared to the similar Conant's Anaconda. Their attractive colors have given Yellow Anacondas a growing following in the hobby. Photo by M. Walls, courtesy of Steve and Rini Mitchell.

often are irregularly fused across the center of the back to produce wide black bands. On the sides are two or three irregular rows of black ocelli or crescents with yellow centers or edges; these often fuse into broken black stripes. Sometimes they extend forward on the neck to almost connect with the head stripes back from the eye.

Adult Yellow Anacondas usually are about 2.5 to 3 meters in length, but there are records of specimens about 5 meters (18 feet) long.

This is a southern anaconda found from Bolivia and western Brazil south through Paraguay and Uruguay into northeastern Argentina. It was first described by Cope in 1862 (*Proc. Acad. Nat. Sci. Philadelphia*, 1862: 70) from

Map of eastern South America showing the general distribution of *E. notaeus*.

Head and midbody views of *E. notaeus*.

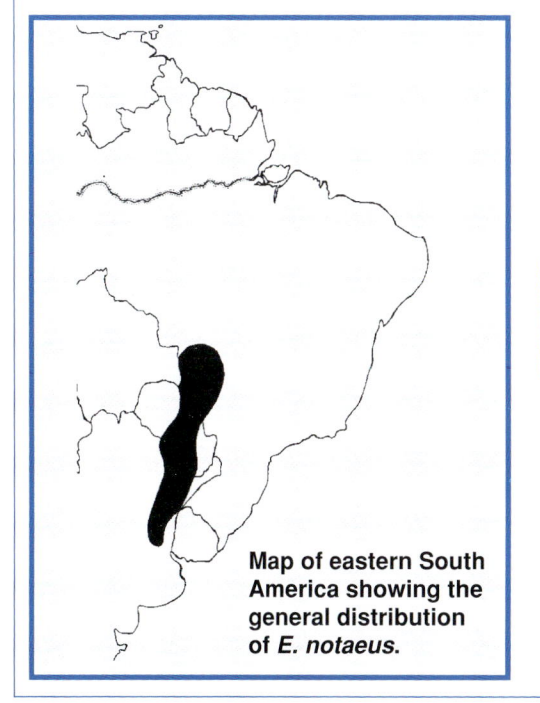

Unlike many snakes, Yellow Anacondas do not become darker as they age. They retain approximately the same contrast in their patterns throughout their lifetime. Photo by R. D. Bartlett.

the Paraguay River. *Epicrates wieningeri* Steindachner, 1903, described from Paraguay, generally is considered the same species, but the holotype is reported to have 244 ventrals and 64 subcaudals, both counts outside the normal range for the Yellow Anaconda, though it has a similar color pattern. The Yellow Anaconda is closely related to *E. deschauenseei* and distinguished only by color pattern, but the two species have different ranges.

In most aspects of their natural history and keeping, Yellow Anacondas are like small versions of Green Anacondas. They are mostly aquatic but sometimes stray a bit from the water and bask more often than Greens. Its smaller size allows it to climb a bit more than Greens, but it still is a largely aquatic and subaquatic species. It feeds on the usual array of mammals, birds, and some fishes and reptiles of appropriate size. Unlike Green Anacondas, it likes a nighttime temperature drop from a high of about 30°C (90°F) to as little as 18°C (65°F) at night. It is likely to spend days at a time in its pond, coming out only at night to

Ventral pattern of a Yellow Anaconda. Photo by M. Walls, courtesy of Steve and Rini Mitchell.

THE TRUE BOAS: BOIDAE

Although they stay smaller than their green cousins, Yellow Anacondas become very large snakes requiring huge quarters and careful management. They are not good snakes for beginning keepers. Photo by I. Francais.

feed. Yellow Anacondas have been bred in good numbers recently. The litters are relatively small, from 10 to 30 young, the newborns some 60 to 70 cm in length. The babies feed soon after birth and are sexually mature in about four years.

Eunectes notaeus is a beautiful boa and just tame enough to handle without too many problems until it reaches full size. It still

Xiphosoma madagascariensis Dumeril & Bibron.

Synonyms: None.

Arboreal Madagascan boas with deep vertical furrows or pits between the supralabials and infralabials. The head is distinct from the neck, the body is distinctly compressed and often ridge-backed, and the tail is short and prehensile. The eye is in contact with two or three

Smaller and hardier than Greens, Yellow Anacondas still are a challenge to house. They need high humidity, warm temperatures, and a large water area. Photo by A. Both.

requires a terrarium setup that is larger than most hobbyists can afford, and it can inflict dangerous bites by accident or intent. Unless you can provide for all its needs, you should not purchase a Yellow Anaconda as a pet.

Genus Sanzinia Gray, 1849 (*Catalogue Snakes British Mus.*: 98). Type species by monotypy

supralabials and is otherwise bordered by 8 to 11 small scales. The nostril is in a large partially divided scale, and there is a pair of distinct internasals on the snout. A single pair of prefrontals may be developed or all the scales on top of the head may be small. The scales of the loreal region are small and in several rows. The mental groove is distinct.

THE TRUE BOAS: BOIDAE

Sanzinia madagascariensis displaying its distinctive blue tongue, a characteristic not found in any of the other boids. The tongue, along with the labial pits and pattern, make this an easy boa to identify. Photo by R. D. Bartlett.

The musculature has been described by Auffenberg (1958) and is said to be quite distinct from that of *Boa constrictor*, probably as much through an adaptation for climbing as through any lack of relationship. The hemipenis probes to eight to ten subcaudals. The hemipenis is weakly forked, the lobes broad and with a strongly projecting flounce near their bases that gives the distal portion of the organ a vaguely diamond shape. The shaft is unornamented and about a third the length of the organ, separated from the expanded distal half by shallow flounces. The sulcus spermaticus is undivided for about 80% of its length, then forks into two short branches that end at the tips of the weakly defined lobes. There are 17 pairs of chromosomes

Map of Madagascar indicating the approximate range of *S. madagascariensis*.

SANZINIA MADAGASCARIENSIS

Madagascan Tree Boa

A pair of internasals is present and sometimes a pair of prefrontals as well (sometimes no or just a single prefrontal scale present). There are 8 to 11 small scales in a partial circle around the eye and some 10 to 12 scales between the eyes across the top of the head (variable). The scales on top of the head often appear distinctly rounded or tubercular. The scales in the loreal region are variable, but often are in three horizontal rows and two or three vertical rows. There may be a somewhat enlarged scale in front of the eye. There are 13 to 15 supralabials, two or three (sometimes one) touching the lower edge of the eye, and 14 or 15 infralabials, all separated by deep furrows or pits.

Sanzinia is the Madagascan equivalent of *Corallus*. The two genera share many characteristics and behaviors. Photo by R. D. Bartlett.

Head and midbody views of *S. madaga-scariensis*.

(2N=34), as in *Acrantophis* and unlike most other boas (*Boa* has 2N=36, *Corallus* 2N=40 or 44 as far as known).

Kluge (1993) synonymized *Sanzinia* with *Boa*, but the genus is so distinct in chromosome number, hemipenis structure, deep vertical pitting between the labials, and reported myology (musculature) that I can see no reason to synonymize the two genera or, for that matter, synonymize *Sanzinia* with *Acrantophis*, which differs in lacking labial pits, hemipenis structure, and general appearance and behavior.

THE TRUE BOAS: BOIDAE

above: Young *Sanzinia* are a bright, brick red, changing to olive green upon maturity. The specimens from the northwestern part of the range stay reddish brown an may be a separate species. Photo by R. D. Bartlett.

below: Although mostly arboreal, Madagascan Tree Boas seem to do the majority of their hunting after dark on the forest floor. Photo by P. Freed

This is a cleanly marked and brightly colored Madagascan Tree Boa that is showing some iridescence. Most individuals are neither as bright nor as easy to handle as this one. Photo by M. Walls.

The dorsal scales are smooth and in 41 to 53 rows at midbody. There are 200 to 234 ventrals and 30 to 48 subcaudals.

Adults and young differ in color and there is at least some variation as well with locality. As a rule, adults are greenish or olive-brown in tone with a yellowish belly that may be plain or marked with small blackish spots. The top of the head usually is marked with small irregular dark brownish specks, and there is a dark brown stripe from the back of the eye to the corner of the mouth, sometimes continuing forward to above the nostril. The labials generally are paler than the top of the head. The trunk carries two series of large dark brown diamonds or lozenges, one on each side, the rows sometimes meeting at mid-back or connected by narrow dark brown bars. Each diamond tends to have an elongate yellow to white stripe or spot in it and may have a wide whitish outer edge as well. Most juveniles are distinctly reddish, gradually assuming the greenish tones of the adult.

Most specimens in captivity come from the humid eastern coast of Madagascar, where juveniles are reddish and adults are distinctly greenish. Specimens from the northwestern part of the island, seldom seen in captivity, are brownish as juveniles and remain brownish as adults; they come from a relatively dry habitat and quite possibly represent a distinct species or subspecies.

Adults commonly exceed a meter in length, and there is a record of a specimen 250 cm long. The tail is about 8 to 10% of the total length.

THE TRUE BOAS: BOIDAE

Sanzinia is less dependent on high humidity in the terrarium than *Corallus caninus* or *Python viridis*. They do best when kept at a relative humidity of 70% or slightly higher but can tolerate occasional drops to 50%. Photo by R. D. Bartlett.

Sanzinia madagascariensis is found only on Madagascar, where it is common along most of the eastern coast, extending around the northern tip of the island some distance along the northwestern coast as well. It was first described as *Xiphosoma madagascariensis* by Dumeril & Bibron in 1844 (*Erpetol. gen.*, 6: 549) from three syntypes. Boulenger (1893) referred it to *Corallus*, and Kluge (1993) referred it to *Boa* along with the python *Python viridis*. The boa spends much of the day several meters up in trees, but it comes to the ground at night to feed on small mammals and perhaps frogs. The tail, though short, is quite prehensile, and the ridge-backed trunk is a typical adaptation of arboreal snakes. They are not choosy about humidity, being found in trees in dry areas, near swamps, and in rainforest conditions. It also adapts well to human interference and may be

Female *Sanzinia* turn very dark when they are gravid; some become almost black. This may be an adaptation enabling them to absorb more heat from the sun making it easier to keep their unborn young at the proper temperature. Photo by K. H. Switak.

Acrantophis. Referring both *Acrantophis madagascariensis* and *Sanzinia madagascariensis* to *Boa* created a problem with homonyms, and Kluge replaced the species name for the Madagascan Tree Boa with a new name, *mandrita*; if *Sanzinia* is held as distinct, as it is here, there is no reason to use the name *mandrita*, and it becomes a synonym of *Sanzinia madagascariensis*.

The habits of *Sanzinia* appear to be somewhat similar to those of found near villages and cultivated fields. Active at night and at dusk and dawn, especially during the rain, it is said to become inactive during the dry season from June to August. It has been said (though difficult to authenticate) that specimens from eastern Madagascar are aggressive while those from the northwest are gentle, but this does not hold true with captive-bred specimens.

In captivity, specimens should be kept individually in a tall, well-

THE TRUE BOAS: BOIDAE

Breeding Madagascan Tree Boas can be difficult. They seem to have low fertility in the terrarium. This could be due to breeding incompatibility between individuals from different parts of the range. Photo by R. D. Bartlett.

planted cage with many climbing branches. The terrarium should be kept at about 28 to 30°C (82 to 90°F) during the day, dropping to about 22°C (72°F) at night. Many adapt easily to mice as a main food, feeding at night and on the bottom of the cage. Breeding may be spurred by a cooling period of about two months (the temperature remaining at 20°C (68°F) or somewhat lower) to duplicate the natural resting period. This brumation may take place at mid-year or during the winter. Males may fight, entwining their tails, tugging at each other, and scraping their opponent's sides with their spurs. Males have larger spurs than females and a more tapered tail. Putting two males and a female together after brumation may lead to combat and more success in mating. Pregnancy may last from five to seven months and produces small litters (1 to 16 young) of large babies that may be 40 to 48 cm in length. The babies usually feed after their first shed at an age of one or two weeks. This species has proved difficult to breed with regularity in captivity, but some breeders produce decent numbers for sale each year. If possible, try to be sure of the origin of any specimens purchased and don't try to interbreed brown and green adults, which might represent different taxa. There are some indications that breeding difficulties may have a genetic basis. Many captive-bred specimens are quite vicious, like most other tree boas and tree pythons, and they do not have a strong following in the hobby.

The Javelin Sand Boa, *Eryx jaculus*, is one of the many sand boas present in the hobby in small numbers. Photo by G. and C. Merker.

The Burrowing Boas: Erycinidae

As you might expect, the relationships of the burrowing boas are uncertain. They appear to be closely related to the true boas, Boidae, but differ in being strongly adapted for burrowing, a specialization not present in the true boas. As such, they have stoutly constructed skulls with strengthened rostral areas to allow easier penetration of loose soil. Typically the rostral shield also is enlarged and projects from the snout, often extending backward to separate the internasal shields. The eyes are small and not protuberant, and they have vertically elliptical pupils. The color patterns usually are simple and the colors on the brownish side, while the tail is short, stout, and ends bluntly unless the terminal scale is developed as a claw-like spine to aid maneuvering in a burrow. The skeleton is a study in compactness, there being few spaces between the skull bones and the premaxillary-frontal bone junction is developed as a type of hinge to both stabilize the rostral area and allow it to flex for burrowing. The posterior vertebrae are oddly developed in most of the species (most simple in *Lichanura trivirgata*), with the neural crest (projection at the mid top of the vertebra) widened and bearing a deep groove. Often the posterior vertebrae are excessively developed and partially fused, with small spiny bone processes that help support the club-shaped mass that often is similar in size and development to the head.

The top of the head typically has a pair of internasals followed by two pairs of parietals, which may be broken into several small scales irregularly placed. The frontal is absent except in *Charina bottae* and is replaced by many small scales. Typically there are many small scales between the nostrils and the eye, without a distinct loreal, and the eye may be surrounded by a circle of many small scales. The supralabials may or may not be in contact with the eye (typically they are separated from it by several rows of

Rubber Boas, *Charina bottae*, have a distinct frontal scale which distinguishes them from the other members of the family. Photo by G. Merker, courtesy R. Straub.

small scales). The mental groove under the jaw may be developed or not, but there seldom are distinct chin shields developed. The ventrals are narrow, the dorsal scales small and rather oval instead of elongated, the anal is entire and often has small scales in front and behind it, and the subcaudals are entire. Commonly the tail ends in a rounded plate-like or thorn-like spine and is less than 10% of the total length. External leg remnants (spurs) are present in both sexes but may be quite small and hidden under scales, especially in females. All the species are live-bearers.

Traditionally three genera have been recognized in this group, which originally was defined as a tribe of the Boidae. The dozen species are quite uniform in development both internally and externally, and I find it difficult to see any characters that will separate the genera *Charina*, *Lichanura*, and *Eryx*. Kluge (1993) has synonymized *Lichanura* with *Charina*, a move that may be correct but which I have not followed here. (Kluge also synonymized the python *Calabaria*, which I consider to represent a full family, with *Charina*, a step that I consider to be very unfortunate and misleading.) It certainly appears that the species *trivirgata* is the most boa-like of the erycinids and assumedly the most primitive species of the family. The neural crests of the caudal vertebrae are distinctly flattened but only shallowly grooved and lack small spiny processes as in most other species of the family. The hemipenes of the three traditional genera are very similar in most respects. The most unspecialized head scalation occurs in *bottae*, which otherwise is quite specialized for burrowing. Frankly, the three groups are so similar, and the species of *Eryx* are so diverse in head form, that I could consider an argument to recognize only one genus (*Eryx*) in the family. I recognize here the three traditional genera, largely because *Lichanura* retains so many primitive features of the skeleton compared to the neighboring *Charina*, and I suspect they have been isolated for many years. However, I would strongly consider a system in which both *Charina* and *Lichanura* were synonymized with the Old World *Eryx*, as the differences among these snakes seem to be more at the specific level than the generic level.

Key to the Genera of Erycinidae

A. A distinct frontal scale present; adults typically unicolor above .... *Charina*

AA. Frontal scale absent, replaced by several small scales; adults typically with a pattern of dark brown stripes or blotches on a paler background .... B

B. Rostral shield prominent; tail relatively short and thick, ending in a plate or spine; Eurasia and Africa .... *Eryx*

BB. Rostral shield rounded and not prominent; tail relatively longer and more slender, slightly prehensile, not ending in a specialized plate-like or spiny scale; southwestern North America .... *Lichanura*

THE BURROWING BOAS: ERYCINIDAE

Genus Charina Gray, 1849 (*Catalogue of the Snakes in the British Museum*: 113). Type species by monotypy *Tortrix bottae* Blainville.

Synonyms: *Wenona* Baird & Girard, 1852; *Pseudoeryx* Jan, 1862 (preoccupied). Both names are based on specimens now identified as *bottae*.

Cylindrical boas of small to moderate size (under a meter in total length) with the head not distinct from the neck. The tail is short, about 10% of the total length, and only slightly tapers to the strongly rounded tip covered with an enlarged plate-like scale. The rostral shield is large and rounded, distinctly protuberant when seen from the side. From above it extends back to partially divide the internasals. The anterior prefrontals commonly are distinct, but the posterior prefrontals usually are broken into three to five scales (often two large scales separated by smaller azygous scales, but sometimes two distinct large prefrontals). The frontal is large and distinct (though sometimes somewhat fragmented), usually somewhat oval in shape. One or two enlarged scales over the eye can be interpreted as supraoculars. There may be small but distinct parietals behind the frontal. The nostril is situated between two nasal shields, the posterior often enlarged. Commonly there is a single scale corresponding to a loreal between the posterior nasal and the one or two preoculars. Typically there is a row of small scales separating the eye from the supralabials. The anterior supralabials may be much higher than the posterior ones. The mental groove is weakly defined, and there may be weakly enlarged chin shields.

The caudal vertebrae are strongly modified, the posterior ones with many small bony frills and ornaments on all the pro-

Charina probably ranges further north than any of the other boas. It is adapted to living in cool to cold conditions and spends large amounts of time in hibernation. Photo by G. and C. Merker.

cesses, the vertebrae partially fused and very variable in details. The neural crest is greatly flattened and deeply grooved, almost splitting the dorsal part of the vertebra into two. There are about 14 maxillary teeth, no palatine teeth, about 13 pterygoid teeth, and about 16 dentary teeth. The coronoid bone is absent or at least poorly developed. The hemipenes probe to about 15 subcaudals in males and are simple, not bilobed. The basal third is smooth, there

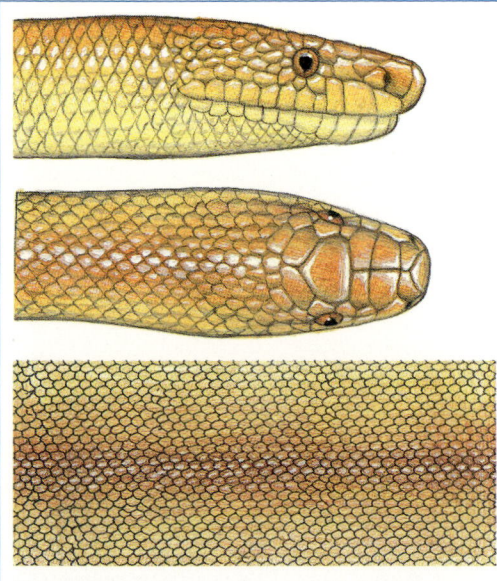

Head and midbody views of *C. bottae*.

CHARINA BOTTAE

Rubber Boa

Recognizing the Rubber Boa is simple because of its nearly cylindrical shape with a blunt, rounded tail and its uniform color. It is the only erycinid that normally has a distinct frontal scale.

The rostral shield is large and protuberant, extending back to nearly separate the large internasals. Though the head shields are very variable individually, typically there are two large and distinct prefrontals, sometimes separated by a small median scale. The frontal is large and seldom broken into two

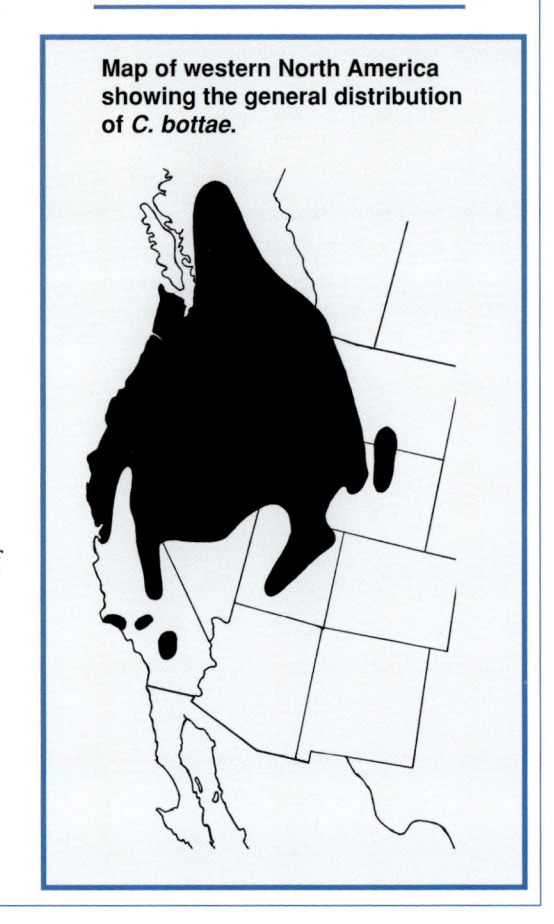

are about four large flounces over the middle third of the organ, and the distal third is rather inflated, smooth, and vaguely looks like a pair of large suckers. The sulcus is simple over most of the organ, bifurcating just before the end of the hemipenis.

Though there can be no doubt that *Charina* is closely related to both *Lichanura* and *Eryx*, *C. bottae* is the only species of the family to retain a frontal scale, assumedly a primitive state, while it has a strongly modified tail. The reduced palatine teeth and coronoid seem to be the culmination of reduction through the family. In sum, the snake bears a confusing mixture of what are probably primitive and specialized characters. The hemipenis looks much like that of *Lichanura* but differs in the more shallowly forked sulcus (probably just a specific character). The presence of a frontal will differentiate it from the other species of the family.

Map of western North America showing the general distribution of *C. bottae*.

THE BURROWING BOAS: ERYCINIDAE

pieces. Posteriorly it is convex to nearly straight. There is a pair of small but distinct parietals in most specimens, these sometimes broken. The anterior nasal may be fused with the internasal or not. Usually there is a single large, squarish loreal, but it may be fused with the prefrontal. There are one or two preoculars and two or three postoculars.

belly is yellowish, unmarked or with small spots or clouds of brown. Newborn specimens are very pale tan to pink, soon becoming darker; they have translucent cream to pale yellow bellies. Occasional specimens have brown specks along the lower scale row at the junction with the ventrals. A "lilac" mutation that appears to represent the absence of yellow

Rubber Boas are secretive snakes that spend much of their time under cover of one type or another. In the terrarium, provide a substrate that allows for burrowing. Photo by G. Merker, courtesy R. Straub.

There are 8 to 12 supralabials, one to three of which may contact the eye or be separated by small scales, and about 11 or 12 infralabials. The dorsal scales are smooth and in 39 to 49 rows at midbody (outside range 32 to 53). There are 182 to 231 ventrals and 24 to 43 subcaudals.

Most specimens are a uniform shade of light brown, often tending toward olive or reddish. The

(axanthic) has been recorded in the wild. These black-eyed specimens were pale grayish purple above, becoming pale purple on the sides and white on the belly. I am not aware that this mutant has been bred in captivity or offered for sale.

Adults commonly are 50 to 70 cm in total length; males are smaller than females. The record appears to be almost 84 cm. The tail is about 12 to 15% of the total length in males, 10 to 13% in females.

Rubber Boas are widely distributed over the northwestern United States and adjacent Canada. The species ranges from southern British Columbia, Canada, southward into central Utah, northern Nevada, and northern California, following the coast and the mountains southward as relict populations into southern California. The species was described in 1835 by Blainville (*Nouv. Ann. Mus. Hist. Nat. Paris*, 4: 289) from a specimen of uncertain origin somewhere in California. Three subspecies have been recognized in the past, but most workers today recognize only two: *C. b. bottae* over most of the range; and *C. b. umbratica* Klauber, 1943, as isolated populations in San Bernadino and Riverside Counties, California. Erwin (1974) made a good argument for recognizing *umbratica* as a distinct, isolated species, but intergrades with *bottae* are supposed to have been found. *C. b. umbratica* is smaller than the nominate subspecies (under 50 cm versus adult at over 50 cm), has the dorsal scales in about 39 rows at midbody (versus typically 42 to 46), averages only 191 ventrals (versus 205), and has the posterior edge of the frontal almost straight (versus convex). Synonyms include *plumbea* Baird & Girard, 1852; *isabella* Baird & Girard, 1852; *brachyops* Cope, 1889; and *utahensis* Van Denbergh, 1920.

Rubber Boas typically are inhabitants of moist coniferous forests and range from sea level to moderate altitudes. They usually are associated with pine, fir, and oak and often are found near streams. They are quite adaptable, however, and in some areas may be found near old home sites, trash dumps, and rather dry grasslands. In drier areas they may be found in silty or sandy areas, often near conifers. Rotten logs and other detritus on the forest floor provide cover, as do rodent burrows. They are confirmed burrowers but also climb a bit. Activity is mostly nocturnal or crepuscular, but sometimes they are abroad on cloudy days. Unlike other boas (except possibly some of the Russian desert forms), they can

Although they are unicolored, there is some variation in Rubber Boas. This especially dark individual was captured in Walla Walla, WA. Photo by K. H. Switak.

THE BURROWING BOAS: ERYCINIDAE

Be careful that the food given to Rubber Boas is not too big. They have small and rather inflexible mouths. Young specimens may need to be fed small lizards, frogs, or deer mouse pinkies. Photo by K. H. Switak.

tolerate cold temperatures and may be active at air temperatures near 10°C (50°F) and have been found crawling over light snow cover; their normal activity temperature is closer to 13 to 18°C (55 to 65°F). They feed on a variety of small mammals, especially shrews and rodents, and also on lizards and perhaps even large invertebrates, killing the prey by constriction. They are gentle snakes that coil tightly when disturbed and hide the head in the center of the coils. Mating occurs in spring when temperatures allow normal activity to resume. The young, usually only one to five in number, are born in August and September, sometimes when snow already is on the ground. They average 20 to 25 cm in total length. In some areas, young born late in the year may have to immediately retreat underground and remain in hibernation or brumation until next spring.

Few hobbyists keep Rubber Boas, and they have gained a poor reputation. This possibly is because wild-collected adults do not adapt to the warm temperatures maintained in most reptile rooms, becoming uncomfortable at temperatures above 21°C (70°F) or so. Captive-bred young may be a bit more adaptable but are difficult to obtain, perhaps because most breeders are located in California, which prohibits trade in native species. Regardless, if kept cool most of the year (about 18°C, 65°F, cooler at night) and provided with a loose substrate (sand/loam/peat moss) with many hiding areas, this species often does well and is a nice, gentle pet that accepts small mice readily. Beware of dehydration, however, because these snakes have thin skins. You may have to soak your specimen once a week to be sure it gets enough water. During the winter the temperature should be dropped gradually to about 10°C (50°F) for one to two months to maintain a natural rhythm. Breeding usually occurs when the snakes, kept separate during brumation, are returned to normal temperatures in the spring and put together. Males are smaller than females, have longer and more slender tails, and have conspicuous curved spurs (often hidden and straight in females). Pregnant females should be maintained at warmer temperatures and give a weak basking light. Young may have to be brumated before they will feed during the next spring, but allow them to eat if they wish. Litters often consist of just one or two young. They mature in about three years and may live more than ten years in captivity.

Genus Eryx Daudin, 1803 (*Hist. Nat. Rept.*, 7: 251). Type species by subsequent designation *Boa turcica* Olivier = *E. jaculus*.

Synonyms: *Clothonia* Daudin, 1803 [*johnii*]; *Cusoria* Gray, 1849 [*elegans*]; *Gongylophis* Wagler, 1830 [*conicus*]; *Neogongylophis* Tokar, 1989 [*colubrinus*]; *Pseudogongylophis* Tokar, 1989 [*jayakari*].

Small to medium boas that seldom reach a meter in length. The head is rather depressed and not distinct from the stout body. In most species the snout is distinctly shovel-shaped and the mouth is countersunk, an adaptation for burrowing in loose sand. The tail is short, commonly only 8% of the total length, and sometimes ends in a heavy, pointed or down-turned spiny scale, though it may be simply conical or bluntly rounded. The rostral scale is prominent and often protuberant or may have a distinctly sharp edge, and it often projects backward to partially divide the internasals. Behind the internasals may be one to three pairs of prefrontals or just a field of small, irregular scales of mixed sizes. The frontal, supraoculars, and parietals are not distinct. The nostril is small, often slit-like, and placed between two nasal shields and followed by several small scales to the eye, without a distinct loreal or (usually) preoculars. The supralabials may reach the eye or be separated from it by small scales. The mental groove usually is distinct, and there may be well-developed chin shields.

The neural crest of the caudal vertebrae is low and flat, with a deep groove, and there are many small bony frills and ornaments on most of the processes of the vertebrae (variation in vertebral characters has been used as a generic and subgeneric character by workers). There are about 10 to 15 maxillary teeth, 3 to 6 palatine teeth, 3 or 4 pterygoid teeth (about 13 in *E. conicus*), and 11 to 13 dentary teeth (about 17 in *E. conicus*). The coronoid is well developed. The hemipenes probe to about 6 to 12 subcaudals in males and are simple, not forked or bilobed. The proximal third of the shaft is smooth, there are about three weak flounces at the center of the shaft, and the distal third is weakly or strongly inflated and is ornamented with sponge-like reticulations. The sulcus forks beyond the middle of the organ, the forks disappearing before reaching the end of the organ.

As usually recognized, *Eryx* is a rather diverse genus. Tokar (1989) recognized two genera and four subgenera for these species, and he may have a point, though usually all the names are synonymized with *Eryx*. Because *conicus* differs so much in both counts of teeth and the strongly keeled scales, as well as many osteological characters, it often has been placed in the full genus *Gongylophis*, though most authors today fail to recognize this genus. Tokar in fact recognized *Gongylophis* as a genus, but he included in it several species in two subgenera: *G. (G.) conicus*; *G. (Neogongylophis) colubrinus*; *G. (N.) muelleri*, the latter two African. Tokar also broke *Eryx* into two subgenera: *E. (E.) elegans*; *E. (E.) jaculus*; *E. (E.) johni*; *E. (E.) miliaris*; *E. (E.) somalicus*; *E. (E.) tataricus*; *E (E.) vittatus*; *E. (Pseudogongylophis) jayakari*. [*E. vittatus* traditionally has been considered a subspecies of *E. tataricus*.] The problem with Tokar's genera and subgenera is that they are based on development of the tooth-bearing bones, number of teeth, and degree of ornamentation of the caudal vertebrae, all characters that vary in nearly a continuum from species to species. It might be better,

Many of the *Eryx* have blunt tails that resemble their heads. This pseudo-head is used to lure predators away from the real one. Pictured is the Brown Sand Boa, *E. johni*. Photo by I. Francais.

instead of breaking *Eryx* into smaller genera, to synonymize *Charina* and *Lichanura* with it, as a case could be made that several species of *Eryx* are as distinct from the type of *Eryx* (*jaculus*) as they are from *bottae* and *trivirgata*. The problem is not aided by the rarity of several species in collections and the almost inaccessible areas occupied by some of the species.

Key to the Species of Eryx

A. Eyes entirely on upper surface of the head, separated by only four rows of scales; tail ending in a curved spine .... *jayakari*

AA. Eyes on dorsolateral surface of head, separated by five or more rows of scales; tail ending bluntly, in a straight spine, or in a curved spine .... B

B. Rostral with a rounded edge; body with scales in 40 or more rows, the scales strongly keeled; head scales strongly keeled; eyes separated by 8 or more scale rows; tail simply pointed .... *conicus*

BB. Rostral with a sharp horizontal edge; body scales usually without strong keels at least anteriorly; head scales not keeled C

C. Top of head with about 12 to 15 scales between the eyes; 44 to 59 dorsal scale rows;

The Rough-scaled Sand Boa, *E. conicus*, has some interesting differences from the other *Eryx*. This has led some herpetologists to place it in its own genus, *Gongylophus*. Photo by R. D. Bartlett.

In this book I have been conservative recognizing species and subspecies, simply following the more recent literature. The species from the southern Russian area remain poorly understood, with a multitude of subspecies of doubtful status described; some may be full species, but probably most are synonyms. The following key probably will not work to distinguish all the variations of the species correctly.

THE BURROWING BOAS: ERYCINIDAE

Ventral head view of the Central Asian Sand Boa, *E. miliaris*. Note the large rostral and deep mental groove. Photo by M. Walls.

ventrals 162 to 197; tail tip sharply pointed .... *colubrinus*

CC. Top of head with only 5 to 9 scales between the eyes .... D

D. Tail ending in a pointed, sometimes curved spine; Africa below Sahara .... E

DD. Tail ending bluntly or in a straight, conical spine; Eurasia and Mediterranean .... F

E. Midbody scale rows 38 to 45; ventrals 174 to 187; subcaudals 16 to 21; five scales between the eyes .... *muelleri*

EE. Midbody scale rows 39 or 40; ventrals 159 to 161; subcaudals 24 to 26; six scales between the eyes .... *somalicus*

F. Adults uniformly brown above or with traces of dark transverse bands; dorsal scales in 54 to 65 rows at midbody; ventrals 194 to 210 .... *johni*

FF. Adults with spotted or blotched pattern above; dorsal scales in fewer than 55 rows at midbody .... *jaculus* complex

G. Prefrontals not developed; dorsal pattern often of open pale blotches down center of back outlined by darker wavy bands; dorsal scale in 43 to 49 rows at midbody; ventrals 164 to 184; subcaudals 20 to 32 .... *miliaris*

GG. Prefrontals developed; dorsal pattern of dark blotches down center of back .... H

H. Prefrontals as large as or larger than internasals; dorsal scale rows 36 to 41 at midbody; ventrals 162 to 184; subcaudals 22 to 45. .... *elegans*

HH. Prefrontals smaller than internasals; dorsal scales in more than 41 rows at midbody I

I. Top of head with scales in more or less regular rows; often three similar scales behind prefrontals; east of Caspian Sea............... *tataricus*

II. Top of head with scales very irregular; two or three scales behind prefrontals, the middle scale smaller than the lateral ones; west of Caspian Sea ....*jaculus*

ERYX COLUBRINUS

Kenyan Sand Boa

The only commonly seen species of sand boa in captivity, *Eryx colubrinus* is easily recognized by its relatively large and stout body and the distinctive head scalation: numerous tiny scales between the eyes and only the internasals developed.

The internasals are the only developed shields on top of the head. The rostral shield is broad and has a sharp horizontal edge. There are 11 to 15 small and irregularly placed scales between the eyes across the top of the head and about 12 to 15 small scales in a circle around the eye. The supralabials number 12 to 14; there are two rows of scales between the eye and the supralabials. There are 19 to 21 small infralabials. The mental groove is weak or absent. The dorsal scales are in 44 to 59 rows at midbody (formula commonly 43/49-53/59-25/29 in specimens from Kenya) and are smooth or weakly keeled (often strongly blackish blotches across the back, the blotches wider than the interspaces. Often the blotches run together to form two broad, irregular broken blackish brown bands outlining a bright orange-tan middorsal stripe. A row of small dark brown or blackish spots is low on the side and often fused into a broken and very irregular band. On top of the tail are five or six narrow blackish bands.

This is a very pale specimen of the Kenyan Sand Boa with reduced brown spotting. These animals exhibit a lot of variation, and breeders are selecting for some interesting and pretty patterns and colors. Photo by G. and C. Merker, courtesy of C. Reinman.

keeled over the vent). There are 162 to 197 narrow ventrals and about 19 to 28 subcaudals. The tail is thick and bluntly pointed, ending in a conically pointed scale. Maxillary teeth 12, palatine teeth 4 or 5; pterygoids 8; dentary teeth 10 to 12.

Though quite variable in coloration and pattern from individual to individual, typically adults are bright orange-tan with large

The top of the head is pale with a broad band across the snout and a narrower stripe from the nape to between the eyes, and there may be a broad dark stripe back from the eye; the head pattern actually is quite variable. The belly is whitish to yellowish and usually unmarked or nearly so. Cultivated color forms exist.

This is a rather large sand boa, adults often exceeding 50 cm in

THE BURROWING BOAS: ERYCINIDAE

Kenyan Sand Boas are the most popular of the sand boas in the hobby. This is not surprising, as they are one of the largest, most colorful, and easiest to breed and care for. Photo by G. Merker, courtesy of R. Straub.

total length. The maximum length appears to be 77 cm. The tail is about 8 to 9% of the total length.

Though I'm calling this species the Kenyan Sand Boa because that is the most familiar name among hobbyists, the species ranges from the mouth of the Nile in Egypt south through eastern Africa to Kenya and Tanzania, with a record from Niger and one doubtful specimen collected in Yemen on the Arabian Peninsula. The range appears to be continuous or nearly so, but three subspecies have been recognized in the literature: *E. c. colubrinus* Linnaeus, 1758 (*Systema Naturae*, Ed. 10, 1: 228, type from Egypt), from Egypt south to Somalia; *E. c. rufescens* Ahl, 1933 (Somalia); and *E. c. loveridgei* Stull, 1932, from southern Somalia to Kenya and northern Tanzania. In theory the subspecies can be distinguished by dorsal and ventral scale counts, but instead they appear to produce a continu-

Head and midbody view of *E. colubrinus*.

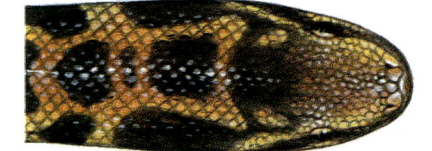

ous and overlapping sequence; the midbody scale row count appears to increase from north to south (*colubrinus* 47-49; *rufescens* 44-50; *loveridgei* 50-59), while the number of ventrals decreases from north to south (*colubrinus* 175-197; *rufescens* 181-194; *loveridgei* 162-185), at least in a general way (data from Scortecci, 1939). I see no reason to recognize subspecies in this species on the basis of published data and consider *loveridgei*, the form supposedly most common in the hobby on the basis of origin of imports, to be a synonym of *colubrinus*; *rufescens* long has been considered a synonym.

For many years this species was called *E. thebaicus* Reuss, 1834, *colubrinus* being considered a synonym of *E. jaculus*. *E. scutata* Gray, 1842, is a synonym. Questionably the taxon described by Jan, 1863, as *E. jaculus* var. *sennariensis* (Sennar, a region of the eastern Sudan) has been considered a synonym, but if so it must be based on an aberrant specimen.

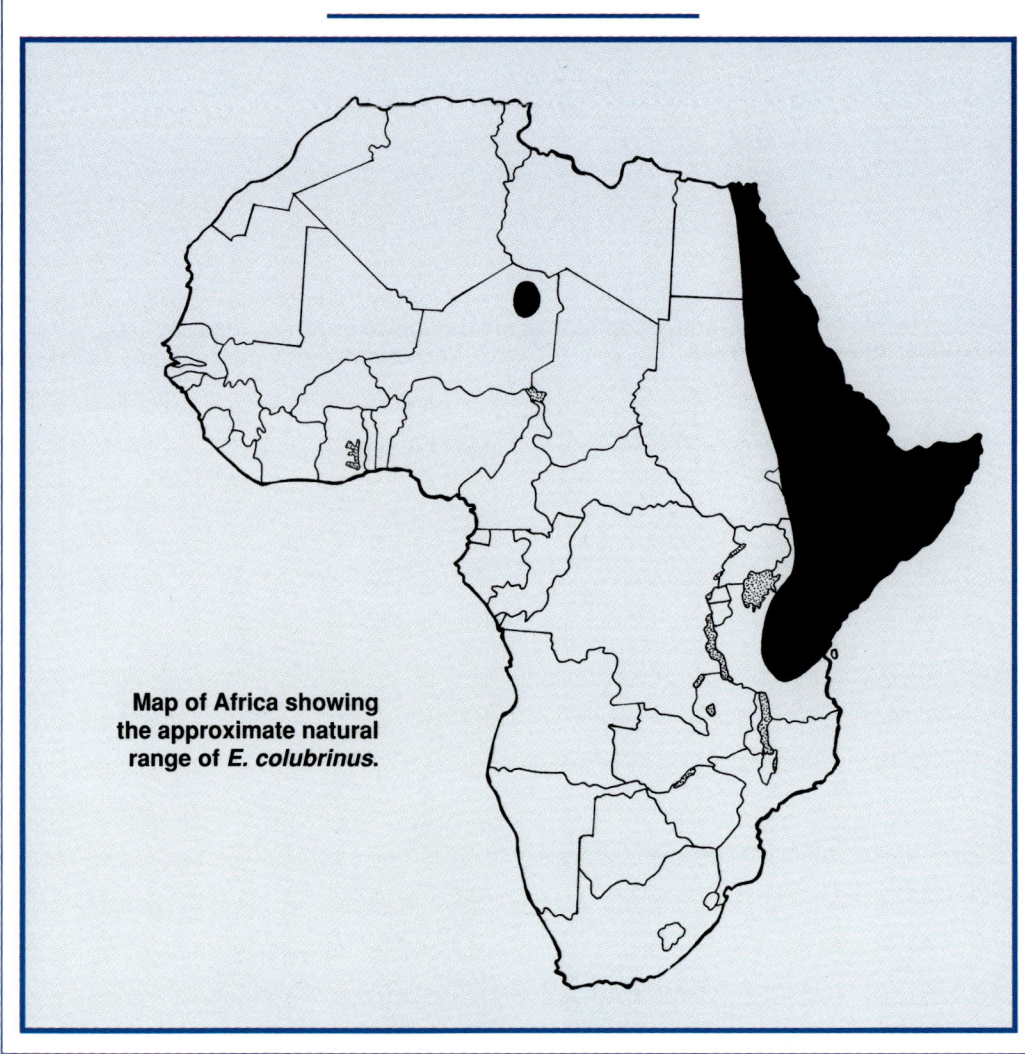

Map of Africa showing the approximate natural range of *E. colubrinus*.

THE BURROWING BOAS: ERYCINIDAE

Kenyan Sand Boas are secretive burrowers that are active at night. They occur in dry habitats ranging from sandy areas to dry savanna with shrubs and feed on a variety of invertebrates and small vertebrates that they find during their rambles under the ground and at the surface. Lizards seem to be the preferred prey, but earthworms, insect larvae, and small mammals are taken by different sizes of boas. Though usually considered inoffensive, they have large teeth and can produce a painful bite if surprised or annoyed.

Like other sand boas, they usually are kept in small terraria, and several specimens can be

Neonatal Kenyan Sand Boa next to an adult. The sand boas tend to have small litters of large young. Photo by I. Francais.

As an example of the variation in *E. colubrinus*, consider these three individuals. All of them were collected in Tanzania and, if subspecies are recognized, are identified as *E. colubrinus loveridgei*. Photo by P. Freed.

kept in one cage. Commonly an under-tank heater keeps part of the terrarium substrate at 32 to 35°C (90 to 95°F), with another area allowed to drop sharply at night. A basking light in one corner may be used on occasion, especially by pregnant females. The substrate should be loose, often just plain smooth large-grained sand, with some partially buried hide boxes and pieces of broken crockery and cork bark. Acclimated specimens often spend much of their time on the surface and will take small mice presented just before the room lights are turned off. A water bowl is not necessary, but a soak once or twice a week may be appreciated, as may an occasional spraying.

Recently Kenyan Sand Boas have been bred in good numbers

Two of the widely produced color phases of Kenyan Sand Boas are the axanthic (black and white) and the amelanistic (tan and yellow) phases. Photo by W. P. Mara.

This individual shows a lot of orange color and reduced brown blotching. By breeding this animal to other mostly orange ones and so on, solid orange Kenyan Sand Boas might eventually appear. Photo by R. D. Bartlett.

THE BURROWING BOAS: ERYCINIDAE

The sand boas prefer rather dry conditions in the wild and in the terrarium. A high relative humidity will lead to health problems such as respiratory and skin infections. Photo by I. Francais.

in captivity. Though some pairs mate in a rather normal way on the surface of the terrarium at night, others restrict their activity to completely below the sand. The male, which has larger spurs than the female (in some females the spurs may be completely hidden under scales and hard to find), comes up under the female and loosely coils about her body, eventually putting his cloaca in contact with hers. The short tails end up projecting vertically through the surface of the sand in some cases. Young are born about four to six months after mating and may number 6 to 15 or more. The young are like small versions of the adults but usually more colorful. Most will take pinkie mice after their first shed. Sexual maturity is reached by three years of age.

Two captive-bred color variants currently are available. The albino form may be striking pink and orange, while the axanthic form often appears black and dull gray. There is considerable variation in the color quality of both variants, and specimens are best purchased after examination of the parents to determine how well the colors will maintain themselves. I find the axanthic form distinctly unattractive, but many keepers like it. There seems to be a trend among breeders to select (perhaps unconsciously) for specimens with reduced blackish blotching and paired bands instead.

Most specimens seen are small, but full adults are thick-bodied, impressive snakes that at first glance may be hard to relate to the small specimens usually seen. Specimens often live for eight to ten years in captivity.

Currently, the Kenyan Sand Boa is the only *Eryx* produced in any color and pattern variants. As the other sand boas are bred in greater numbers, new color morphs are sure to become established. Photo by W. P. Mara.

THE BURROWING BOAS: ERYCINIDAE

ERYX CONICUS

Rough-scaled Sand Boa

One of the most distinctive little boas, *E. conicus* may be recognized by the presence of strongly keeled scales on top of the head and over the entire upper body. The keeling and several oddities of the skeleton have led to some workers placing the species in a distinct genus, *Gongylophis*, but recent interpretations are against ranking it as a separate genus.

The rostral shield is broad but not especially sharp-edged. The internasals are large and are the only developed shields on top of the head. There are 8 to 10 small scales from eye to eye across the top of the head, 10 to 15 scales around the eye, and one or two rows of scales between the eye and the supralabials. There are 11 to 14 supralabials and 14 to 17 infralabials. There is no trace of a mental groove. Except for the scales of the lower sides, the dorsal scales and scales on top of the head bear raised pimple-like keels that are especially strong on the tail. The dorsal scales are in 45 to 55 rows at midbody (rarely as few as 40). There are 161 to 182 ventrals and 17 to 24 subcaudals.

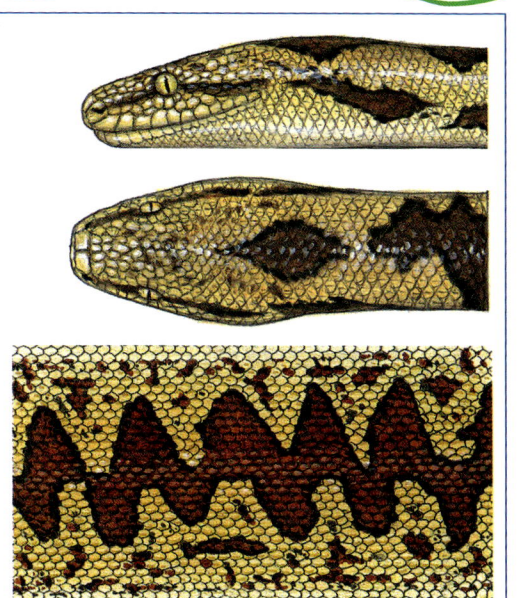

Head and midbody views of *E. conicus*

Most specimens are a pale yellow or tan to grayish, sometimes with a reddish tinge along the center of the back. There are many large irregular dark brown

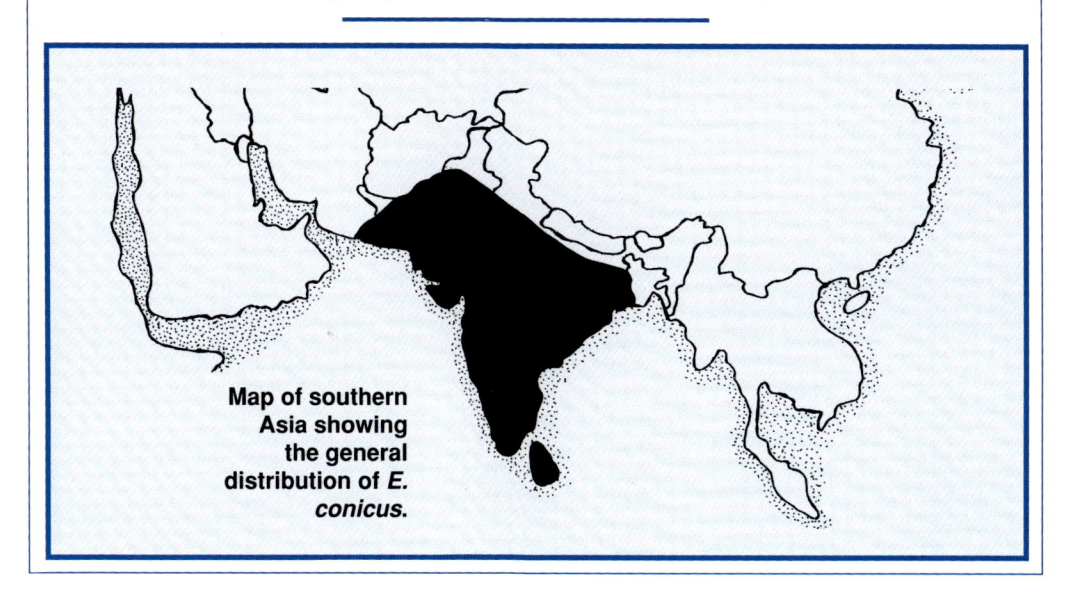

Map of southern Asia showing the general distribution of *E. conicus*.

Head of *E. conicus*. Note the heavy keeling of the scales. Photo by R. D. Bartlett.

or reddish brown blotches on the back, these often fused into short zigzag bands. The smaller blotches on the sides often are elongated and partially fused as well. The belly is white, rarely with small grayish spots.

Adults commonly are 50 to 60 cm in total length, occasionally with large females reaching almost 90 cm in length. The tail is very short and tapers to a blunt point; it is only some 6 to 7% of the total length.

Eryx conicus is a common snake over almost all but extreme northern India and Pakistan. It also occurs in Sri Lanka and should occur in eastern Iran and also in Bangladesh, though I am not aware of records for these countries. It was described by Schneider in 1801 as *Boa conica* (*Hist. Amph.*, 2: 268) from Tranquebar, southern India. Synonyms include *viperina* Shaw, 1802; *ornata* Daudin, 1803; and *bengalensis* Guerin-Meneville, 1830. The doubtful subspecies *brevis* Deraniyagala, 1951, from Sri Lanka probably is not distinct.

This is a very secretive burrower in nature, inhabiting both sandy and silty areas with shrubs and even standing water. They come up only at night or after heavy rains flood their burrows. As usual, they feed mostly on small mammals but also take lizards. This is a species commonly used by snake charmers because of its strong resemblance to the rightly feared Russell's Viper, *Vipera russelli*, one of the most deadly snakes in India. When picked up it flattens the head and makes a slashing strike

The pattern of *E. conicus* resembles that of the highly venomous Russel's Viper that occurs within its range. This may provide some protection from predators. Photo by I. Francais.

THE BURROWING BOAS: ERYCINIDAE 173

This is a very stocky Rough-scaled Sand Boa, possibly a gravid female. Female sand boas may spend many hours basking under a light, keeping their body temperature near 38°C / 100°F. Photo by G. and C. Merker, courtesy of C. Reinman.

Young Rough-scaled Sand Boas are slightly brighter in color than adults. This one has a warm, yellowish cast to it that, unfortunately, likely will fade as the animal ages. Photo by K. H. Switak.

to the side, producing a painful bite. Young are born in June and July in Pakistan. and measure about 20 cm in total length.

Often seen in captivity, though not nearly as common as the Kenyan Sand Boa, *Eryx conicus* is easy to keep, hardy, long-lived (often surviving 20 years), and requires little in the way of caging and food. Adults and young both feed readily on frozen, thawed mice of the appropriate size, though pregnant females may not feed during the six months or so of their pregnancy. As often is the case in sand boas, males have longer, more slender tails than females and obvious spurs (the spurs of females may be very small and completely hidden under scales). Pregnant females often use a basking light. Most litters contain from 8 to 12 young, though larger litters (to 17) have been recorded. Young are more brightly colored than adults but with similar patterns. I'm not aware of color variants being bred so far, but I believe that albinos have occurred. There are few breeders of this species, but it seems that selective breeding might improve the color quality of specimens, emphasizing the yellow and pale reddish tendencies of some specimens. Except for a tendency to strike when first handled, this is an excellent species for the enthusiast.

Sand boas are content to live in small sweater boxes, as long as they are kept warm and dry. Photo by I. Francais.

ERYX ELEGANS

Elegant Sand Boa

The Elegant Sand Boa is one more of the poorly known species related to *E. jaculus* occurring in the Afghanistan-southern Russian deserts. It differs from the other species in the larger dorsal scales, 41 or fewer around midbody as compared to commonly 45 or more in the related *E. jaculus*, *miliaris*, and *tataricus*.

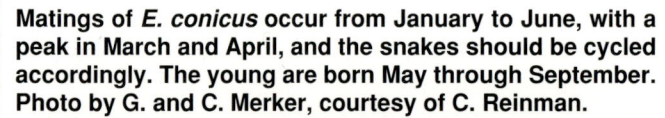

Matings of *E. conicus* occur from January to June, with a peak in March and April, and the snakes should be cycled accordingly. The young are born May through September. Photo by G. and C. Merker, courtesy of C. Reinman.

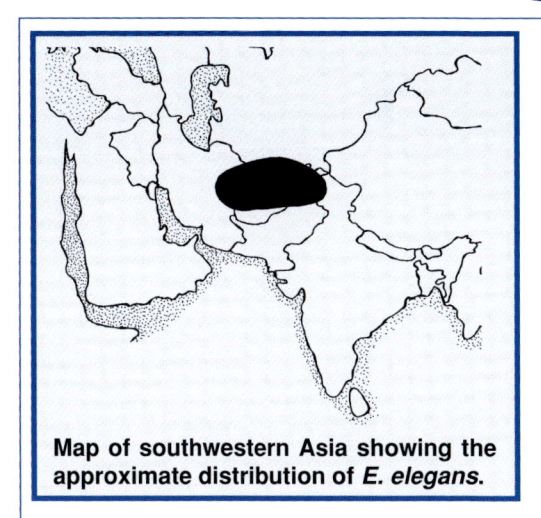

THE BURROWING BOAS: ERYCINIDAE

Map of southwestern Asia showing the approximate distribution of *E. elegans*.

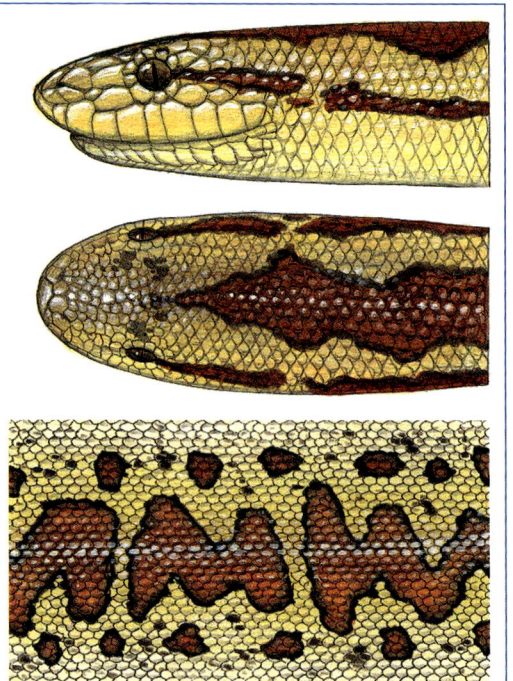

Head and midbody views of *E. elegans*.

The rostral shield is broad, with a sharp horizontal edge. The internasals are large and are followed by a pair of prefrontals of about equal size. The top of the head is covered with irregular scales, with 7 between the eyes across the top of the head, about 9 scales around the eye, and usually only one row of scales between the eye and the supralabials. There are 9 or 10 supralabials. The mental groove is developed. The dorsal scales are smooth, occasionally keeled above the cloaca, and in 35 to 41 rows at midbody. There are 159 to 184 (rarely to 149) ventrals and 22 to 45 subcaudals (a tremendous range, but females tend to have lower counts than males).

This species is grayish to pale olive in color with rather small dark brown rounded spots down the middle of the back and small spots on the sides. The blotches may be distinctly outlined with black. The head is pale, with at most traces of a dark band behind the eye. The belly is white to pale yellow with many black spots.

Adults reach about 40 cm in total length. The tail is relatively long, 10 to 15% of the total length.

E. elegans was described by Gray in 1849 (*Catalogue of Snakes British Museum*: 107) as *Cusoria elegans* based on a specimen from Afghanistan. It ranges from Turkmenistan and northeastern Iran across Afghanistan supposedly into northwestern India, but this area is of course badly collected and the details of the range are uncertain. *E. jaculus czarewski* Nikolsky, 1916, described from the Kopet-Dag region of Iran, is considered to be a synonym though it has a distinctly lower ventral count (149 to 169) than typical specimens (159 to 184). This species exhibits a tremendous range of scale counts and obviously deserves more study.

I've seen little on the natural history of this species, but it seems to be found in dry, high deserts and savannas subject to great temperature extremes. It is considered rare, but of course the remoteness of the range and political difficulties in the area may simply make collecting difficult.

ERYX JACULUS

Javelin Sand Boa

This was the first sand boa kept in the terrarium because it occurs in eastern Europe and at one time was commonly collected for the hobby there and in northern Africa. Today, however, European populations are largely protected or extirpated and only a few specimens are being shipped out of Egypt and occasionally points further east. It is the westernmost species of a complex including *E. tataricus, miliaris,* and *elegans,* and is difficult to distinguish from those species. In the hobby it is likely to be confused with the much more common *E. colubrinus,* which also may be shipped out of Egypt, but that species has much smaller scales on top of the head, with a dozen or more between the eyes, while there are only 5 to 9 between the eyes in *E. jaculus.*

The rostral shield is prominent and sometimes quite produced, with a sharp horizontal edge and a long backward extension to partially separate the large internasals. A pair of small prefrontals is present, often with a third scale between them. There are 5 to 7 (rarely 9) scales between the eyes across the top of the head, 7 to 14 small scales in a circle around the eye, and one row of scales between the eye and the supralabials. There are 10 to 14 supralabials. The mental groove is developed. The dorsal scales are in 45 to 54 rows at midbody (rarely as few as 40, seldom more than 50) and are smooth except posteriorly, where they may be weakly keeled. The ventrals number 161 to 205, the subcaudals 19 to 36 (females have much shorter tails than males and thus lower subcaudal counts). As in most of the similar sand boas, the tail is thick and bluntly conical.

Coloration varies considerably depending on local conditions, but generally the boa is tan to orange-tan or yellow with many dark brown spots of very irregular shape down the middle of the back and smaller spots along the

Head and midbody views of *E. jaculus*.

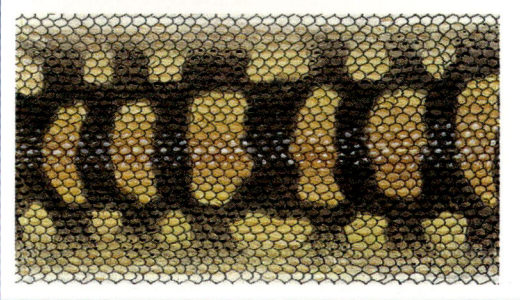

THE BURROWING BOAS: ERYCINIDAE

Photo of *E. jaculus* showing the orange color of the ventral surface. The belly color of this species ranges from white to pink to orange and may be plain or spotted. Photo by P. Freed.

sides. The blotches often fuse into short stripes and larger blotches. On the nape the blotches may form a pair of elongated spots that converge toward the top of the head. Usually there is a dark brown stripe back from the eye. The belly varies from white to orange or pink and may have dark brown or blackish spots or be plain. Solid brown as well as bluish, green, and pinkish specimens have been recorded, these colors sometimes prominent in local populations.

Most adult Javelin Sand Boas are over 50 cm in total length, and the record appears to be about 80 cm. The tail is 8 to 12% of the total length.

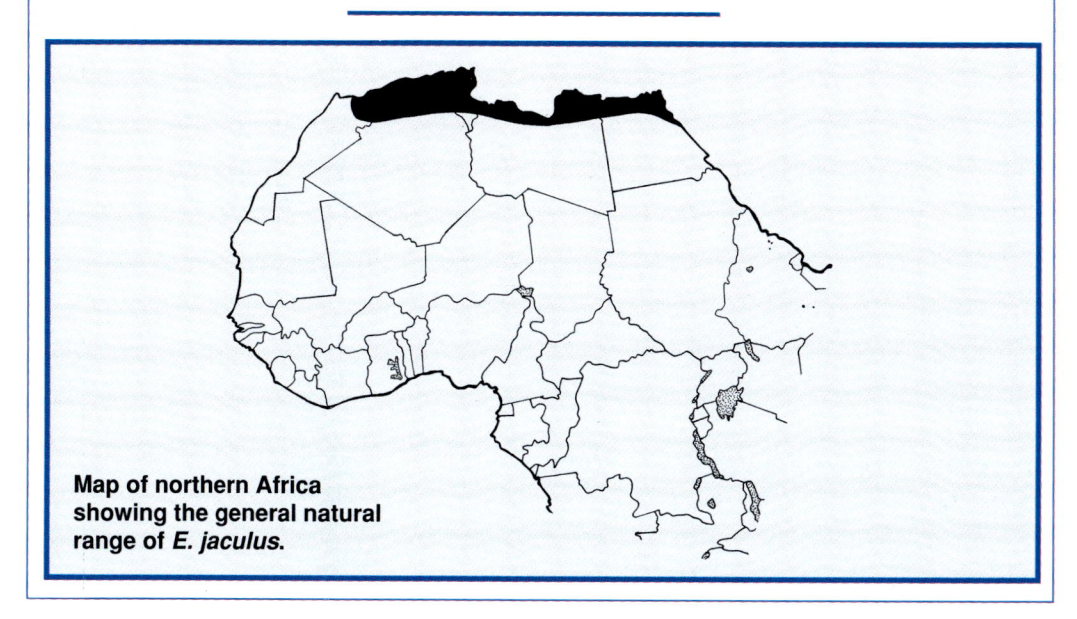

Map of northern Africa showing the general natural range of *E. jaculus*.

Javelin Sand Boas are difficult to distinguish from some of the other Asian sand boas, such as *E. miliaris* and *E. tartaricus*. Hobby animals may be misidentified. Photo by C. Banks.

Map of western Asia and eastern Europe showing the general distribution of *E. jaculus*.

A wide-ranging species, the Javelin Sand Boa is found from Russian states on the shores of the Caspian Sea south into Israel, Syria, Iraq, and northern Saudi Arabia. It occurs across Turkey into eastern Europe in the Balkans (where locally extirpated) and the Greek islands and mainland. It also occurs across northern Africa from Algeria and Morocco to Egypt. Records from Mongolia and China seem to apply to *E. tataricus* or similar species. Over this range specialists have distinguished three subspecies that are individually very variable and usually impossible to distinguish unless the collecting locality is known (which makes one doubt their validity; there appear to be no gaps in either distribution or morphology between the subspecies). These are: *E. j. jaculus*, from northern Africa into the Middle East and Iran; *E. j. turcicus* (Olivier, 1801) from the Balkans and Greece as well as eastern Turkey; and *E. j. familiaris* Eichwald, 1831, from western Turkey, the Georgia-Armenia area, to northwestern Iran. *E. j. jaculus* and *E. j. turcicus* tend to have a large scale dividing the prefrontals and touching the internasals, while *E. j. familiaris* lacks this third scale or, if present, the scale does not touch the internasals. Some authors do not distinguish *E. j. turcicus* from the nominate subspecies. The species was described by Linnaeus in 1758 as *Anguis jaculus* (*Systema Naturae*, Ed. 10, 1: 228) from Egypt. Synonyms that have accumulated over the years include *cerastes* Linnaeus, 1758; *teherana* Jan, 1865; *proprius* Carevsky, 1916; and *urmianus* Rostombekov, 1928.

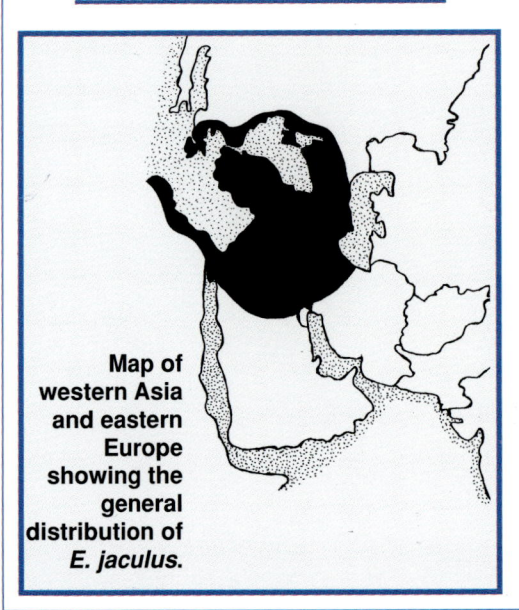

THE BURROWING BOAS: ERYCINIDAE

This sand boa occurs in the usual dry, sandy deserts and savannas over much of its range, but it also occupies more heavily vegetated areas with loose soil in eastern Europe. It is a strong burrower and often also is found in the burrows dug by small rodents, its major food. Additionally it eats lizards, small birds, and even carrion. This is a long-lived species, with specimens often living over 15 years in captivity.

It can be kept much like *E. colubrinus*, with a few specimens in a relatively small, warm, terrarium with sand as the substrate and hiding place. The sand should be deep enough to allow the snakes to dig freely. Though some keepers feel that strict adherence to a complicated photoperiod and temperature regime is necessary, others feel the snakes are not nearly so sensitive. Since the area in which they occur often has cold winters (especially the European and southern Asian populations), a two-month cooling during the winter with reduced light might not be a bad idea. Specimens from North Africa, however, may do well at more or less constant temperatures and lighting over the entire year (allow the temperature to drop at night, of course, as for most desert animals).

Males may compete for females, so it is best to keep them separately most of the year. A mating

Due to development and over-collection, the Javelin Sand Boa is threatened throughout the northern and eastern parts of its range. Several countries protect it, and this snake is seldom available to the average hobbyist. Photo by V. Jirousek.

Some commercial breeders produce a few Javelin Sand Boas every year. They are as easy to care for as the other and boas and hopefully will become more available. Photo by G. and C. Merker, courtesy of C. Reinman.

trio of two males and one female may produce best breeding results. The specimens should be put together in early spring and separated after several matings have been noted over the next month or so. Litters are small, usually less than ten young. The young and adults feed well on small mice, with large females even taking rat pups. Males may not feed for several months when looking for females to breed. Males have obviously longer and more tapering tails than females, and females usually are longer and thicker than males. Maturity is reached in about three years.

Because this species has been over-collected in eastern Europe, it has disappeared from much of its range and seldom is common anywhere in the area. Specimens still are taken (illegally, mostly) in the Greek islands. Egypt occasionally exports specimens to Europe and probably the American market as well, but specimens from further east in the range are rarely seen. In America this is not a familiar species, few specimens reaching the hands of hobbyists, and those that do may be confused with *E. colubrinus*.

ERYX JAYAKARI

Arabian Sand Boa

This truly unique sand boa probably deserves its own genus and is the type of the Tokar subgenus *Eryx (Pseudogongylophis)*. It can be recognized immediately by the greatly flattened head and the small eyes (with oblique vertical pupils) that are placed distinctly

THE BURROWING BOAS: ERYCINIDAE

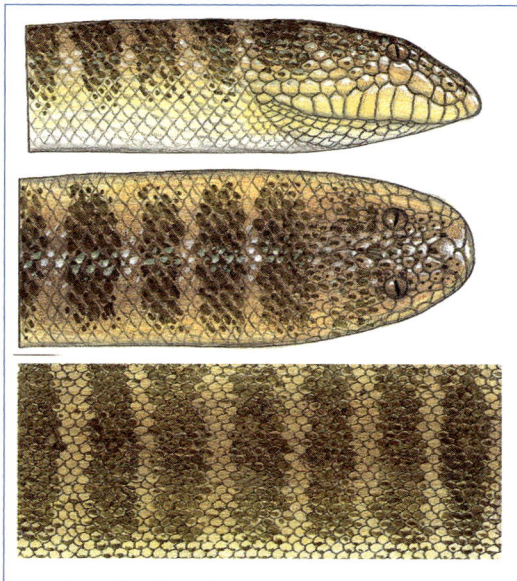

Head and midbody views of *E. jayakari*.

Map of the Arabian Peninsula showing the general distribution of *E. jayakari*.

on top of the head instead of the sides.

The rostral is broad and has a sharp horizontal edge. It projects somewhat from the flattened snout. The internasals are rather small and are partially separated by both the rostral in front and a median scale at the back. There are 4, sometimes 5, scales between the eyes on top of the head, 9 or 10 scales around the eye, and one large scale separating the eye from the supralabials. The supralabials number 11. The mental groove is present but not very distinct. The dorsal scales are smooth and in 37 to 51 rows at midbody. There are 158 to 184 narrow ventrals and 16 to 24 even narrower subcaudals. The tail is short and thick but ends in a heavy claw-like spine that often is distinctly curved downward.

Arabian Sand Boas are plainly patterned, being pale grayish brown above with many irregular dark brown cross-bands and scattered white spots. The head is mostly pale with a few dark brown spots. The belly is white.

Adults are 30 to 40 cm in total length, occasionally reaching 50 cm. (There is an incomplete specimen known that may have been 64 cm long.) The tail is very short, only 6 to 7% of the total length and almost as thick as long.

This is the common sand boa of the Arabian Peninsula. (It probably is the only species, as the single record of *E. colubrinus* is doubtful.) It is found in loose sands everywhere south of a line from Kuwait to about 100 km north of Jeddah and may be quite common. It barely enters the corner of Iran. The species was described by Boulenger in 1888 (*Ann. Mag. Nat. Hist.*, (6) 2: 508) from Muscat. *Eryx fodiens* Annandale, 1913, is a synonym.

Wholly nocturnal in an area where rains are rare, the Arabian Sand Boa appears to be a lizard specialist, feeding almost exclu-

E. jayakari is a strange sand boa that is rarely seen in the hobby. If you acquire one, keep it on sand in a very dry terrarium. Temperatures should be high in the daytime with a large drop at night. Photo by R. D. Bartlett.

sively on small geckos and perhaps avoiding skinks and other lizards with hard skins. It has lived for almost 12 years in captivity. Such a sand specialist is unlikely to be found in many terraria in the near future, but it is not impossible that it could appear in the hobby on occasion.

ERYX JOHNI

Brown Sand Boa

Though not colorful, the Brown Sand Boa makes an excellent pet and has some popularity in the hobby, with a few young being produced each year. It is the only species of the genus that normally is uniformly colored as an adult (exceptional specimens of most other sand-boas may be brown) except for traces of narrow, even cross-bands.

Head and midbody views of *E. johni*.

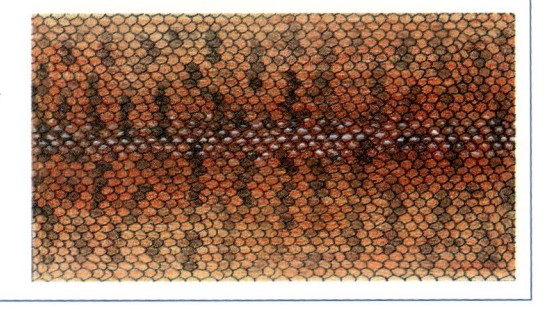

THE BURROWING BOAS: ERYCINIDAE

Brown Sand Boas have a wide and shovel-like rostral scale indicative of their strong burrowing habits. They inhabit rocky areas with hard soils and are adapted to burrow in such difficult terrain. Photo by R. D. Bartlett.

The rostral shield is wide and protuberant, with a sharp edge. The internasals are large, and there is a distinct pair of prefrontals. There are 6 to 9 small scales between the eyes across the top of the head, 9 to 12 scales around the eye, and one (sometimes two) rows of scales between the eye and the supralabials. There are 10 or 11 supralabials (rarely 9 or 12) and 13 to 18 infralabials. The mental groove is distinct. The dorsal scales are smooth to weakly keeled, more strongly keeled posteriorly, and in 53 to 67 rows at midbody (usually 55 to 60). There are 190 to 210 ventrals

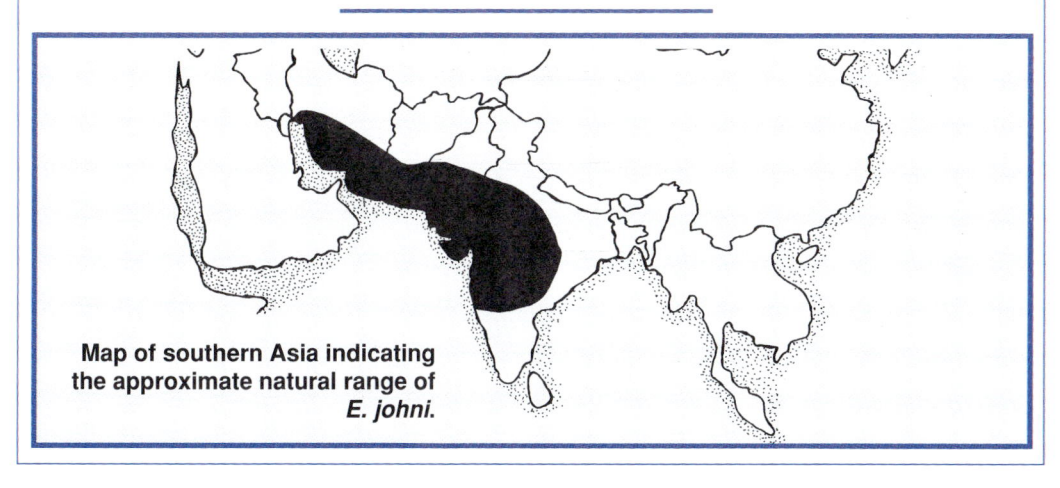

Map of southern Asia indicating the approximate natural range of *E. johni*.

(females with more ventrals, commonly 209 versus 199 in males) and 20 to 40 subcaudals (commonly 28 to 40, somewhat more scales in males than females). The tail ends bluntly in a rounded plate. The spurs are well developed in males, smaller in females.

Adults and juveniles differ in pattern and sometimes color. Young specimens are pale tan to dark reddish brown and have 11 to 17 dark blackish brown narrow cross-bands over the back, plus 2 to 5 similar bands on the distinctly paler tail. The belly is creamy white with dark gray and yellowish spots. With growth the dark cross-bands usually disappear into the background color, which becomes increasingly darker. Typical adults are dark brown, somewhat paler on the tail, where traces of banding may be visible. It has been suggested that dark reddish brown juveniles become the darkest brown adults. Occasionally adults retain relatively strong dark bands on the body, and rarely uniformly pale tan adults are seen. With age the belly also becomes darker. The different colors and patterns do not appear to be correlated with geography.

Adults are over 60 cm in total length, and there are records of large females a full meter long. The tail is short, only about 8% of the total length, and may actually be wider than the head.

The Brown Sand Boa ranges over dry, often cold, deserts and plains from western Iran across Pakistan over northern and central India. The species first was described by Russell in 1801 (*Indian Serp.*: 18, as *Boa Johni*)

By far, Brown Sand Boas are not the most attractive of snakes, but are desirable terrarium animals, being hardy, docile, easily cared for, and medium-sized. Photo by K. H. Switak.

THE BURROWING BOAS: ERYCINIDAE 185

Juvenile Brown Sand Boas are pretty snakes, but you must remember that most animals become solid brown. Purchase one because they make good pets, not for the juvenile colors. Photo by K. H. Switak.

from Tranquebar, India, an area from which it no longer can be collected and well to the south of the known modern range. *Eryx persicus* Nikolsky, 1907, from Khuzistan, Iran, is considered a synonym or weakly defined subspecies found from Iran over Pakistan into northern India.

In Pakistan this is a species of low-lying clay plains with grass and scattered shrubs. It is not common in sandy areas and may be absent from rocky areas. They are nocturnal and seldom seen except after rains, when they may wander aboveground. They seem to feed mostly on mice, shrews, and perhaps other small mammals and birds. Because of their large size they can constrict quite large prey. In

The young of *E. johni.* are quite large for the genus, being up to 23 cm / 9 inches long at birth. They can take fuzzy-sized mice for their first meal. Photo by P. Freed.

Brown Sand Boas prefer very dry keeping conditions. For this species and many of the other *Eryx*, some keepers house them without water bowls. They place a water bowl in the cage for only a few hours a week. Photo by G. Merker, courtesy R. Straub.

Pakistan young snakes about 23 to 25 cm long are found in August and September, probably indicating when birth occurs. Sexual maturity may not be reached for five years at a length of about 60 to 65 cm. They grow slowly even if heavily fed. The tail is held above the coiled snake when it is disturbed and serves to distract predators from more important parts of the body, especially the head that is hidden deep within the coils.

This species can be kept much like *E. colubrinus*, but it tolerates lower temperatures and more varied substrates. Breeding occurs on occasion in captivity, producing very desirable specimens for specialists. Though not colorful, this is a very interesting species that has proved hardy and easy to care for. It commonly lives 10 or

This adult male has retained some bright banding on his tail. Specimens from the western parts of the range often stay banded, although the contrast of the bands does fade as the animal matures. Photo by R. D. Bartlett.

THE BURROWING BOAS: ERYCINIDAE

15 years, and there are records of almost 20 years in captivity. Even large adults are gentle and easy to handle, seldom showing the annoying biting in which some large Kenyan Sand-Boas may indulge. Highly recommended though still expensive and hard to obtain as captive-breds.

ERYX MILIARIS

Central Asian Sand Boa

This widely distributed species is very similar to *E. tataricus* and *E. jaculus* in most respects, and these species long were considered one. I am not sure that I could distinguish these species, especially considering that each shows tremendous variation in head scalation. The middorsal scale rows are a bit larger than in the others and the prefrontals are more poorly developed.

The rostral shield is large and has a sharp horizontal edge. The internasals are well developed, but the prefrontals are not obvious. There are 6 to 9 irregular scales between the eyes and 10 to 14 around the eye. The dorsal scales are smooth or weakly keeled posteriorly and are in 43 to 49 rows at midbody. There are 164 to 184 ventrals and 20 to 32 subcaudals (females tend to have lower counts than males).

Like the related species, this is a brownish boa with a dark brown stripe back from the eye and a pair of dark brown broken stripes converging on the nape. Often the middle of the back is paler than the sides, the usual dark brown

Head and midbody views of *E. miliaris*.

blotches being partially fused into irregularly scalloped bands. Other specimens have the typical dark middorsal blotches of related species. The belly is whitish to pinkish, often with small black spots.

Adults commonly are 50 cm in total length, and the species may reach 67 cm in length. The tail is 8 to 10% of the total length.

The Central Asian Sand Boa ranges over much of dry Asia from the northern coast of the Caspian Sea to Inner Mongolia and adjacent northern Chinese provinces, south to Afghanistan and Turkmenistan. Over this large range it is not commonly collected (for obvious reasons considering the harshness of the country and political problems). Many subspecies have been described, but presently none is considered to be valid. This confusion of names certainly helps make the species difficult to characterize and dis-

This is a pale and cleanly marked specimen of *E. miliaris*. Most are darker and have less well defined markings. This one also lacks the yellowish spots that most of these snakes bear between the dark bands. Photo by G. and C. Merker, courtesy C. Reinman.

tinguish from *E. jaculus* to the west and the sympatric *E. tataricus*. The species originally was described by Pallas in 1773 as *Anguis miliaris* (*Reise ver. Prov. russ. Reich.*, 2: 718) from near the Caspian Sea in the southwestern part of the range. Synonyms include: *koslowi* Bedriaga, 1907; *roborowski* Bedriaga, 1907; *nogaiorum* Nikolsky, 1910; *rarus* Carevsky, 1916; *tritus* Carevsky, 1916; *incerta* Carevsky, 1916; *bogdanovi* Carevsky, 1916; and *rickmersi* Werner, 1930. It appears that almost every specimen collected before 1949 was described as a distinct taxon.

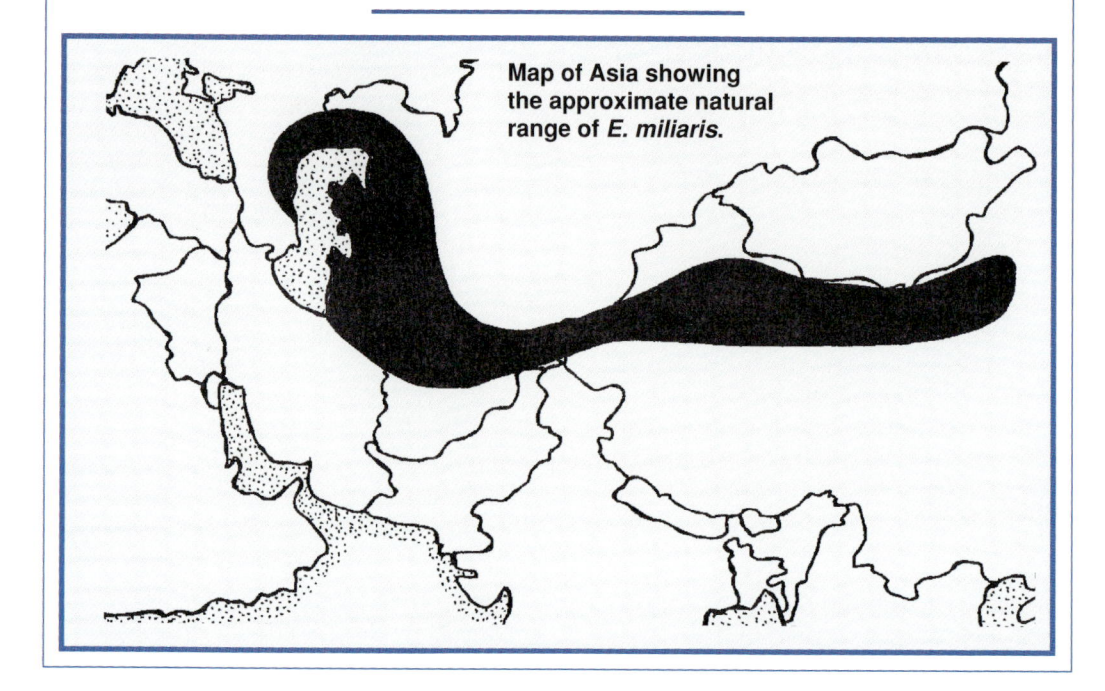

Map of Asia showing the approximate natural range of *E. miliaris*.

THE BURROWING BOAS: ERYCINIDAE

Head of *E. miliaris*. The eyes of this species are slightly larger than those of the very similar *E. tartaricus* which occurs in the same range.

Young Central Asian Sand Boas are tiny animals, rarely being more than 13 cm / 5 inches long. They can be difficult to feed and may refuse mice until adulthood. Photos by R. D. Bartlett.

Central Asian Sand Boas are one of the nippier of the sand boas, but, with frequent handling, they normally will tame down. Photo by M. Walls.

Like the other sand-boas, this species is found in loose, dry substrates and is active mostly at night. It probably feeds mostly on lizards. Most of the range consists of desert subject to tremendous daily and seasonal variation in temperature. I am not aware of many specimens being kept in captivity in private hands. It has been bred on rare occasions, producing three to seven young.

ERYX MUELLERI

West African Sand Boa

Though widely distributed across northern Africa below the Sahara, *E. muelleri* is not a well-known species and appears not to enter the terrarium hobby. It can be recognized by the large terminal spine on the tail that usually is distinctly curved and claw-like, plus scale counts.

The rostral shield is broad with a sharp horizontal edge. Only the internasals are well-developed, the rest of the head being covered with small, irregular scales, often the scale behind the center of the internasals enlarged. There typically are 5 scales between the eyes, 9 or 10 scales around the eye, and a single row of scales separating the eye from the supralabials; 9 supralabials are present. There is no mental groove. The dorsal scales are smooth and in 38 to 45 rows at midbody. There are 174 to 187 ventrals and 16 to 21 subcaudals.

Typical specimens are yellowish above with large, usually round, dark brown blotches down the middle of the back, these sometimes partially fused into short zigzag middorsal bands. Smaller brown blotches alternate with the middorsal blotches. The belly is whitish to pinkish. Sometimes the back is largely dark and the dark coloration extends onto the belly.

Adults are 30 to 40 cm in total length, occasionally reaching 50 cm. The tail is about 8 to 9% of the total length.

Originally described by Boulenger (1892, *Ann. Mag. Nat. Hist.* (6) 9: 74) as *Gongylophis muelleri* from Sennar in the eastern Sudan, the species is now known to be distributed from western Africa below the Sahara across the continent to the Sudan, but it is not collected often. Two subspecies, perhaps

Midbody view of *E. muelleri.*

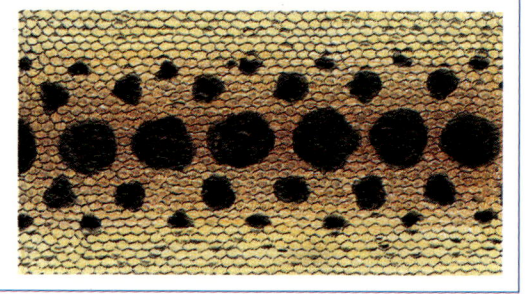

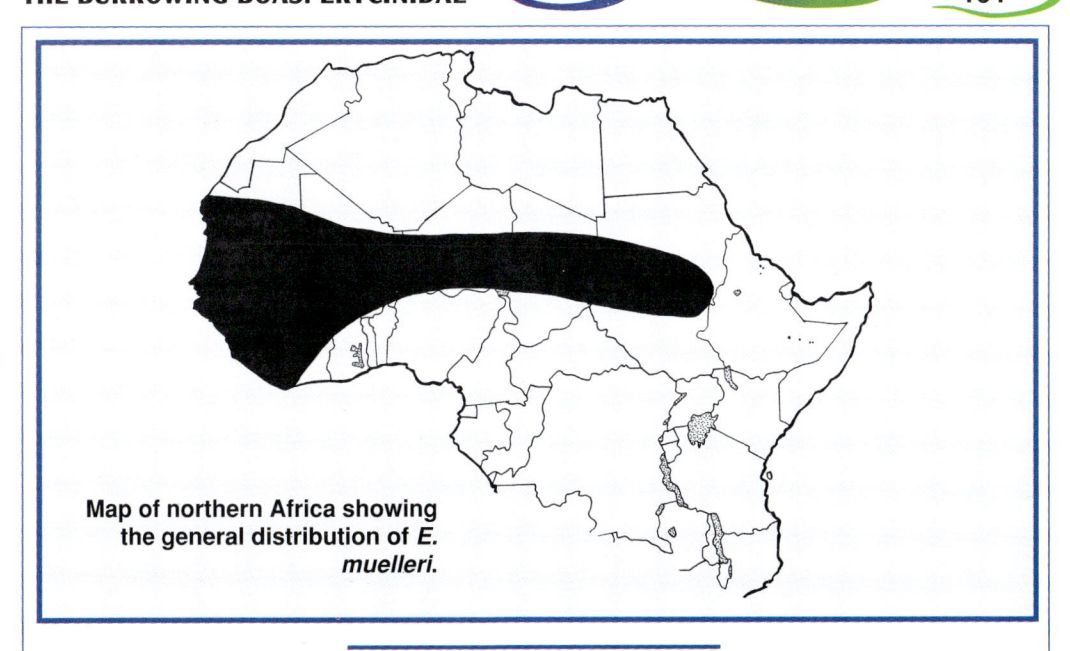

THE BURROWING BOAS: ERYCINIDAE

Map of northern Africa showing the general distribution of *E. muelleri*.

not distinct, have been recognized: *E. m. muelleri* from Mauritania and Senegal (including the Ivory Coast) east to Sudan; and *E. m. subniger* Angel, 1938, from southwestern Mauritania and western Mali. Much of the northern part of the range of the species has been devastated by recent droughts, overpopulation, and political and economic problems of late, and the status of the survival of the species might be considered uncertain.

The species seems to prefer dry savannas and sub-desert conditions. It probably is nocturnal and most active after rains, feeding on lizards and probably small mammals. I've seen little on its natural history, and I've never seen it mentioned in private hands, though I see no reason why it should not occasionally be exported from Senegal or neighboring countries and misidentified as *E. colubrinus*.

ERYX SOMALICUS

Somali Sand Boa

This small sand boa from Ethiopia and Somalia is very poorly known, only a few specimens being in collections. It appears to be similar to the West African *E. muelleri*, but Tokar relates it to the *jaculus* group (subgenus *Eryx*) while placing *mueller* with *colubrinus* in subgenus *Neogongylophis*. It probably is sympatric with *E. colubrinus* and occurs not far from the range of *E. muelleri*. I've described it strictly in comparison with the latter species.

Midbody view of *E. somalicus*.

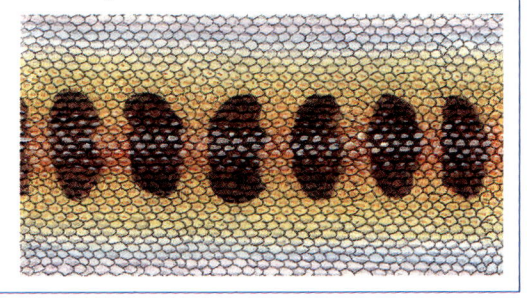

Map of Africa showing the approximate natural range of *E. somalicus*.

spots. Some specimens are very dark.

The largest specimen mentioned appears to be almost 40 cm in total length. The tail is about 9% of the total length.

Poorly known, specimens of *E. somalicus* have been recorded from southern Somalia (near Mogadishu) north to southern Ethiopia. Present political and economic conditions make it unlikely the species will be imported for the hobby trade unless some reach the market through visiting military. The species was described by Scortecci, 1939, from three specimens from Mahaddei Wen and the vicinity of Mogadishu, Somalia.

ERYX TATARICUS

Tartar Sand Boa

Tartar Sand Boas belong to the group clustered around *E. jaculus*, and like most of them it is poorly defined and difficult to recognize as well as extremely variable. It is best separated from *E. jaculus* by range, occurring east of the Caspian Sea.

The rostral shield has a sharp horizontal edge, the internasals are prominent, and there may be two small prefrontals or a series of three or four smaller scales in their place. Often the scales behind the prefrontals are in more or less even rows. There are 7 to 9 small scales across the top of the head between the eyes and 10 to 14 scales in a circle around the eye; a single scale usually separates the supralabials from the eye. There are 11 or 12

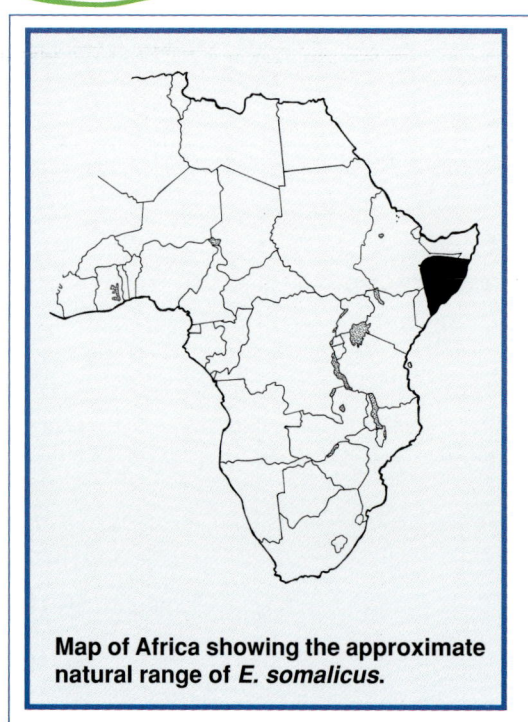

The rostral shield is large and projecting. There are 6 scales between the eyes across the top of the head, about 11 in a circle around the eye, and one row of scales between the eye and the supralabials. The dorsal scales are in 39 or 40 rows at midbody. There are 156 to 161 ventrals and 22 to 25 subcaudals, plus a large curved terminal spine.

Compared to *E. muelleri*, there are fewer ventrals and more subcaudals, as well as supposedly one more scale between the eyes. *E. colubrinus* has about a dozen scales between the eyes.

These boas appear to be yellowish or orange above with large rounded dark brown or reddish brown blotches over the back. The belly is white, as are the lower sides. and there may be a narrow pinkish band down the center of the belly outlined by small dark

THE BURROWING BOAS: ERYCINIDAE 193

supralabials and about 16 infralabials. The mental groove is present. The dorsal scales are smooth, though they may be weakly keeled posteriorly, and are in about 45 to 59 rows at midbody (varying down to 43 rows in some populations, with most counts between 50 and 59). The ventral count varies from 169 to 213, and there are 17 to 45 subcaudals; females have distinctly lower counts than males in most populations.

As in the other species of the complex, these are brownish to tan boas with many (around 50) rather small and irregular dark brown blotches running down the middle of the back, with alternating smaller spots on the sides. There is a dark line back from the eye, and the blotches on the nape tend to form a pair of short stripes that converge toward the head.

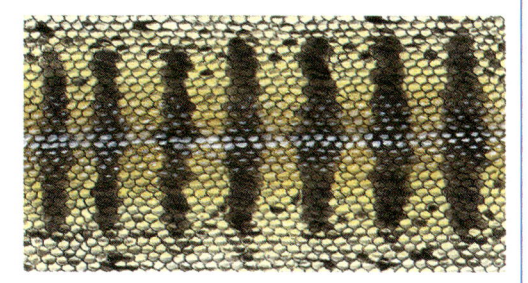

Head and midbody views of *E. tartaricus*.

The belly is cream to pinkish, with or without black spots.

This is a large sand boa, with adults often exceeding 50 cm in

Tartar Sand Boas are perhaps the largest members of the genus, reaching lengths of just over 1 meter / 39 inches. Adults can take rather large prey and have been known to constrict multiple animals at one time. Photo by G. and C. Merker, courtesy of C. Reinman.

E. tataricus is difficult to distinguish from the other snakes in the *jaculus* complex. It tends to be the darkest of the group and has less protruding eyes than *E. miliaris*. It is best separated from *E. jaculus* by locality. Photo by R. D. Bartlett.

total length, the record appearing to be about a meter in length. The tail is about 10 to 12% of the total length.

E. tataricus has a wide range in dry, sandy areas from western China and Pakistan over southern Russian states to Iran and Afghanistan. The species was described by Lichtenstein in 1823 (*Verz. Doubl. zool. Mus. Berlin*: 104). Many subspecies have been described for this species, and some authors recognize three distinct subspecies on the basis of scalation and scale counts. Others feel that the snake exhibits so much variation as to be unbreak-

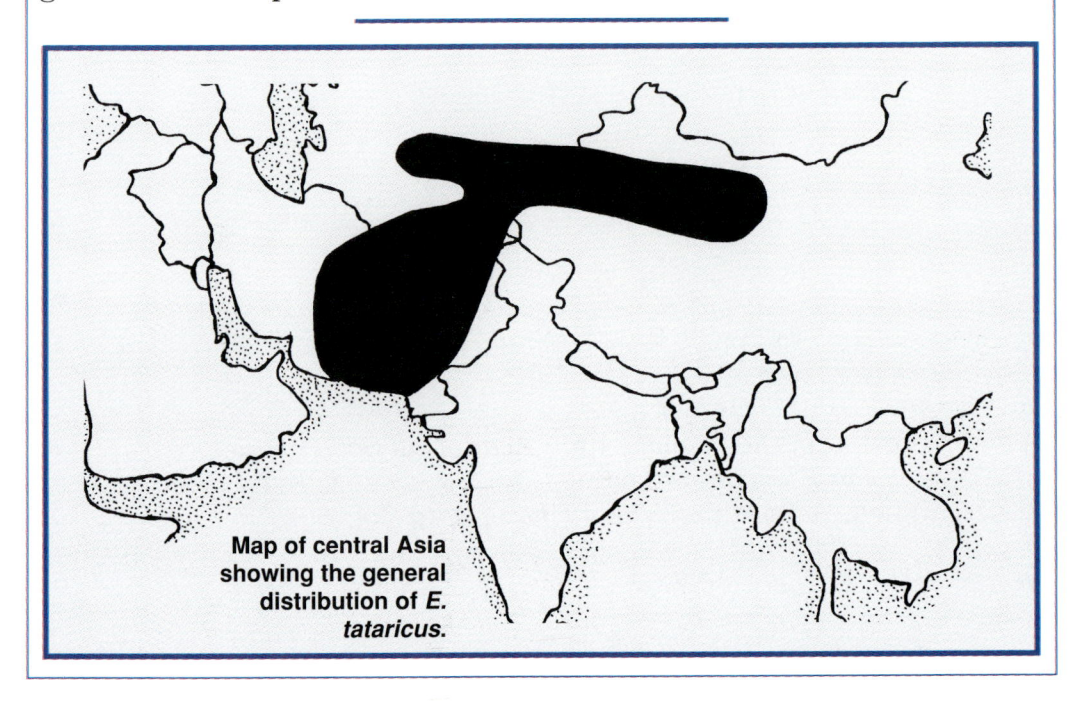

Map of central Asia showing the general distribution of *E. tataricus.*

Female Tartar Sand Boas tend to have large litters (up to 30 young) of large young. The newborns measure 12 to 20 cm / 5 to 8 inches. Photo by G. and C. Merker, courtesy of C. Reinman.

able into subspecies. There is evidence from osteology that two species may be found under this name, but more research is needed. If subspecies are recognized, they are: *E. t. tataricus* from Iran and southwestern Russian states; *E. t. speciosus* Carevsky, 1916, from Tadzhikistan into Afghanistan (perhaps); and *E. t. vittatus* Chernov, 1959, from western Pakistan, western China, Afghanistan (perhaps), and supposedly westward into Iran (thus overlapping the range of the other two subspecies). Tokar, 1989, considered *vittatus* a full species, but there has been no recent and complete review of the species. Its relationships to *E. jaculus* remain undetermined, though there may be a gap in distribution between the two taxa.

As with most sand boas, it is a species of dry, open deserts and shrubby savannas that is nocturnal and most likely to be found after infrequent rains. When collected they coil into a loose ball and raise the tail tip above the coils like a head. Specimens are known to eat small rodents, which they kill by constriction. They probably also take lizards. I am not aware of this species being bred on a regular basis, but it is reported to have lived over eight years in captivity. It should be kept much like *E. colubrinus* and *E. jaculus*. Captives have produced litters of over 30 young.

Genus Lichanura Cope, 1861 (*Proc. Acad. Nat. Sci. Philadelphia*, 1861: 304). Type species by monotypy *L. trivirgata* Cope.

Synonyms: None.

Medium-sized boas (occasionally exceeding a meter in length) with the head somewhat widened behind the jaws and slightly wider than the neck. The tail is over 10% of the total length, tapers much as in many colubrids, and does not end in a specialized scale; it is slightly prehensile. The rostral shield is broad and rounded, not very prominent from above, but projects backward to partially separate the internasals. Behind the internasals are one or two pairs of prefrontals and many small scales of varied sizes and shapes; there is no distinct frontal or supraoculars. The nostril falls between two nasals that commonly are followed by three or four rather large and squarish scales before the one to many prefrontals. Usually the supralabials are separated from the eye by a row of small scales. There are no distinct chin shields, and the mental groove is weakly defined or absent.

The neural crests of the caudal vertebrae are flat and broad but only shallowly grooved, the processes of the caudal vertebrae lacking many fine irregular bony elaborations. There are about 16 maxillary teeth, more than usual for the family, only a few palatine teeth, about 11 pterygoid teeth, and about 18 dentary teeth. The coronoid bone is present. The hemipenes probe about 10 subcaudals in males. They are very weakly bilobed at the tip, smooth over their basal half, bear about 5 or 6 flounces that are strongly developed, and are smooth over the distal third. The sulcus bifurcates at about the midpoint of the organ, the forks ending at the tips of the lobes.

Close-up views of *L. trivirgata*. *top*: Head of a Rosy Boa. The rostral does not normally separate the internasals as it does in other members of the family. *center*: Vent of a juvenile male Rosy Boa. The spurs on each of the vent are visible but not greatly developed. *bottom*: Tail of a Rosy Boa. Note the blunt end. Rosy Boas do not have any special scale modifications such as the spines borne by some of the *Eryx*. Photos by M. Walls.

THE BURROWING BOAS: ERYCINIDAE

The smooth distal third of the hemipenis vaguely looks like a pair of large suckers.

Lichanura appears to be the primitive genus of the Erycinidae, lacking the greatly modified tail of the other members of the family and generally having more teeth. As mentioned, the genus has been synonymized with *Charina*, but the two genera appear distinctive enough to consider separate genera as long as both are left separate from *Eryx*. *Charina*, for instance, lacks an obvious coronoid bone and palatine teeth (the tooth-bearing portion of the palatine also is absent) while having a strongly modified, rounded tail with many fine bony frills and ornaments on the caudal vertebrae as well as a deeply grooved neural crest. Presently only one species is recognized in the genus *Lichanura* and there are anything from three to six subspecies recognized by various authorities.

Although Ball Pythons are more famous for their predilection for rolling into a ball when frightened, Rosy Boas often do this as well. Photo by W. P. Mara.

The head scalation is discussed above. There are 7 to 11 scales around the eye. The dorsal scales are smooth and in 35 to 45 rows at midbody. Ventral scales number 218 to 244, and there are 39 to 51 subcaudals (the high subcaudal count echoing the long, tapered tail).

LICHANURA TRIVIRGATA

Some Rosy Boas have little contrast in the pattern like this one. This an individual from Baja California and placed in the subspecies *roseofusca*. Photo by K. H. Switak.

Rosy Boa

In recent years the Rosy Boa has become one of the most popular captive-bred boas in the United States. Its distinctive but variable striped pattern is attractive, it feeds well on mice, and it is hardy.

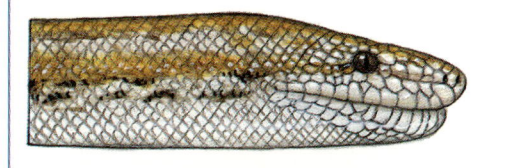

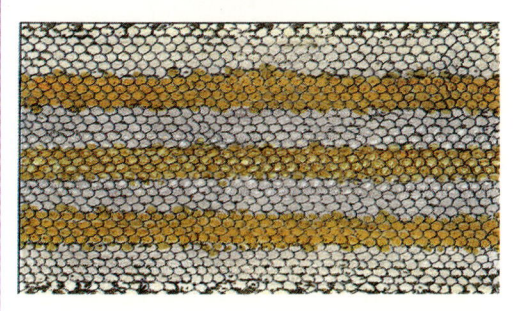

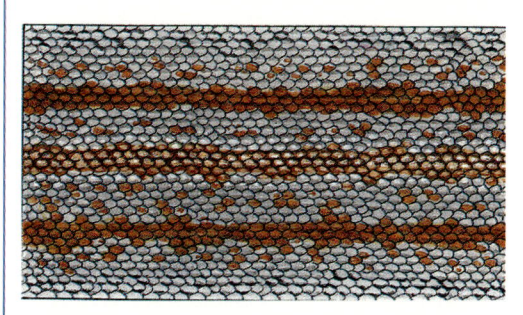

THE LIVING BOAS

Coloration and pattern vary considerably, but typically the background is bluish gray, pale brown, terra-cotta, or creamy yellowish. There are three broad dark stripes extending from the eyes and tip of the snout to near the tip of the tail. The stripes may be deep blackish brown, dark reddish brown, pale brown, rose, or rather pinkish. The stripes also vary from having nearly uniform edges to being very jagged with indistinct edges. The belly is pale yellow to pale gray, often with scattered darker brownish spots. Young specimens are similar to adults but typically paler with more distinct patterns. Occasional specimens are uniformly brown of one shade or another with virtually no dorsal pattern visible. Distinctive color patterns may be strongly associated with local populations and subspecies.

Adults commonly are 60 to 80 cm in total length, with some specimens reaching a meter. The

Above: Head and midbody views of *L. trivirgata*. The midbody views are representative of the variation present in this species. Some individuals are almost unicolored with no visible striping.

Right: Map of the southwestern U.S. and northwestern Mexico showing the general distribution of *L. trivirgata*.

THE BURROWING BOAS: ERYCINIDAE

199

Despite what breeders may say they are selling, the names used for Rosy Boas in the hobby are not to be trusted. The taxonomy is very complicated, and few herpetologists agree on which names are valid. The top animal is from Bagdad, Arizona and could be considered *arizonae* or *gracia*. The bottom animal is from an unknown locality, but its colors match the typical specimens from Baja. It is assigned to the subspecies *trivirgata*. Top photo by K. H. Switak. Bottom photo by R. D. Bartlett.

The general color pattern borne by this snake seems to be the most common form in the hobby today. This animal comes from northeastern Baja and matches the locality and color of the subspecies *roseofusca*. Photo by K. H. Switak.

record length appears to be a bit over 1.1 meters. The tail is long for an erycinid, commonly 13 to 15% of the total length.

The Rosy Boa is a species of the deserts and oases of the extreme southwestern United States and adjacent Mexico. It is found over most of southern California, southwestern Arizona, all of Baja California, western Sonora, and several islands in the Gulf of California. Over this rather limited range it has a discontinuous distribution, with many local and isolated populations. As such, it presents great taxonomic difficulties because almost every large or small population currently may not be sharing genes with neighbors and may be genetically and morphologically distinct. Recognition of subspecies thus is problematic in this species, because there are many localized forms that are just as recognizable, if not more so, than the formally named taxa.

The species was first described by Cope in 1861 as a new genus and species (*Proc. Acad. Nat. Sci. Philadelphia*, 13: 304) from Cape San Lucas, Baja California. From that point on the taxonomy of the species has been a long listing of new names. Included in the synonymy (some perhaps valid subspecies) are: *roseofusca* Cope, 1868; *myriolepis* Cope, 1868; *orcutti* Stejneger, 1889; *simplex* Stejneger, 1889; *gracia* Klauber, 1934; *bostici* Ottley, 1978; *saslowi* Spiteri in Bartlett, 1987; and *arizonae* Spiteri, 1993. Of the nine names assigned to this species, as many as seven currently are considered recognizable subspecies by some, as few as two

THE BURROWING BOAS: ERYCINIDAE

This is an attractive animal from southern California. Although assigned to *myriolepis*, this Rosy could just as easily be considered *gracia*, depending on which name you recognize. Photo by G. and C. Merker.

by others. For the most current survey of the subspecies, see the controversial article by Spiteri, 1993; the conclusions of Spiteri are accepted by few academic herpetologists.

Frankly, my personal interpretation of variation in this species, based on the literature and also on the many localized color forms being bred by hobbyists, is that no subspecies should be recognized at this time. It would be better to categorize specimens by the locality from which they came and not use formal names. The form from the southern half of the Baja peninsula is most distinctive in its clean-edged blackish brown stripes on a very pale creamy tan background color, but even it varies considerably in tone and in width of the stripes, seeming to gradually become paler bright brown in the central part of the peninsula (*saslowi*). In the northwestern part of the peninsula many specimens tend to have the stripes poorly contrasted from the background color; these have been called *roseofusca*. In southern California the stripes tend to have irregular edges but are distinct from the background color; the colors of both stripes and background vary considerably. This form, which contains many localized variants, traditionally has been called *gracia*, though recently the name *myriolepis* has been resurrected for the form and *arizonae* proposed for the slightly differentiated populations from western

Without locality data, it is basically impossible to assign subspecies to most Rosy Boa specimens. This animal is identified as *roseofusca* by the photographer. Photo by R. D. Bartlett.

THE BURROWING BOAS: ERYCINIDAE

Albino Rosy Boas are a rarity in the hobby and command high prices. Thus far, all of these beautiful snakes are from southern California stock assigned to the subspecies *roseofusca*. Photo by K. H. Switak.

Arizona. The name *bostici* has been applied to a form very like the lower Baja *trivirgata* from Cedros Island in the Gulf of California. My advice to hobbyists—and to herpetologists—would be to use these names cautiously because all are so variable, there are wide zones of supposed intergradation between most of the forms, and within each so-called subspecies there are local populations that do not "fit" the definition of the subspecies that is supposed to occupy the area. I consider all the names to be synonyms of a species without formal subspecies.

Rosy Boas are desert snakes typical of dry, often rocky areas with hot days, cool nights, and low humidity. They usually are found near permanent or temporary bodies of water but also may be found in crevices between rock jumbles far from surface water. (Their attraction to water is one reason for the isolation of the many small populations of the species.) They hide by day under logs and other

This Rosy Boa from San Bernadino, California has very reddish stripes that are clearly defined. It is identified as *myriolepis*, but it only barely resembles the *myriolepis* on the earlier page. Photo by P. Freed.

Rosy Boas are among the most easily kept of the snakes discussed in this volume. They are content with a small terrarium, a deep substrate, warmth, and occasional meals. Photo by I. Francais.

Keeping captive-bred specimens of the Rosy Boa has become very popular, and many specimens of probably over a dozen color forms are bred each year. They do well kept individually or in small groups in small terraria with a loose substrate (everything from sand to wood shavings has been used successfully). Keep the terrarium at about 24°C (75°F), allowing the temperature to drop a bit at night. Use an under-tank heating pad or something similar to keep one corner of the terrarium at about 32 to 38°C (90 to 100°F). A basking light is not necessary (though some specimens learn to become active during the day and will use a light), and normal room lighting is sufficient. Adults and most young feed readily on frozen and thawed mice of appropriate size.

debris, in rodent burrows, and in cracks and crevices in the rocks, coming out at night to wander from rodent burrow to rodent burrow in search of food. They are very efficient constrictors and may hold and kill two rodents at a time. Mating occurs in the spring, with the young being born in late summer or early autumn. The young are few in number (one to five) and fairly large, often 25 cm or more in total length. They are like the adults but cleaner and brighter in color and pattern.

Handling Rosy Boas is usually not a problem. They tend to be docile snakes that rarely bite. Photo by K. H. Switak.

Breeding works best if the animals are brumated for six to eight weeks during the winter. The temperature is allowed to slowly drop to a nearly constant 13°C (55°F) and the hours of light are reduced to near-total darkness. After the brumation period the temperature and lighting are slowly returned to normal and the sexes are put in with each other. Males have prominent spurs compared to females and somewhat more tapered tails. Mating

THE BURROWING BOAS: ERYCINIDAE

should occur almost immediately. Males are not combative. Pregnant females may prefer warmer temperatures and may even bask regularly. The young usually are born in August or September, occasionally as late as December, and usually take their first meals after shedding. Some young may not feed until the next spring, however. Maturity is reached in three years or less, and the boas may live almost 20 years in captivity.

There is some controversy as to whether real albinos exist in the breeding programs for this species. A few wild-collected albinos have been taken, but most supposed albinos darkened with age and seem to represent some other type of mutation. A few breeders, however, swear that they are breeding true albinos lacking melanin. So far, however, most albinos look like faded specimens and are not especially attractive. Perhaps more attractive variants will appear shortly. Breeders often keep pure strains of Rosy Boas representing specific localities and may selectively breed these lines for brighter colors and cleaner patterns. As a general rule, it is best not to try to interbreed specimens with different patterns, as muddy, undesirable color schemes may result. It should be noted in passing that specimens (and their offspring) from Baja California are the results of illegal exportations; see Mellink, 1995, *Herp. Nat. Hist.*, 3 (1):95-99.

Confirmed desert-dwellers, Rosy Boas will do poorly in humid conditions. Some keepers recommend only allowing them a water bowl a few hours a week in order to keep the relative humidity low. Photo by G. Merker.

The Cuban Dwarf Boa is the only member of the family that appears in the hobby in any great numbers. Photo by K. H. Switak.

THE DWARF BOAS: TROPIDOPHIIDAE

The dwarf boas or wood snakes are very strange little snakes known only from the tropics of the New World, with most of the species on the Caribbean Islands. All are small and rather slender snakes, seldom approaching a meter in total length, that have small heads with rather rounded snouts, and have the dorsal scales in few rows for boas, usually only 21 to 29 at midbody. At first glance the snakes look much like colubrids, but the ventral scales are relatively narrower than in most colubrids and males have small spurs near the vent that often are hidden under a flap of scales; females may lack spurs. The eyes often are fairly large and protuberant, the pupil vertically elliptical. The family is defined technically by a group of anatomical characters that link the species to the colubrids, especially the presence of a well-developed tracheal lung and the absence of the left lung (which is present in almost all other boas and pythons); there are major differences in the arterial system as well and in the kidneys of two of the four genera (*Tropidophis* and *Trachyboa* lack the lobes typical of kidneys of other boas).

As a rule, a typical snake of this family has a short tail that is prehensile, a wide head distinct from the neck, and a large frontal scale on top of the head with one or two pairs of prefrontals (or a large rounded scale replacing them). The scales typically are smooth, but several species have strong keels on the scales, and the genus *Trachyboa* is among the most heavily keeled of all snakes. The anterior teeth in the jaws are not much longer than those farther back, and the teeth gradually become shorter posteriorly. The short, blunt tail often is the best character for putting a snake in this family, when used in combination with the vertical pupil shape and a glance at the head scalation.

The dwarf boas have proved to be uncommon to rare snakes whose secretive nocturnal life styles have made them difficult to collect. They spend the day under a great variety of cover, including rocks, termite mounds, and bromeliads, coming out at night to feed on a variety of frogs and lizards plus the occasional small rodent. They are constrictors, though weak ones, and even constrict frogs before swallowing them. Most species are terrestrial and prefer the vicinity of swamps and streams, but some species inhabit very dry savannas; a few are mostly arboreal, living in bromeliads, orchids, and mosses on trees several meters from the ground. The young of dwarf boas often have yellow tail tips that serve as lures to attract small lizards within striking range.

All the tropidophiids seem to be live-bearers, though some literature erroneously suggests that *Trachyboa* lays eggs. The litters are small and the young are tiny, making them almost impossible to maintain in captivity. The rarity of these snakes, their reliance on frogs and lizards as food, and the difficulty of rearing the young have made them uncommon pets in the terrarium hobby, and the whole family is unfamiliar to all but advanced hobbyists. The species that live on the American mainland all appear to be rare and seldom are collected even when they are known to occur in a specific locality.

Traditionally the Tropidophiidae (also spelled Tropidopheidae and Tropidophidae) has been associated with the Bolyeriidae, the split-jaws from Round Island in the Indian Ocean, the two groups approaching the colubrid level of development through reduction of dorsal scale rows and standardization of the head scales, plus reduction of the external spurs. However, the Bolyeriidae have a uniquely jointed upper jaw, unusual vertebrae, and a distribution so different from the tropidophiids that I suspect the relationship is one of convenience rather than sharing of an ancestor. Split-jaws lay eggs (as far as known) and tropidophiids give live-birth (as far as known; the life history of many species remains uncertain), but this probably is just a coincidence. Split-jaws are treated in my book on the pythons.

Recently it has been suggested that the jaw musculature and various aspects of scalation and internal anatomy (including the very asymmetrical placement of the cloacal glands and the presence of lobes on the kidneys) indicate that the genera *Ungaliophis* and *Exiliboa* are more closely related to each other than they are to *Tropidophis* and *Trachyboa*. It even has been suggested that they should form their own family, the Ungaliopheidae. Of course, there also are major differences between *Tropidophis* and *Trachyboa*, and perhaps the next study will suggest that each genus should be put in a unique family. For the moment, the dwarf boas seem a fairly uniform group easily defined on the basis on lung development and general appearance and probably sharing a common ancestor, so I keep them all in one family, Tropidophiidae. It seems likely that the genera are relicts of a larger group, now extinct, that represented various specializations from the true boa level to the colubrid level and thus showing different combinations of advanced and primitive characters.

Four quite distinct genera are recognized in the Tropidophiidae, with *Exiliboa* being discovered only in 1967 (when a single female was taken). The genus *Boella* was described as a new genus of Tropidophiidae but proved to be based on a mislabeled specimen of *Epicrates inornatus*. The

THE DWARF BOAS: TROPIDOPHIIDAE

Ungaliophis continentalis has unique head scalation, with the prefrontals forming a large oval shield. This combined with the pattern should make identifications easy. Photo by R. Kayne.

possibility exists that other species and perhaps genera of tropidophiids are yet to be discovered on the American mainland, while it is almost certain that several undescribed *Tropidophis* occur in the Caribbean. I've tentatively recognized 23 species in the family for this book, but admittedly there are at least three or four more described subspecies of Caribbean *Tropidophis* that appear to be isolated and distinctive and thus probably deserving of specific level treatment. In these cases I've just mentioned the possibility of a change of status because it seems likely that the area between the questionable taxa has not been adequately collected and intermediate specimens may appear at a later date; I realize that this is inconsistent but it also is practical at the moment.

Key to the genera of Tropidophiidae

A. Rostral scale reduced or absent; top of head with very irregular scales; all head scales strongly keeled .... *Trachyboa*

AA. Rostral scale present, obvious; top of head with regular scales, including frontal and prefrontals; scales keeled or not . B

B. Prefrontals fused into a large oval shield (azygous prefrontal) as large as or larger than frontal; loreal present .... *Ungaliophis*

BB. Prefrontals in one or two pairs, never a large oval shield; loreal present or absent C

C. Loreal present; internasals fused into a large oval shield .... *Exiliboa*

CC. Loreal absent (fused to preocular); internasals paired .... *Tropidophis*

Genus Exiliboa Bogert, 1968b (*Amer. Mus. Novitates*, No. 2354: 2). Type species by monotypy *E. placata* Bogert, 1968.

Synonyms: None.

A small tropidophiid with the head moderately distinct from the body and with small external spurs in both sexes. The nostril is located within a single nasal scale, the rostral is distinct, and the internasals are fused into a large azygous plate (rarely with seams breaking it into two or three irregular scales). There is a pair of squarish prefrontals (sometimes fused and sometimes separated by a small irregular scale), and the frontal is rather triangular or five-sided. The supraoculars are large, one over each eye. A large squarish loreal (rarely two) separates the nasal from the single preocular. The cloacal scent glands are strongly staggered, one much further from the vent than the other.

A single species of very restricted distribution has been found so far.

EXILIBOA PLACATA

Oaxacan Cloud Boa

This little, almost uniformly grayish or blackish boa is known only from two cloud-forest areas in Oaxaca, southern Mexico. Though apparently not uncommon, the remoteness of its range and the logistic difficulties of collecting in the area prevented its earlier discovery.

The Oaxacan Cloud Boa is immediately recognizable by the combination of the dark color above and below, common presence of a white spot over the entire anal scale, and the fused internasals plus a distinct loreal.

Supralabials 7 (very rarely 6), 2 entering the orbit; infralabials 7 (very rarely 6 or 8). Scales smooth, dorsal rows typically 19-19-17 (19 one head length behind the head, 19 at midbody, 17 one head length before the vent),

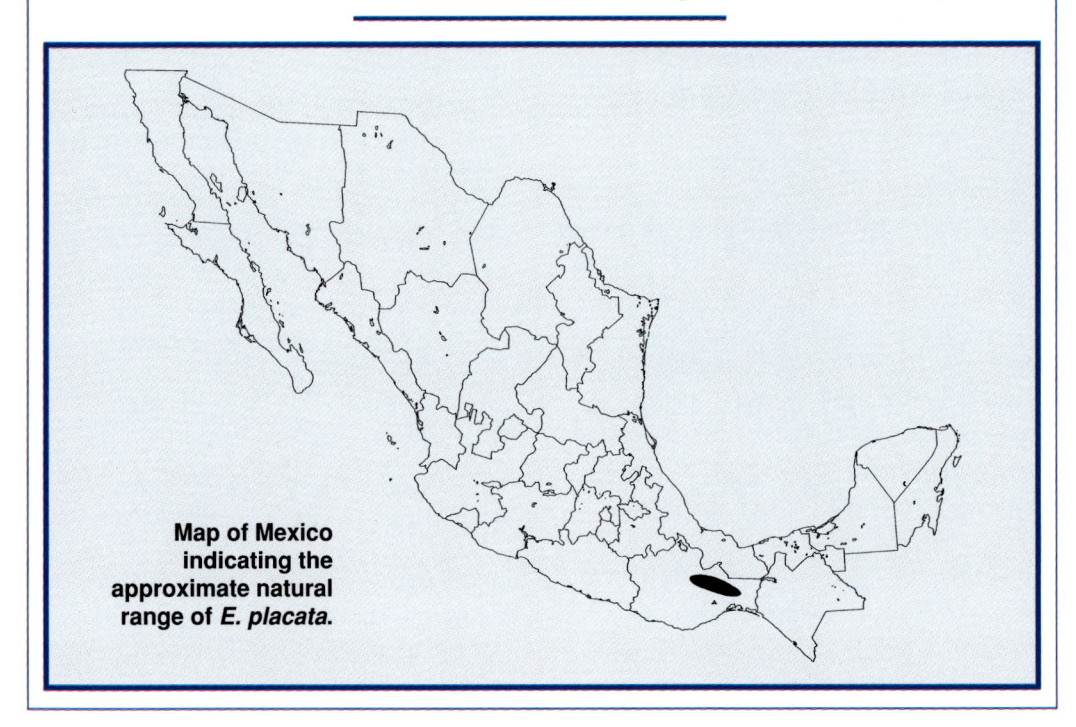

Map of Mexico indicating the approximate natural range of *E. placata*.

THE DWARF BOAS: TROPIDOPHIIDAE

occasionally 17/18-21-15/16. Ventrals 152 to 160 in males, 160 to 168 in females; subcaudals single, 27 to 31 in males, 24 to 28 in females. Typical tooth counts (each side): maxillary 19, palatine 7, pterygoid 11, dentary 19.

There are 18 pairs of chromosomes (2N=36), with 16 macrochromosomes and 20 microchromosomes. The chromosomes may differ from those of other boids in the positioning of secondary constrictions. The hemipenis (based on drawing in Dowling, 1975) is slender and ends in shallow but distinct forks that are terminated in short awns. There are about five strong flounces on the distal two-thirds of the shaft, the basal third of the shaft smooth. The sulcus spermaticus forks at about 75% of the length of the organ.

This snake is almost uniformly dark gray to blackish above and below, sometimes with a faint paler stripe from the back of the eye to the angle of the jaws. The skin between the scales is pale, especially anteriorly between the lower scale rows. There almost always is a large white blotch over the anal scale (rarely in front of the scale) and there may be a white spot at the side of the tail as well; the spurs are white in both sexes.

Adults commonly are 40 to 45 cm in total length, with the record apparently 469 mm. The tail is about 10 to 12% of the total length.

So far *Exiliboa placata* is known only from the cloud forests of the Sierra Juarez range of Oaxaca,

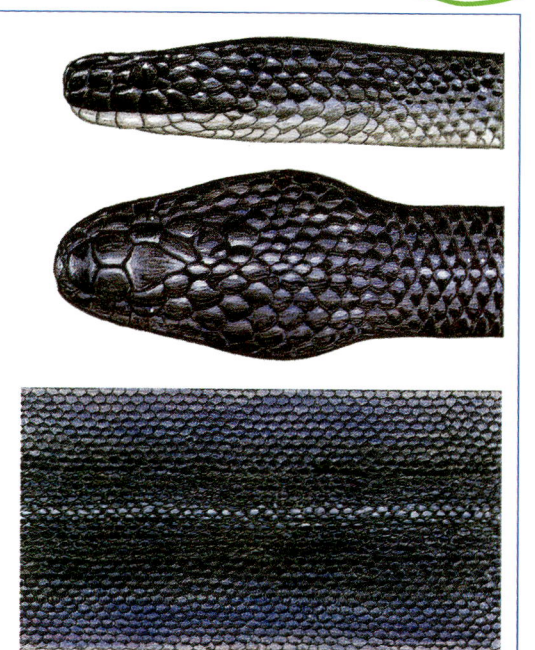

Head and midbody views of *E. placata*.

Mexico, plus similar habitats in the Sierra Mixe nearby. There it occurs in rocky areas with numerous subterranean crevices on steep slopes at about 2000 to almost 2400 meters elevation.

Oaxacan Cloud Boas are typically found under rocks and logs in sunny clearings in their moist, cold habitat. They are active mostly at night, when the temperature may be only 15°C (59°F), and temperatures seldom exceed 20°C (68°F). It is not uncommon to find two or more specimens under a single rock, so they apparently are not territorial boas. The snakes feed mostly on small frogs (*Eleutherodactylus*) and their eggs plus salamanders (*Pseudoeurycea*). Predators in the area (weasels and opossums) may be deterred by a very strong-smelling and adhesive yellowish cloacal gland secretion.

In nature, the young (which are about 10 cm in total length) are born in September and October. Litters seem to vary from 8 to 16 young, with larger females bearing more and larger young than smaller females. Breeding in captivity (as opposed to pregnant females giving birth) seems not to have been reported.

Presently this species is not available to hobbyists and rarely has been kept even by zoos and museums. The snake is very sluggish at all times, in keeping with the low temperatures of its natural habitat. When picked up or disturbed it tends to form a tight ball with its head hidden in the coils. It has been kept in small cages furnished with sphagnum moss and a rock or piece of wood under which to coil. It shows no tendency to climb. Obviously in the terrarium it should be kept cool (18 to 20°C, 65 to 68°F) and dark. Specimens have fed poorly in captivity but will take small frogs and their eggs (remember that the *Eleutherodactylus* species lay their eggs on the ground, not in water). Mice have been refused. Most of what is known about the species is to be found in the original description and in Campbell & Camarillo R., 1992.

Genus Trachyboa Peters, 1860 (*Monats. Konig. Akad. Wiss. Berlin*, 1860: 200). Type species by monotypy *T. gularis* Peters, 1860.
Synonyms: None.

A group of small, very stout, and "stiff-bodied" ground-dwelling boas from tropical America. The head is moderately distinct from the body and there are small external spurs only in the male. The rostral scale is small or indistinct and not the usual vertical scale reaching and separating paired internasals. The nasal scales are distinct and each is pierced by a nostril. The top of the head is covered with many small scales of varied sizes, not easily interpreted as prefrontals, frontals, etc. There are many scales between the eye and the nasal scale. The scales of the head and body are strongly keeled. The openings of the cloacal scent glands are adjacent to the vent.

Two poorly understood species that seldom have been collected are contained here. Variation in these species is not understood, and it is possible that more species are hidden among the variants of the described species.

TRACHYBOA BOULENGERI

Horned Spiny Boa

Perhaps the most unique small boa, *T. boulengeri* was described by Peracca in 1910 (*Ann. Mus. Zool. Univ. Napoli*, 3[12]: 1) from a single specimen supposedly from Brazil. No specimens have ever been recorded from Brazil since, and it is assumed the type locality is incorrect. This is the only truly spiny-scaled boa.

A small brown boa readily recognized by extremely rough keeling on the body and on the head, with the internasals compressed into small horns and the scales of the top and sides of the snout rough and irregular. The two uppermost scales above the eye (supraoculars) also are compressed and horn-like. In *T.*

THE DWARF BOAS: TROPIDOPHIIDAE

gularis the head scales are merely roughly keeled; the two species differ in scale counts as well.

Supralabials 10 to 12, roughened, none typically touching the eye; infralabials about 13. Scale rows at midbody 23 to 33, the scales strongly keeled. Ventrals 131 to 141; subcaudals single (as is anal scale), 20 to 28. Sexual dimorphism in scale counts is suspected but not proven.

The head is brown, sometimes with paler blotches on the snout or between the eyes. There may be two irregular rows of large black spots or cross-bands over the belly; the tail may be clean yellow below.

Adults appear to seldom exceed 40 cm in total length, the tail about 10% of the total length.

This is a rain-forest species known from localities from

The yellow tail tip on this Horned Spiny Boa may be used to lure frogs and other prey. Not all individuals exhibit this coloration, so the significance is not certain. This individual is from Ecuador. Photo by P. Freed.

The Horned Spiny Boa is basically a dull brown snake with a rosy yellow belly. In well-marked specimens (especially juveniles) there is a series of large yellowish blotches down the middle of the back and about five series of small black spots along the sides, these often with a small reddish or yellowish area near each spot. Panama and Colombia as well as Ecuador, all on the Pacific slope.

It seems that this species lives in litter in and near moist rain forests. It is secretive, active at night, and can be found under logs and detritus of various types. Probably it hides in small animal burrows as well, but it seldom climbs. Food in nature is uncer-

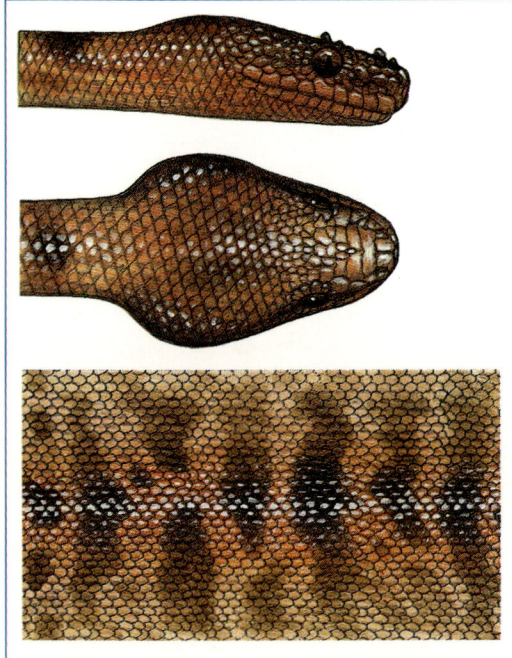

THE LIVING BOAS

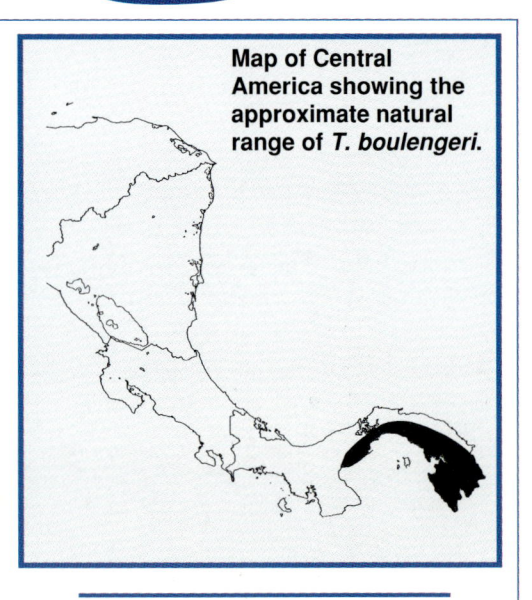

Map of Central America showing the approximate natural range of *T. boulengeri*.

Head and midbody views of *T. boulengeri*.

tain, but probably it consists mostly of small frogs and lizards.

Only a few specimens of the Horned Spiny Boa have been kept in captivity, and it is not a very satisfactory species. An adult can be kept in a small terrarium with a few centimeters of loam and sphagnum, a water bowl, and leaves and pieces of bark for cover. A temperature of about 25°C (77°F) or a bit less is satisfactory, and no light is necessary or appreciated. The bottom of the terrarium should stay moist through regular sprayings.

The snakes are very sluggish in captivity, move little, and may be difficult to feed. They eat small (under 5 cm) frogs at night, usu-

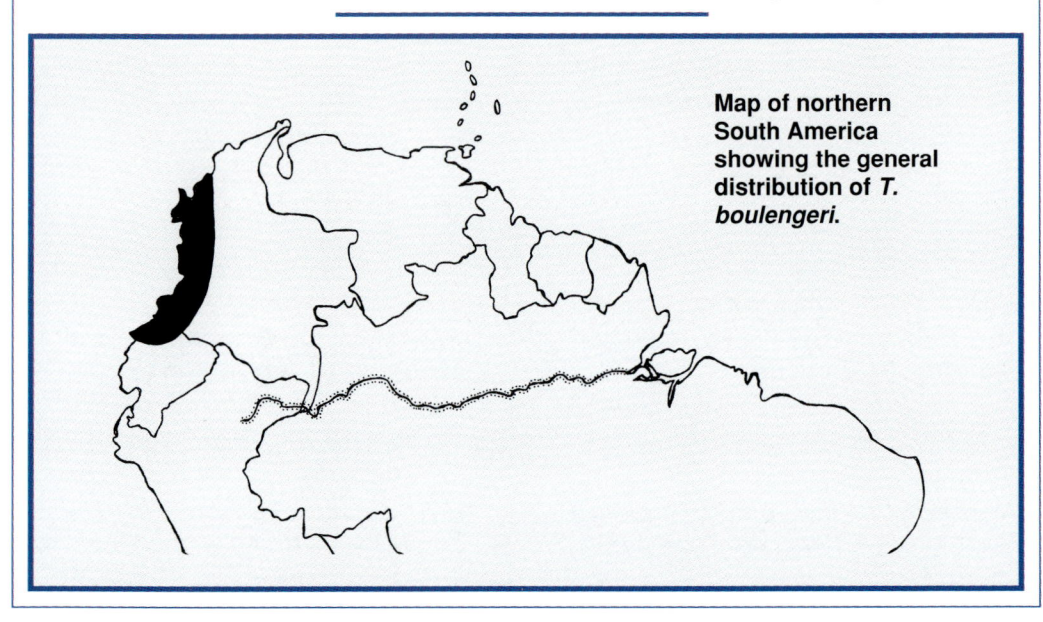

Map of northern South America showing the general distribution of *T. boulengeri*.

THE DWARF BOAS: TROPIDOPHIIDAE

Close-up view of the head of *T. boulengeri*. Notice the horns adorning the supraocular and nasal areas. This character immediately sets it apart from other boas. Photo by R. D. Bartlett.

ally only one or two per week. They also may eat tadpoles and small fishes. The prey is constricted. When touched, the snakes may either form a tight flat coil with the head at the center or go into rigor, the body stretched out straight and stiff for several minutes. If kept too warm or allowed to dry out, the snakes quickly die.

Young are about 12 to 13 cm long and are pencil-thin. The length of pregnancy is unknown, but large embryos have been found in a female collected in April. Litters are small, just five or six young. The young feed on very small frogs and tadpoles placed in very shallow water. They seldom feed well and usually die in a few weeks. Young have horns similar to the adult but have a much more contrasting and colorful pattern.

TRACHYBOA GULARIS

Keeled Spiny Boa

The Keeled Spiny Boa is very similar to the Horned but differs in scale counts. Additionally, the scales of the head, though roughly keeled, lack distinct horns over the eyes and snout. The scales on the snout may be strap-like and resemble regular prefrontals to some extent, but scalation still is very irregular.

Supralabials about 13, one usually entering the orbit; infralabials about 13. The keeled dorsal scales are in 29 to 31 rows at midbody. There are 146 to 153 ventrals and 23 to 30 single subcaudals. The ventral scales provide complete separation from *T. boulengeri*.

This is a dull brown boa with a darker brown head and indistinct large paler brown to yellowish

Head and midbody views of *T. gularis*.

blotches along the middle of the back. On the sides are two rows of blackish spots, the lower one often extending onto the edge of the belly. The belly is yellowish. It can be assumed that young are more strongly marked.

Adults are up to 40 cm in total length, the tail about 10% of the total length.

Trachyboa gularis remains known only from the relatively dry coastal area of Ecuador, the types coming from the vicinity of Guayaquil. The synonym *multimaculata* Rosen, 1905 (*Ann. Mag. Nat. Hist.* [7], 15: 169) was described from Balao, Ecuador.

Virtually nothing has been recorded for this species in its natural habitat. It does not appear to be a rain-forest resident, probably being found under debris in and at the edge of rather dry forests. I am not even certain that this species has been proved to give birth to living young, though this seems likely. Specimens probably can be kept much

Rarely seen and even more rarely kept, the Keeled Spiny Boa is a mysterious little snake. It is rare even in museum collections, and most aspects of its natural history are unknown. Photo by R. D. Bartlett.

THE DWARF BOAS: TROPIDOPHIIDAE

This specimen of *T. gularis* bears very distinct spotting that is not present on all individuals. Like many snakes, they sometimes roll up when threatened. Photo by R. D. Bartlett.

like *T. boulengeri* but a bit drier and warmer.

Genus Tropidophis Bibron in Sagra, 1840 (*Hist. fisica, pol. y natural de la Isla Cuba. IV. Seg. part.-Reptiles y Peces*: 125; see Smith & Grant, 1958, *Herpetologica*, 14(4): 215-222, for this dating). Type species by monotypy *Boa melanurus* Schlegel, 1837.

Synonyms: *Erycopsis* Fitzinger, 1843 [*melanurus*]; *Leionotus* Bibron in Sagra, 1843

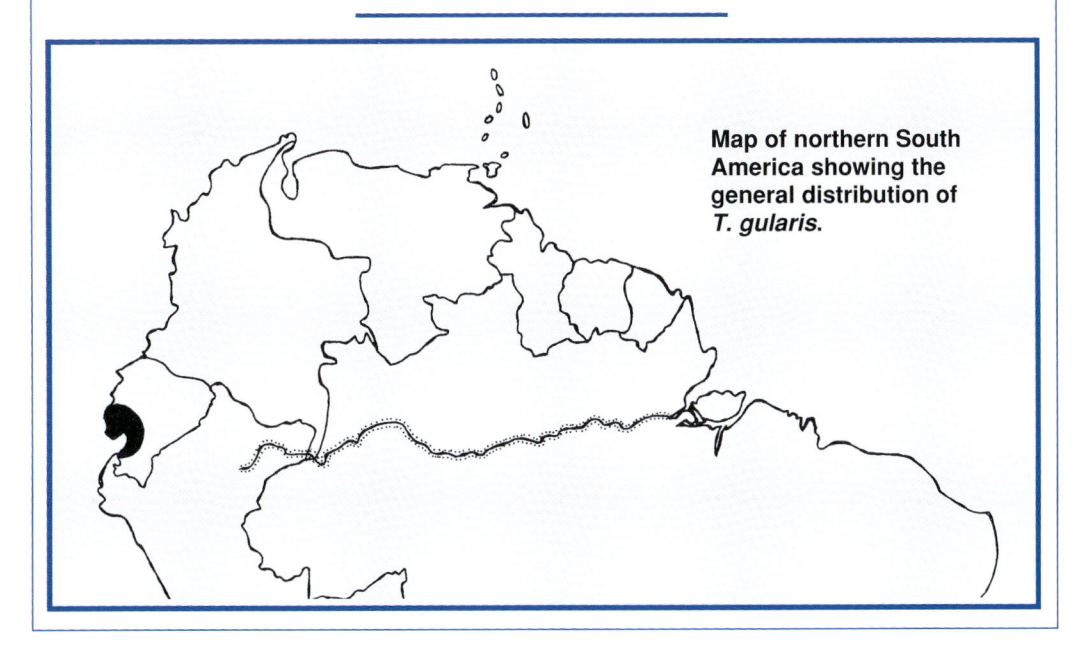

Map of northern South America showing the general distribution of *T. gularis*.

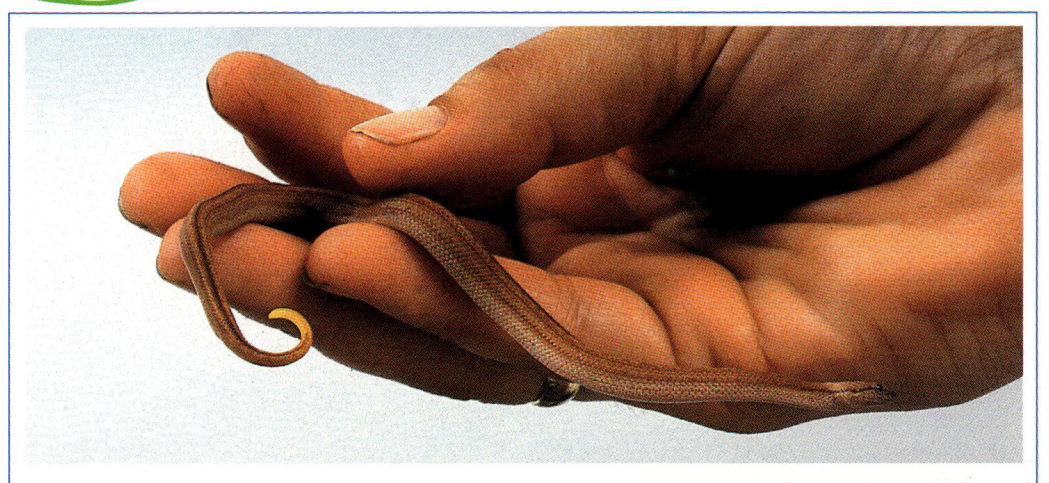

Part of the reason the *Tropidophis* are bred infrequently is the small size of the young. Their minuteness makes them very hard to feed. *T. melanurus* is pictured. Photo by I. Francais.

[*maculatus*]; *Notophis* Hallowell, 1856 [*melanurus*]; *Ungalia* Gray, 1842 [*melanurus*].

Slender-bodied tropidophiid snakes with the head wider than the neck, the eye with a vertically elliptical pupil, left lung absent but tracheal lung large, and kidneys not lobulated. The head scalation is very consistent in the genus, with a pair of internasals in contact at the midline; two pairs of prefrontals (rarely fused into one pair); two nasal scales on each side, the nostril situated between the scales; and no distinct loreal scale (fused to the large prefrontal). There are 21 to 29 dorsal scale rows, the scales either smooth, weakly keeled, or strongly keeled. External spurs are present only in males and are absent even in males of at least one species. The cloacal scent glands are both placed close to the cloacal opening. The anal and subcaudals are unpaired.

Currently the taxonomy of this genus is, in a word, impossible. Only one key presently exists to all the species of the genus, but it does not work. A key to the Caribbean species depends at least in part on geography for its major couplet. Tentatively I recognize 18 species in *Tropidophis*, three on the South American mainland that are virtually unknown and 15 on the Caribbean islands. I've elevated two forms on Jamaica to full species rank on the basis that they do not intergrade with any other known taxa and seem to be quite isolated; using this criterion it might be reasonable to elevate several other putative subspecies to specific rank if it can be ascertained that they really are isolated and the gaps between their ranges are not due to lack of collecting. Complicating the matter even more are the facts that a large number of the species are restricted to Cuba, presently difficult of access because of politics and possibly being destroyed by agricultural practices, and numerous poorly defined and often nominal subspecies have been described. Several undescribed

THE DWARF BOAS: TROPIDOPHIIDAE

taxa probably exist. On the South American mainland these are among the rarest of snakes and are virtually never collected. Their secretive and nocturnal habits make them difficult to find even on very small Caribbean islands where they are known to be fairly common.

Husbandry

Perhaps fortunately, few of these little snakes are available to hobbyists, and they are almost never bred in captivity. Though they seem to be easy to maintain, they almost never are imported.

loam, sand, and peat moss, along with some leaves and bark shreds. Provide many hiding spots, including pieces of cork bark, piles of rocks, and hollow logs. Slender species like to climb. An under-tank heating pad should keep one part of the terrarium so the ground reaches about 28°C (82°F) during the day and drops a few degrees at night. Though many of the species are found in quite dry habitats, always spray part of the terrarium heavily each day to be sure the substrate stays moist; give the snakes both thermal and humidity gradients.

Due to the small size of most of the *Tropidophis*, they often make good candidates for naturalistic terrarium. They generally will not crush plants or displace decorations. Photo by I. Francais.

The large *Tropidophis melanurus* and the smaller *T. haetianus* occasionally appear in the hobby and have been bred in captivity; zoos occasionally culture other species. Because they are small (seldom reaching a meter in total length), one or two specimens can be kept in a 30-gallon long terrarium with a mesh lid. The bottom should be a deep mix of

It seems that all species (as far as known) feed mostly on frogs and lizards in nature. They are nocturnal and sometimes are found crossing roads and paths in search of prey. They need no special lighting as far as known, though a low-wattage ceramic heat light may be used if the temperature drops too much. Feed at night so the snakes can hunt while in the dark as usual. It may be difficult to provide a continual supply of frogs and lizards of the right size, so some keepers have tried to switch them over to pinkie mice with limited success. Try scenting the mice by rubbing them with a lizard, pouring a blenderized lizard suspension over a mouse, or mixing small pieces of mouse and lizard tails (bloody) and gently tapping the snake on the snout with them. Some individuals learn to accept mice nicely, but most don't. Frogs and lizards usually are just grabbed and swallowed, but mice are weakly constricted. There are persistent rumors that some dwarf boas will take mealworms and crickets, but I suspect these are just stories. However, young *Tropidophis* are very small snakes and it seems likely that some may take insects as well as the usual small frogs and hatchling lizards. They have fed on salamanders in the terrarium (of course there are no salamanders in the Caribbean).

When picked up, *Tropidophis* species are gentle and do not strike, but they often secrete a strong-smelling cloacal discharge and try to coil so the head is hidden. They also exhibit autohemorrhaging, where blood vessels on the gums and sometimes the eye burst and drops of blood come to the surface. In lizards that have a similar habit, the blood apparently smells unpleasant to predators. These snakes also exhibit physiological color changes, being able to slowly change color tone from pale (often reddish) to dark (often almost black). This of course means that the spotting may be difficult to see and also may appear dark or pale depending on mood of the specimen. Curiously, the split-jaw (Bolyeriidae) *Bolyeria dussumieri* exhibits a similar ability, which is uncommon in snakes.

Little is known about reproduction of dwarf boas in captivity (or in nature, for that matter). Males have external spurs that are absent in females, but they are very small and often hidden under scale flaps so they are easy to overlook. When probing, a male probes about ten subcaudals. The hemipenes of *Tropidophis* seem to be quite variable in structure, but all are deeply forked with the sulcus dividing at the fork of the organ. Each branch is covered on its distal half with fine flounces. In some species at least, the tip of each branch is itself shallowly forked, producing a quadrifurcate condition (Gibson, 1970). The dwarf boas are of course livebearers, and litters numbering between four or five and over 20 are recorded. The newborns are just 15 cm or so in length and very slender. Breeding may not be seasonal on at least some Caribbean islands, and it is thought that gestation lasts some 10 to 12 weeks. The young are difficult to feed and often starve. In most (all?) species the tails of young are bright yellow and probably serve as lures to attract small prey within striking range. Most specimens have lived only a few years in captivity (usually less than

THE DWARF BOAS: TROPIDOPHIIDAE

eight years), which may not reflect natural life-spans.

Identification

As mentioned, it is very difficult to identify the species of this genus with any confidence. The following summary largely follows the discussion by Hedges and Garrido (1992), though it has obvious short-comings. Hedges and Garrido recognized what might be considered four species groups, more for convenience than as indicating actual relationships.

Pardalis Group

These are rather stout species of small size (less than 50 cm total length with one exception) and with many (25 to 90) small spots on the back. The spots tend to be arranged in 6 to 12 rows over the back. The dorsal scales may be keeled or smooth and are in 21 to 29 rows at midbody. Most species have between 140 and 190 ventral scales (one exception to 208). Included species: *canus, haetianus, jamaicensis, maculatus, nigriventris, pardalis, pilsbryi, stejnegeri, taczanowskyi.*

Semicinctus Group

These are the gracile dwarf boas, with slender, compressed bodies and protruding eyes. The dorsal spots are large and few (18 to 29), often developed as saddles, and are in just 1 to 4 rows across the back. The dorsal scales are smooth. There are many ventrals, from 195 to 225. Included species: *feicki, semicinctus, wrighti.*

Melanurus Group

These are the largest *Tropidophis*, adult at lengths over 50 cm and reaching a meter. The dorsal spots are in 4 to 12 rows across the back and from 37 to 61 down the back; the rows of spots on either side of the midline (paravertebrals) are enlarged. The dorsal scales are keeled and in 25 to 27 rows at midbody. The ventrals number 183 to 217. Included species: *caymanensis, melanurus.*

Unplaced Species

Four species don't fall comfortably into the above groups. *Tropidophis greenwayi* from the Caicos may be related to *T. canus*. *T. paucisquamis* from southern Brazil is remote in range from the rest of the genus but has been considered related to *T. maculatus*. *T. fuscus* has a pointed head with protuberant eyes but was considered by the describers to not be related to the Semicinctus Group because of low scale counts that might associate it with the Melanurus Group; Hedges and Garrido placed it in its own species group. Additionally, *T. battersbyi* has been associated with both the Semicinctus and Pardalis Groups, especially the former.

I will not attempt to present a key to the species of *Tropidophis* as it would be futile and of no real use to the hobbyist. However, a listing by geography and species group might be of interest.

Pardalis Group

Bahamas and Turks & Caicos: *canus*

Cuba: *maculatus,*

nigriventris, pardalis, pilsbryi
(*haetianus*—introduced?)
        Jamaica: *jamaicensis, stejnegeri*
        Hispaniola: *haetianus*
        South America: *taczanowskyi*

Semicinctus Group
        Cuba: *feicki, semicinctus, wrighti*

Melanurus Group
        Cuba: *melanurus*
        Caymans *caymanensis*

Unplaced Species
        Bahamas and Turks & Caicos: *greenwayi*
        Cuba: *fuscus*
        South America: *battersbyi, paucisquamis*

The fact that nine species, half the genus, are restricted in distribution to Cuba (plus one odd group of records that may represent an introduction) does not make identifications any simpler.

In the following species discussions, I have kept the information short and very basic. For more detailed descriptions see Tolson and Henderson (1993), but that book does not include the South American species. Schwartz and Henderson (1991) also provide an excellent summary of the structure, distribution, and natural history of the Caribbean species. I've made no attempt to present the distinguishing characters of the supposed subspecies except where they might be sufficiently distinct and isolated to be recognized as full species at a later date. Identifications in this genus may require comparison with identified specimens, and getting a good name on a single specimen without locality data may be almost impossible. Dark specimens may eventually lighten up if kept in the dark; preserved specimens may have to be held under water to show the pattern.

TROPIDOPHIS BATTERSBYI

Battersby's Dwarf Boa

This species seemingly remains known from a single male in rather poor condition supposed to have been collected in Ecuador in 1875 (Laurent, 1949). The specimen was described as brown with 6 rows of spots across the back, the paravertebrals largest, the ventrals smallest, alternating or not and confluent or not. There are about 38 series of spots down the back. There is a large dark spot covering the parietals and the posterior part of the frontal plus three smaller spots at the anterior edge of the frontal.

The dorsal scales are smooth and in 23 rows at midbody (formula 21-23-17). There are 200 ventrals and 41 subcaudals. The infralabials and supralabials both number 11, 3 in contact with the eye. The parietals are irregular, the frontal is indented at about the middle, and the anterior prefrontals are larger than the posterior prefrontals.

Laurent compared the species to *T. wrighti* of Cuba, separating it by the presence of keeled scales in *wrighti* and smooth scales in *battersbyi* as well as 21 to 23 dorsal scale rows in *wrighti*. However, *wrighti* usually also has smooth scales and agrees in counts with *battersbyi*, even to

THE DWARF BOAS: TROPIDOPHIIDAE

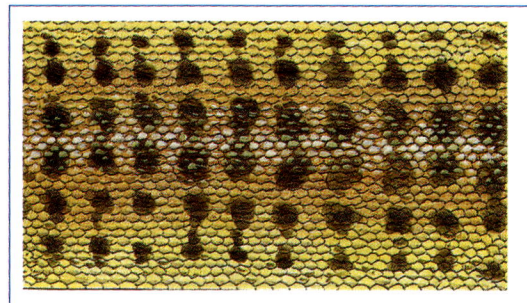

Midbody view of *T. battersbyi*.

the point of both having 12 maxillary teeth. *T. wrighti* has a pattern of just four rows of large blackish spots across the back, rather than six, and has 10 labials rather than 11. The locality for the type of *battersbyi* is uncertain and it appears to have never been retaken in South America. Perhaps it represents a Cuban specimen with wrong data and just at the extreme of variation of *T. wrighti* or perhaps just distorted by preservation.

TROPIDOPHIS CANUS

Bahaman Dwarf Boa

This is a small spotted boa from the Bahamas that has keeled or smooth scales in 23 or 25 rows at midbody, usually fewer than 190 ventrals, and dark blotches in 6 to 12 rows around the body. The occipital spots are absent. Pardalis Group.

Supralabials 9 or 10, infralabials 9 to 12. The midbody scales are keeled or smooth and in 23 or 25 rows at midbody. There are 146 to 191 ventrals and 22 to 37 subcaudals.

Dorsally the Bahaman Dwarf Boa is grayish to brownish with about 10 rows of blackish blotches around the body. The blotching is very variable in number (from 6 to 12 rows) and size and shape. There are 38 to 90 paravertebral blotches. The belly is cream to dull orange with many grayish spots in young, the spots becoming less distinct in older specimens. There is a dark line from the back of the eye that extends onto the side of the nape and then breaks up to become part of the spotting pattern. Large adults may be dark with little or no obvious pattern.

Adults reach a bit over 40 cm in total length.

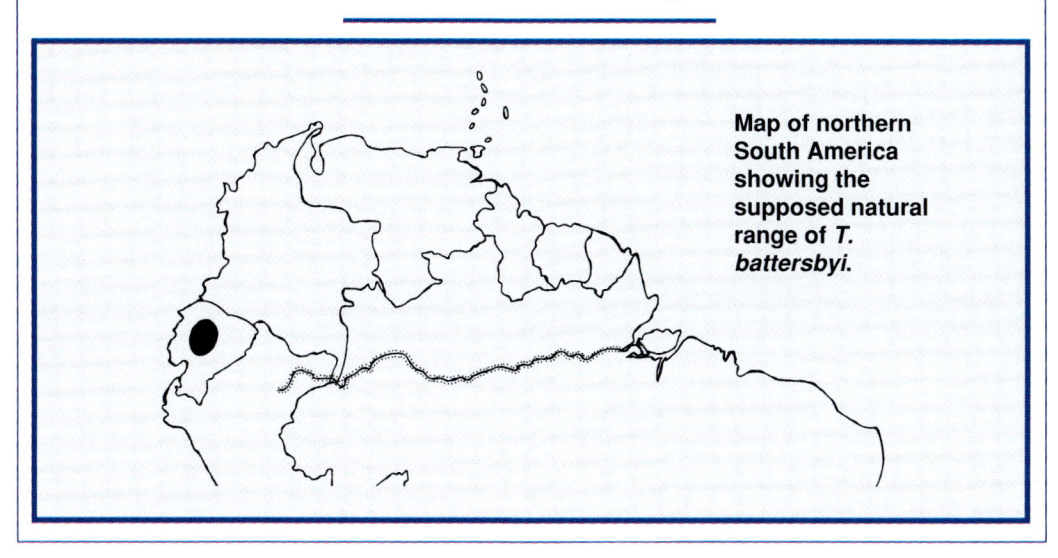

Map of northern South America showing the supposed natural range of *T. battersbyi*.

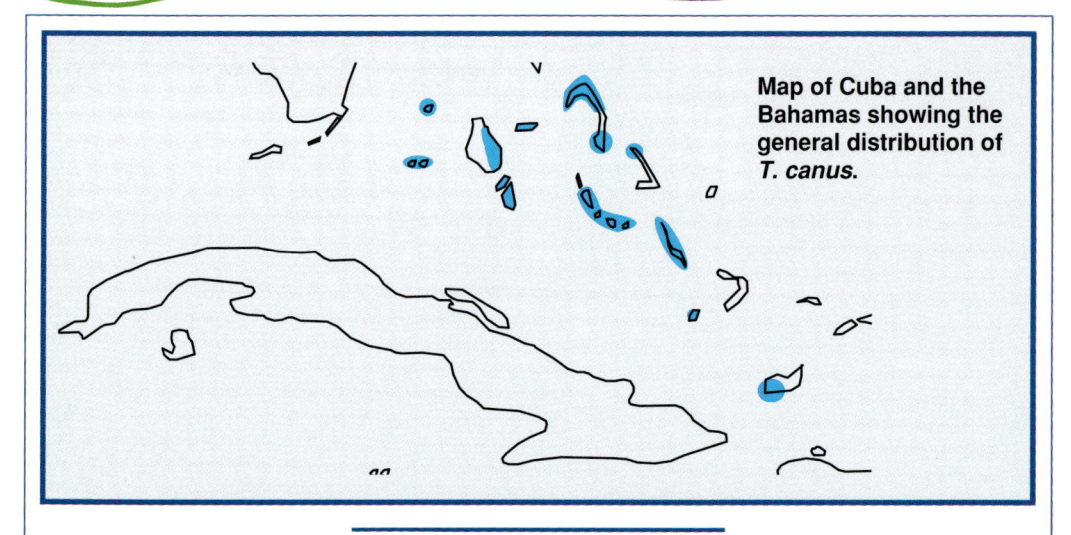

Map of Cuba and the Bahamas showing the general distribution of *T. canus*.

Four subspecies are recognized, all from the Bahamas. *T. c. canus* is from Great Inagua Island; *T. c. androsi* Stull, 1928, is from Andros Island; *T. c. barbouri* Bailey, 1937, is from many small islands and cays in the central Bahamas, including Eleuthera, Cat, Exuma Cays, and Ragged Islands; *T. c. curtus* (Garman, 1887), is from the Biminis and Cay Sal Bank. The species was described by Cope in 1868 as *Ungalia cana* (*Proc. Acad. Nat. Sci.*

This is *T. canus curtus* from the Biminis and Cay Sal Bank. These little inhabitants of dry island forests are almost never seen in the hobby. Photo by R. D. Bartlett.

THE DWARF BOAS: TROPIDOPHIIDAE

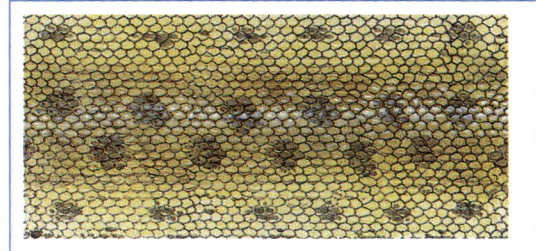

Midbody view of *T. canus*.

Philadelphia, 1868: 129) from Inagua Island.

As might be expected from its occurrence on low, small islands, this species lives in and near dry woods and often occurs near the shore. It is found under logs and rocks, is terrestrial and nocturnal, and tends to come out after rains. It feeds mostly on anoles but also takes frogs and other lizards.

TROPIDOPHIS CAYMANENSIS

Caymans Dwarf Boa

A relatively small species, the Caymans Dwarf Boa is a member of the Melanurus Group from the Cayman Islands south of Cuba. It differs from the Cuban *T. melanurus* in being somewhat smaller (average 37 cm in *caymanensis* and 60 to 80 cm in *melanurus*), commonly having a scale formula of 23/25-25/27-17 (25-27-19 in *melanurus*), having a pale (often yellowish) tail tip in adults (dark in adult *melanurus*), and by having the paravertebral spots distinct and squarish (irregular and indistinct in *melanurus*).

Supralabials 10; infralabials 12 or 13. Dorsal scale rows keeled or smooth, usually in 25 (sometimes 27) rows at midbody. There are 183 to 212 ventrals and 31 to 39 subcaudals.

Head and midbody views of *T. caymenensis*.

The overall coloration is pale gray to tan with a rufous tinge. The head is strongly marked with brown, including bands through the eyes, across the snout, between the eyes, and a large dark trapezoid behind the eyes. The paravertebral spots are large and squarish, chocolate brown, and number 54 to 61 down the back. There are two series of small and indistinct spots on the lower sides; the belly is cream and virtually unmarked to heavily blotched with dark. Often there are narrow pale and dark stripes visible between the paravertebral spots and the lower series of spots. The tail tip is yellow in young and remains light in most adults.

Adults average about 37 cm in total length. The maximum size is a bit over 56 cm.

Three subspecies are recognized. *T. c. caymanensis* inhabits

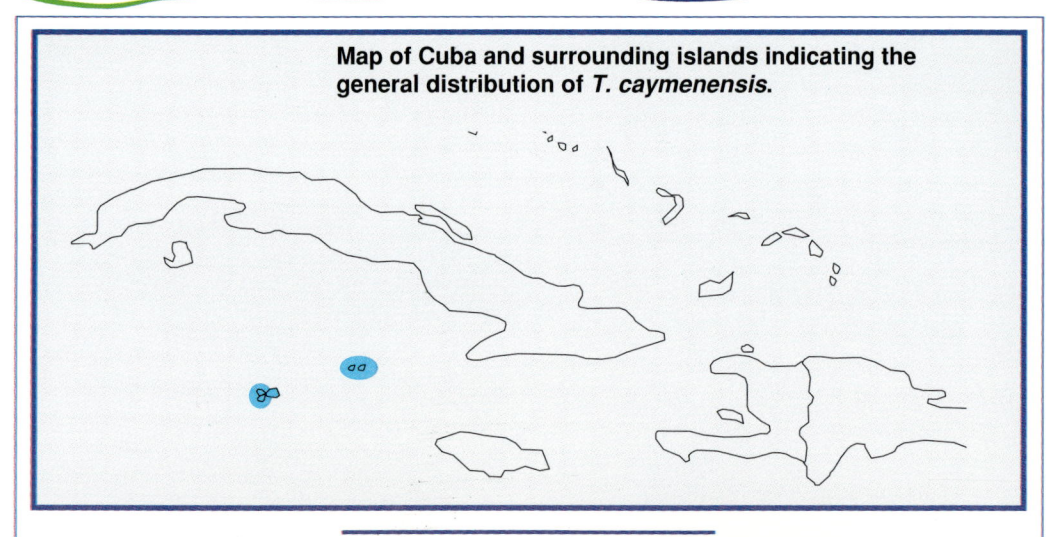

Map of Cuba and surrounding islands indicating the general distribution of *T. caymenensis*.

Grand Cayman; *T. c. parkeri* Grant, 1941, occurs on Little Cayman; and *T. c. schwartzi* Thomas, 1963, is from Cayman Brac.

This species occurs under limestone rocks and logs and under the dead leaves of agave plants in relatively dry and often open areas, sometimes next to the ocean. Though usually terrestrial, it has been found over 2 meters above the ground. Nocturnal, it feeds on the available frogs and anoles.

TROPIDOPHIS FEICKI

Saddled Dwarf Boa

One of the three most contrastingly patterned *Tropidophis*, this species is a member of the Semicinctus Group. The body is slender, the eyes protuberant. It differs from the other species of the group (*T. semicinctus* and *T. wrighti*) by having the dark blotches fused into saddles that extend completely across the back, while the other species have paired and

Head and midbody views of *T. feicki*.

often partially fused blotches that seldom extend completely across the back.

There are 8 to 10 supralabials and 10 to 12 infralabials. The dorsal scales are smooth and typically in 25 rows at midbody (rarely 23); the middorsal scale row may be enlarged. There are 217 to 235 ventrals and 34 to 41 subcaudals.

THE DWARF BOAS: TROPIDOPHIIDAE

If it were imported, *T. feicki* would most likely become a popular snake in the hobby due to its attractive pattern. Because of their small size, raising neonates might present a problem. Photo by V. Jirousek.

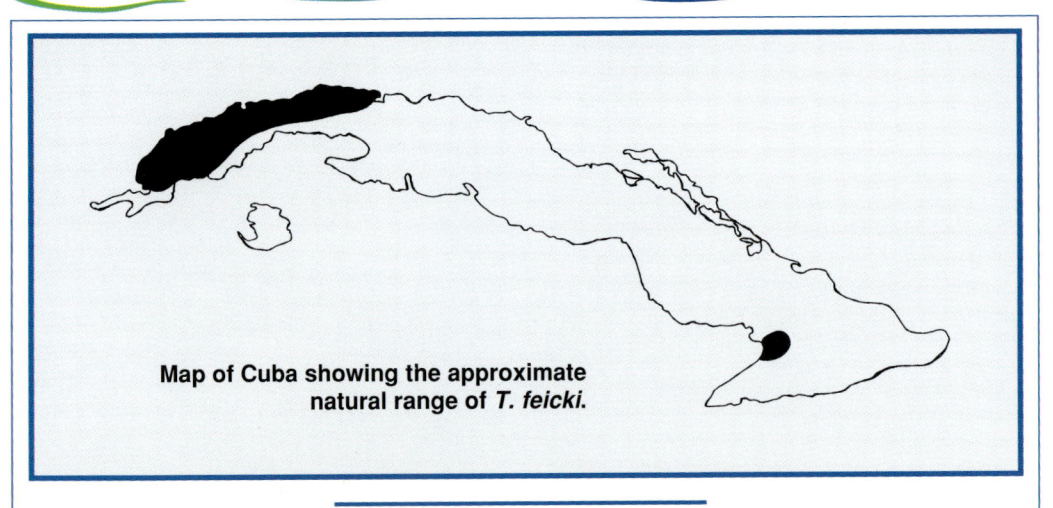

Map of Cuba showing the approximate natural range of *T. feicki*.

This beautiful little boa is pale gray, almost cream, with a yellowish head bearing large occipital spots. Over the back are 17 to 26 wide, relatively regular iridescent dark brown saddles that may extend from one edge of the belly to the other. The belly is creamy, with the dorsal saddles extending slightly onto the ventrals posteriorly.

Adults are over 40 cm in total length, the tail about 10% of the total length. The largest known specimen was 50.5 cm long.

Restricted to western Cuba, it shares its range with *T. semicinctus* but not *T. wrighti*. It was described by Schwartz in 1957 (*Amer. Mus. Novitates*, No. 1839: 3) from three specimens taken in Pinar del Rio Province.

This is a species of relatively dry uplands with limestone cliffs, caves, and loose rock. Though mainly terrestrial, it commonly is found a meter to two above the ground, assumedly foraging for lizards and frogs. Nocturnal, it is paler at night than during the day, showing a distinct physiological color change.

TROPIDOPHIS FUSCUS

Brown Dwarf Boa

This recently described species from eastern Cuba has the slender, compressed body shape and protuberant eyes of a member of the Semicinctus Group but has only 160 to 185 ventrals. Its uniformly dark brown coloration almost completely hides the rows of small dark spots. It was placed in its own species group by the describers and here is considered an Unplaced Species. The species of the Semicinctus Group have more ventrals and a pale background color with large dark blotches and saddles.

The anterior prefrontals are much larger than the posterior ones. The parietals are large but may have fragmented edges. The dorsal scales have weak keels and are in 23 rows at midbody (scale formula 23-23-16/19). The ventrals number 160 to 185, and there are 32 subcaudals in one specimen and 32 in the other with an incomplete tail.

The two described specimens of the Brown Dwarf Boa are uni-

THE DWARF BOAS: TROPIDOPHIIDAE

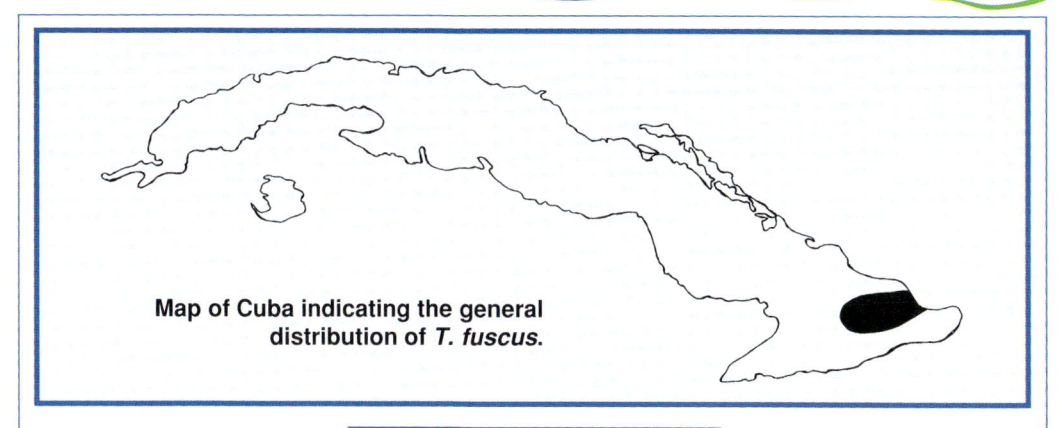

Map of Cuba indicating the general distribution of *T. fuscus*.

formly dark brown above, the belly paler but with large brown blotches. There are traces of about 43 to 46 paravertebral blotches down the back and eight rows of indistinct dark spots and blotches around the body; the dark blotches are not readily visible.

An adult female was almost 34 cm long, while an adult male was over 25 cm in total length, the tail about 10 to over 12% of the length.

This species was described from Minas Amores and Cruzata, Guantanamo Province, Cuba, at from 76 to 500-700 meters elevation. The original description appears in Hedges and Garrido, 1992 (*Copeia*, 1992: 820).

So far *T. fuscus* is known only from two specimens taken in pine woods beneath a log and a large rock during the day. The female holotype carried four or five embryos. It is assumed from the slender shape that the species is at least partially arboreal and is nocturnal. This is the sixth species of *Tropidophis* described from this region of eastern Cuba.

TROPIDOPHIS GREENWAYI

Caicos Dwarf Boa

The Caicos Dwarf Boa is one of the Unplaced Species, though it has been suggested that it might be related to *T. canus*. In addition to its very isolated range, it has a very low number of ventrals.

There are 9 or 10 supralabials and 9 to 12 infralabials. The dorsal scale rows are smooth and in 25 or 27 rows at midbody. Ventrals number 156 to 165, the subcaudals 26 to 30.

This is a dark little boa, generally appearing dark reddish brown to chocolate above with irregular

Head and midbody views of *T. fuscus*.

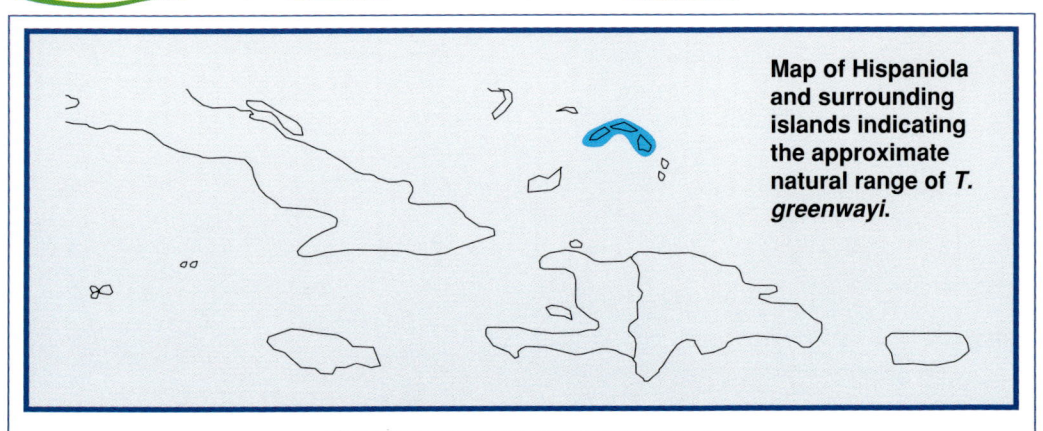

Map of Hispaniola and surrounding islands indicating the approximate natural range of *T. greenwayi*.

blotches or spots in 8 to 10 rows around the body. The paravertebral spots may be fairly distinct and number 27 to 49 along the back. The top of the head usually is brown, sometimes peppered with yellowish or grayish dots. Although newborns may have cream bellies, most adults have reddish brown bellies with two rows of darker brown blotches that may be outlined in white. The tail tip is yellowish in young, becoming dark in many older adults.

Adults commonly are 25 to 35 cm in total length, with a record of 37 cm.

T. greenwayi is a seldom seen little snake about which little is known. Cryptic and nocturnal, they pass unnoticed through the forest. Photo by S. Minton.

THE DWARF BOAS: TROPIDOPHIIDAE

Midbody view of *T. greenwayi*.

Tropidophis greenwayi is found only on the small islands and cays of the Caicos group north of Hispaniola and southeast of the Bahamas. These are small limestone islands with a sparse flora and fauna. The species was described by Barbour and Shreve in 1935 (*Proc. New England Zool. Club*, 16: 2) from a specimen from Ambergris Cay. Two subspecies are recognized, *T. g. greenwayi* from Ambergris Cay, the only known location (where possibly extinct?), and *T. g. lanthanus* Schwartz, 1963 (*Breviora, Mus. Comp. Zool.*, No. 194: 1) from five or six islands and cays in the Caicos Bank.

Nothing seems to be reported on the natural history of this species, but it can be assumed that they feed on lizards and are nocturnal like the other Caribbean dwarf boas.

TROPIDOPHIS HAETIANUS

Haitian Dwarf Boa

The Haitian Dwarf Boa is a Hispaniolan species of the Pardalis Group. Like most other species of this group, it lacks truly remarkable characters, but it often can be recognized by the indistinct dark spots in 8 to 10 rows around the body, 25 to 27 (usually) rows of smooth scales at midbody, and fewer than 200 ventrals.

There are 9 or 10 supralabials and 10 or 11 infralabials. The parietals typically are not in contact. The dorsal scales are smooth and in 25, 27, or rarely 29 rows at midbody. There are 170 to 194 ventrals and 27 to 39 subcaudals.

This species is able to change its color from light to dark. The occipital spots are absent. Generally the background color is some shade of brown, varying from nearly black to bright rufous, and the dark spots are not clearly defined. There are 8 to 10 rows of spots around the body, the paravertebrals numbering 36 to 61 down the back and usually rather large and distinct. The spots on the lower sides may be

Head and midbody views of *T. haetianus*.

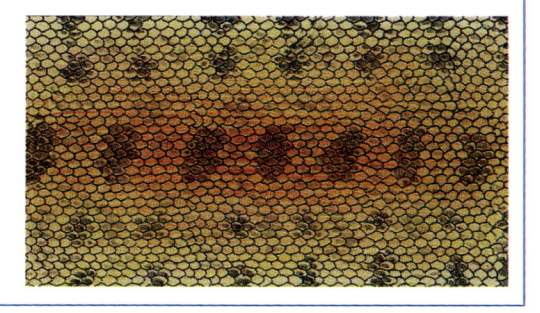

Imported Haitian Dwarf Boas often fail to acclimate to captivity. Generally, they do not accept mice and must be fed anoles or treefrogs. Parasites may also be a factor. Photo by R. D. Bartlett

weak or absent, and there may be fine yellow or white flecking on the sides. The tail tip tends to be dark in adult snakes. The belly often is pale with a suffusion of brown and reduced spotting at the edges.

Most adults are about 35 to 45 cm in total length. The record appears to be 55 cm for a female of the nominate subspecies.

As used here, *Tropidophis haetianus* is found over the entire island of Hispaniola, including the outlying islands. The one record for Cuba is tentatively considered to be based on an introduced

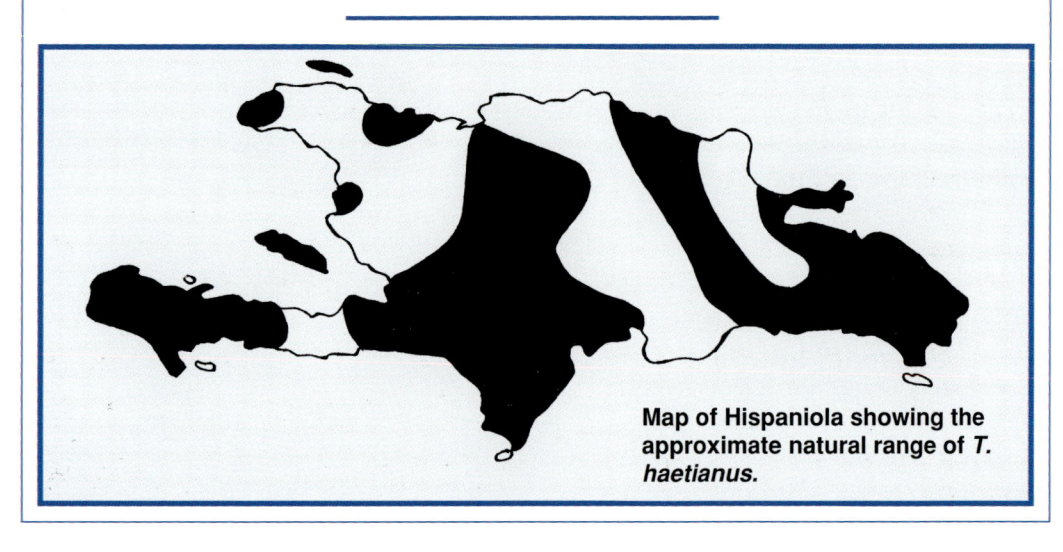

Map of Hispaniola showing the approximate natural range of *T. haetianus.*

THE DWARF BOAS: TROPIDOPHIIDAE

specimen, and the former subspecies from Jamaica are considered to belong to two distinct species, *T. jamaicensis* and *T. stejnegeri*. Three Hispaniolan subspecies are recognized, though they appear to be expressions of a cline. *T. h. hemerus* Schwartz, 1975, is recognized from the extreme eastern Dominican Republic, while *T. h. tibronensis* Schwartz, 1975, occurs

This common dwarf boa is nocturnal and feeds on the usual variety of lizards and frogs, which it kills by constriction. It typically is found in rather dry, open habitats and adapts well to fields and villages, often being found near old home sites. It also occurs in termite mounds. Generally terrestrial, it often has been found in old wells and water tanks and

Some Haitian Dwarf Boas show some pretty iridescence and may have scattered violet and/or green flecks. Captive-breeding rarely occurs, so selection for brighter colors is not likely to happen in the near future. Photo by R. D. Bartlett.

on the Tiburon Peninsula, the long projection from the southwestern portion of the island. The rest of the island is occupied by *T. h. haetianus*. Cope originally described the species in 1879 as *Ungalia haetiana* (*Proc. Amer. Phil. Soc.*, 18: 273) from Port-au-Prince and Gonave Island. *Tropidophis conjunctus* Fischer, 1888, from Cap Haitien, is considered to be a synonym of *T. h. haetianus*.

near streams. Litters number from six to nine young about 16 cm long. This species appears in the terrarium on occasion.

TROPIDOPHIS JAMAICENSIS

Jamaican Dwarf Boa

As used here, *Tropidophis jamaicensis* (new comb.) is removed from *T. haetianus* and given full specific status. Though

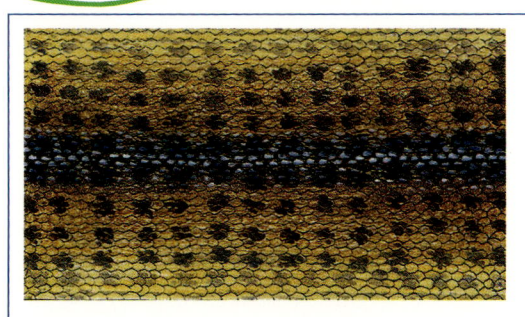

Midbody view of T. jamaicensis.

it shows only minor differences from the Hispaniolan species and from the other Jamaican species, *T. stejnegeri*, it seems impossible that any gene exchange could occur between these three taxa today.

The Jamaican Dwarf Boa differs from *T. haetianus* in generally having a pale tail tip even in adults (remnant of the juvenile yellow tail), the parietals in contact (usually not in contact in Hispaniolan snakes), and often a ventral pattern of a well-defined pale band down the center of the belly. The ventrals number 166 to 181, the subcaudals 28 to 37. The dorsal scales are smooth and usually in 25 rows at midbody (keeled and in 27 rows in *T. stejnegeri*) and 17 rows before the vent. There are about 12 maxillary teeth (commonly 15 in *T. haetianus*). There is a strong tendency to 9 or 10 supralabials. The basic color is pale to dark brown with 10 rows of spots around the body. Adults reach about 35 cm.

T. jamaicensis is found in southern Jamaica. Two subspecies are recognized here: *T. j. jamaicensis* Stull, 1928 (new comb.) southern Jamaica except the Portland Peninsula; and *T. j. stulli* Grant, 1940 (new comb.) restricted to the Portland Peninsula at the central southern edge of the island. The species was first described by Stull in her 1928 revision of the genus (*Occas. Papers Mus. Zool., Univ. Michigan*, No. 195: 12) as *T. maculatus jamaicensis*.

As far as known, it is nocturnal and occurs both under rocks and in low branches of epiphyte-covered trees. Presumably it feeds on the usual assortment of lizards and frogs. It probably is much like *T. haetianus* in its natural history.

TROPIDOPHIS MACULATUS

Freckled Dwarf Boa

This small species of the western part of Cuba is a member of the Pardalis Group. Though similar in many respects to *T. pardalis, nigriventris,* and *pilsbryi*, it has a more conspicuous pattern, occipital spots, and a high ventral count.

In this species, the dorsal scales are smooth or weakly keeled and are in 25 rows at midbody. There are 189 to 208 ventrals and 24 to 41 subcaudals.

The brownish to reddish back has 6 to 10 rows of blotches around the body (usually 8), the blotches generally quite distinct.

Map of Jamaica showing the general distribution of T. jamaicensis.

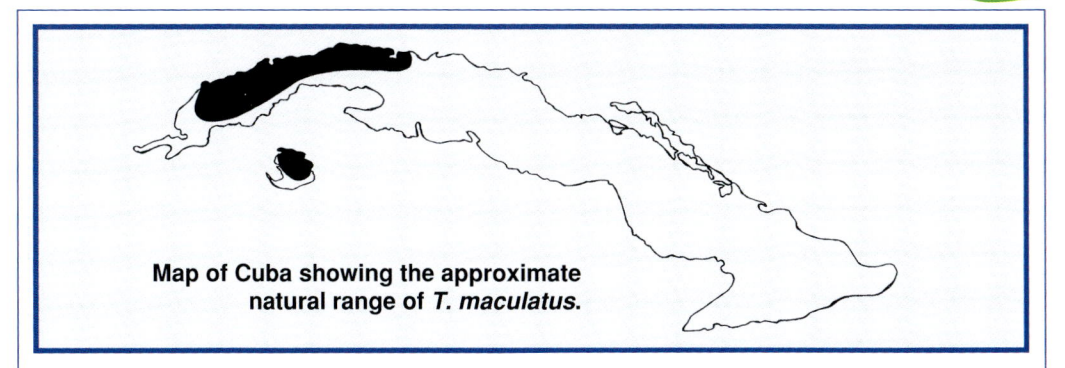

THE DWARF BOAS: TROPIDOPHIIDAE

Map of Cuba showing the approximate natural range of *T. maculatus*.

The paravertebral blotches are moderate but very distinct and number 33 to 54 down the back. The belly is pale with paired dark blotches at the sides.

Adults commonly are over 30 cm in total length, and the record seems to be over 39 cm.

This rather indistinct species is found over western Cuba and the Isle of Pines. It was first described by Bibron in Sagra in 1843 (*Hist. fisica, pol. y natural de la Isla Cuba. IV. Reptiles y Peces*: 212).

Head and midbody views of *T. maculatus*.

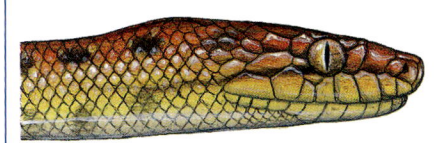

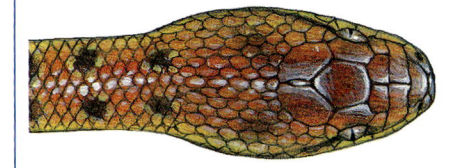

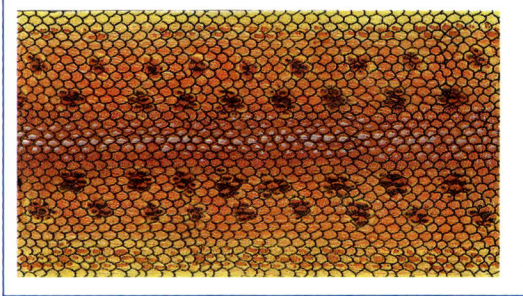

For many years it was badly confused with *T. pardalis* and its other relatives. *T. distinctus* Jan, 1864, and *Ungalia dipsadina* Cope, 1868, are considered to be synonyms.

This is a nocturnal, secretive species of dry, open woodlands. Little has been recorded about its natural history, and there is so much confusion as to its identification that older references are difficult to place.

TROPIDOPHIS MELANURUS

Cuban Dwarf Boa

The biggest species of the genus, the Cuban Dwarf Boa sometimes exceeds a meter in total length. It is perhaps the most commonly seen species in the terrarium hobby as specimens have reached Europe in some numbers, and it is also being bred for the American market. All its scale counts are high for the genus, and it usually has heavily keeled scales. It belongs to the Melanurus Group.

There are 9 or 10 supralabials and 11 to 14 infralabials. The dorsal scales commonly are keeled (but sometimes are smooth) and are in 27 to 29 rows

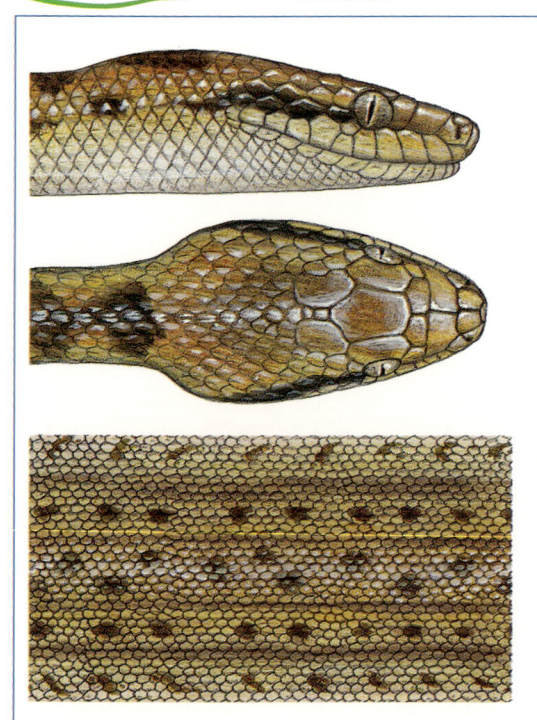

Head and midbody views of *T. melanurus*.

at midbody (rarely 25 rows). There are 183 to 217 ventrals and 29 to 39 subcaudals.

The color and pattern are so variable that descriptions are meaningless, but generally the back is some shade of iridescent brown, gray, or reddish with anywhere from 4 to 12 rows of spots around the body. Usually at least the paravertebral spots are distinct, and commonly many of the spots are picked out with white to yellow scales. Often there appears to be a pale zigzag stripe down the middle of the back. A dark stripe back from the eye may extend back along the lower side of the neck, and the top of the head may be uniformly dark or have a rectangular blotch and various lines and specks. Some specimens have orange outlines about the paravertebral spots, and uniformly orange-backed morphs are being bred in captivity.

Adults commonly are over 80 cm in total length. The record is at almost 106 cm.

T. melanurus is found over almost all of Cuba and also on neighboring Navassa Island. Presently four subspecies are recognized, but one (*dysodes*) seems doubtfully distinct. The subspecies are: *T. m. melanurus* found over almost the entire

Typically, Cuban Dwarf Boas are gray to brown animals with an indistinct pattern of faint dorsal stripes and rows of spots. Many variations in color and pattern are common. Photo by K. H. Switak.

THE DWARF BOAS: TROPIDOPHIIDAE

Gold phase Cuban Dwarf Boas are attractive animals. As can be expected, breeders produce greater numbers of this phase than of the other colors. Photo by K. H. Switak.

Collected in Guantanamo Bay, this Cuban Dwarf Boa is assigned to the subspecies *melanurus*. Visible is the pale but spotted belly exhibited by most specimens. Photo by R. D. Bartlett.

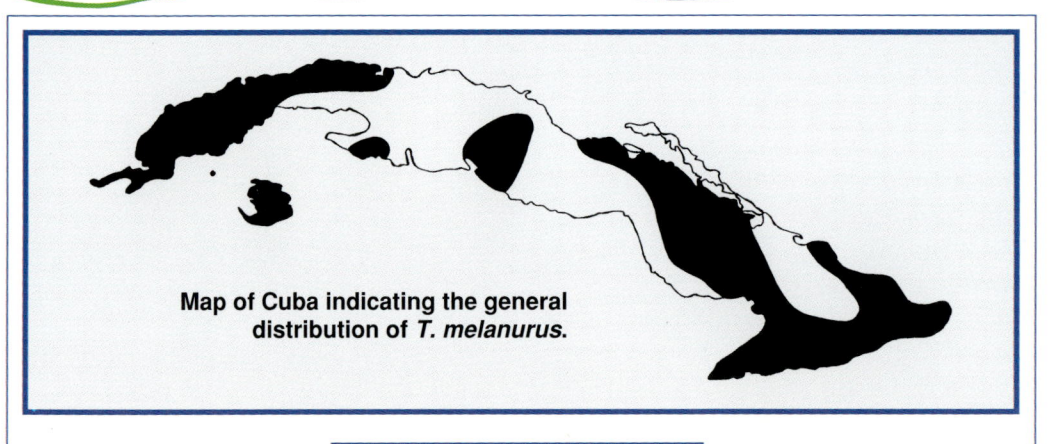

Map of Cuba indicating the general distribution of *T. melanurus*.

island of Cuba; *T. m. bucculentus* Cope, 1868, from Navassa Island; *T. m. ericksoni* Schwartz and Thomas, 1960, from the Isle of Pines; and *T. m. dysodes* Schwartz and Thomas, 1960, from near La Coloma, Pinar del Rio. The species was first described (as *Boa melanura*) by Schlegel in his *Essai Phys. Serp.*, 2: 399. *Notophis bicarinatus* Hallowell, 1856 is a synonym of the nominate subspecies.

Perhaps the most commonly seen *Tropidophis*, this species is found over a great variety of habitats, from rain forests to dry areas with caves and town gardens. It often is found near wells, water tanks, streams, and other moist situations, but apparently it is not at all choosy. It often occurs near man. As expected for the genus, it is nocturnal, secretive, and mostly terrestrial. Frogs and lizards comprise most of the diet, and it even eats toads. There are reports of it feeding on small rodents and even on birds, which might be reasonable considering its large size. Like other species of the genus, it can change color, with active snakes in the dark being paler than those held in the light. Litters consist of about six to eight young. It has been bred in captivity on a regular basis lately and is the most widely seen dwarf boa in the terrarium.

T. melanurus is a habitat generalist and does well in disturbed areas, farmland, and near human dwellings. This adaptability makes them rather undemanding to keep in the terrarium. Photo by K. H. Switak.

THE DWARF BOAS: TROPIDOPHIIDAE

TROPIDOPHIS NIGRIVENTRIS

Black-bellied Dwarf Boa

The common and scientific names of this species are misleading, as not all specimens have dark bellies. This species is very similar to *T. pardalis* and *T. pilsbryi* but usually differs in scale counts and details of the pattern. Pardalis Group.

There are 9 or 10 supralabials and 9 to 11 infralabials. The scale rows are in 23 or 25 rows at midbody and are smooth. There are 144 to 172 ventrals and 25 to 33 subcaudals. The two subspecies associated under this name are distinct in scale counts.

Like so many other dwarf boas, this is a medium to dark brown snake with small darker spots. Typically there are 6 or 8 rows of spots around the body and 37 to 46 paravertebral spots along the back. The paravertebrals are rather small and not always distinct. The lowest row of blotches may be expanded onto the belly or the belly may be clean. Commonly the belly is suffused with brownish pigment. The chin and throat are dark

Midbody view of *T. nigriventris*.

brown in most specimens, and the top of the head also is brown, with a blackish stripe back from the eye.

This is a rather small species that reaches only 35 cm in total length.

The two subspecies have restricted and widely separated distributions in central Cuba. If they truly are isolated, they perhaps would be better considered full species. Both forms are quite rare in collection and poorly known, so the possibility of incomplete collecting exists. *T. n. nigriventris* Bailey, 1937 (*Proc. New England Zool. Club*, 16: 45) comes from eastern Camaguey Province and has 144 to 150 ventrals; the lowermost dark blotches are expanded to cover almost the entire belly. In contrast, *T. n. hardyi* Schwartz and

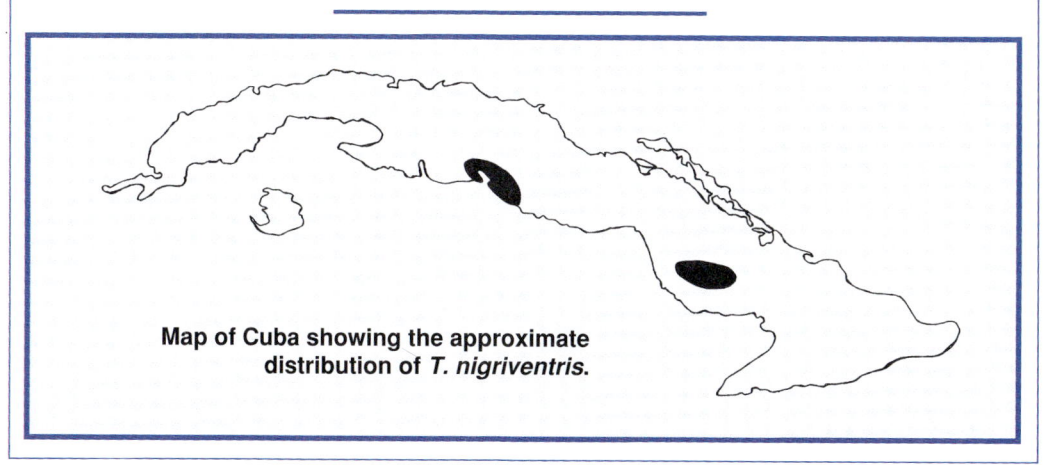

Map of Cuba showing the approximate distribution of *T. nigriventris*.

Garrido, 1975 (*Proc. Biol. Soc. Washington*, 88: 86) has 153 to 172 ventrals and the belly largely pale because the lower row of spots is small and not expanded; it is known from Cienfuegos and Sancti Spiritus Provinces almost 200 km to the east of *T. n. nigriventris*.

The species occurs in rather dry habitats and has been collected at night under rocks.

TROPIDOPHIS PARDALIS

Six-spot Dwarf Boa

A well-marked specimen of the Cuban *T. pardalis* looks much like a motley *T. wrighti*, but it has much lower ventral counts. The eyes may even appear protuberant in some specimens, but the body is never so slender as in the Semicinctus Group species.

The dorsal scales are smooth and is 23 or 25 row at midbody. There are 136 to 165 ventrals and 23 to 34 subcaudals.

This boa can be dull brown but sometimes is bright rufous brown. The head may be bright brown with a broad pale collar over the nape. The spots are in 6 (sometimes 8) rows around the body, and there are 25 to 42 paravertebral spots along the back. Often the paravertebrals are large and rounded, and they may be partially fused across the midline. The creamy yellow belly usually is covered with large dark brown blotches. The tip of the tail even in adults is yellowish.

A small species, the largest recorded specimen is about 34 cm long.

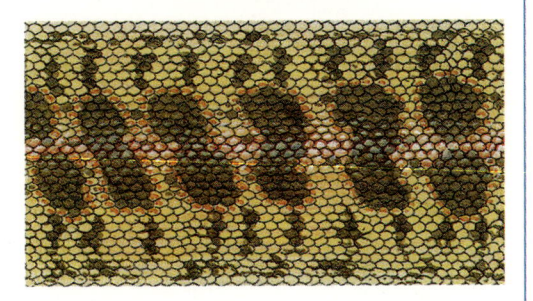

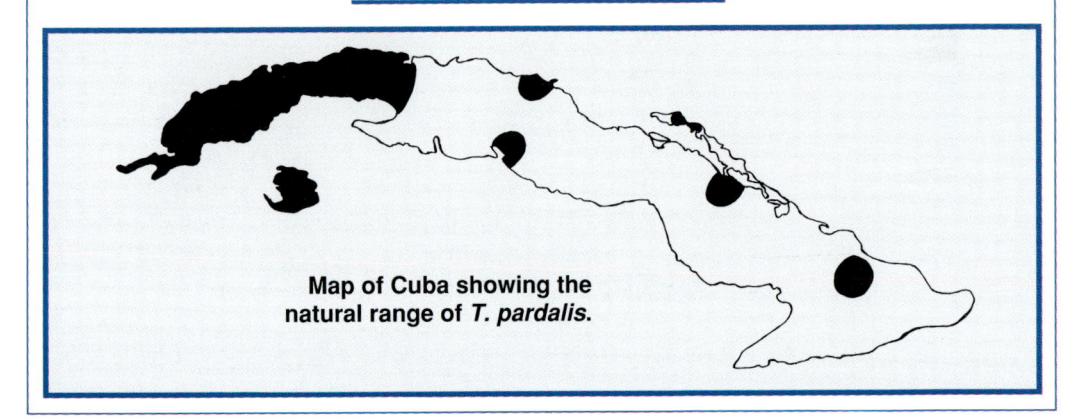

Head and midbody views of *T. pardalis*.

Map of Cuba showing the natural range of *T. pardalis*.

THE DWARF BOAS: TROPIDOPHIIDAE

T. pardalis is not present in the hobby, and there is no information about their captive needs. There are no records of captive breeding of this species. Photo by V. Jirousek.

Specimens assigned to *T. pardalis* have been recorded over most of Cuba and the Isle of Pines, but most have come from the western third of the island; the species is very rare in the eastern half of Cuba, and there is some doubt as to the allocation of these specimens. The species was first described by Gundlach in 1840 as *Boa pardalis* (*Arch. Naturgesch., Berlin*, 6:1: 359).

Like other Cuban *Tropidophis* with large ranges, *T. pardalis* occurs in a variety of habitats from rain forest to dry, open savannas, but it possibly prefers rocky parks and areas near water. Nocturnal, it usually is terrestrial but can climb. It probably feeds mostly on anoles and also on frogs.

TROPIDOPHIS PAUCISQUAMIS

Brazilian Dwarf Boa

Apparently restricted to southeastern Brazil, this species has only 21 dorsal scale rows at midbody, the scales smooth and with an enlarged middorsal row; it is an Unplaced Species. *T. wrighti* has large black blotches in just four rows and is Cuban. The supposedly Ecuadorian *T. battersbyi* has 200 ventrals in the female and 23 dorsal scale rows.

There are two pairs of internasals, 9 or 10 supralabials (3 entering the eye), and 9 infralabials. The parietals are small. There are about 178 ventrals (females) and 37 to 40 subcaudals. There are 19 maxillary teeth.

Midbody view of T. paucisquamis.

The Brazilian Dwarf Boa is brown above with round, indistinct dark spots in six rows across the back, the lowest row of spots large and extending onto the yellowish belly. The belly has two rows of large black spots that sometimes connect to form black cross-bands. There are small dark spots on the frontal and a dark line back from the eye.

Adults reach at least 32.5 cm in total length, the tail about 12% of the total length.

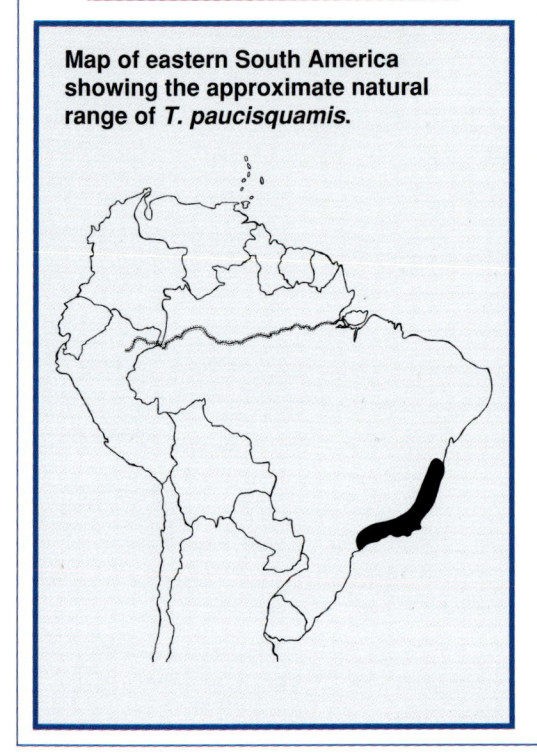

Map of eastern South America showing the approximate natural range of T. paucisquamis.

T. paucisquamis appears to be restricted to southeastern Brazil, occurring in at least the states of Espirito Santo, Rio de Janeiro, and Sao Paulo. There is a doubtful record from Peru. The species was described as *Ungalia paucisquamis* by Mueller in 1901 (in Schenkel, *Verhandl. Naturf. Ges. Basel*, 13: 154) from an unknown locality. *Ungalia braziliensis* Andersson, 1901, is the same species. I've seen nothing on the natural history of this species, but I've probably missed some Brazilian literature.

TROPIDOPHIS PILSBRYI

Pale-spot Dwarf Boa

Another of the very poorly known Cuban *Tropidophis*, this member of the Pardalis Group is difficult to separate from *T. pardalis, maculatus*, and *nigriventris*. It has large spots like *pardalis* but higher scale counts.

There are 10 or 11 supralabials and 11 or 12 infralabials. The dorsal scales are weakly keeled (stronger over the vent) and in 23 to 27 rows at midbody. There are 160 to 183 ventrals and 29 to 35 subcaudals.

A grayish to brown species, the rather large dark spots are in 8 to 10 rows around the body, the spots at the edge of the belly restricted to the belly and not extending beyond the lowermost dorsal scale row. The paravertebral spots are large and dark, often fused across the midline, and number 36 to 50 along the back. The top of the head is dark with traces of rectangles or bands, and there may

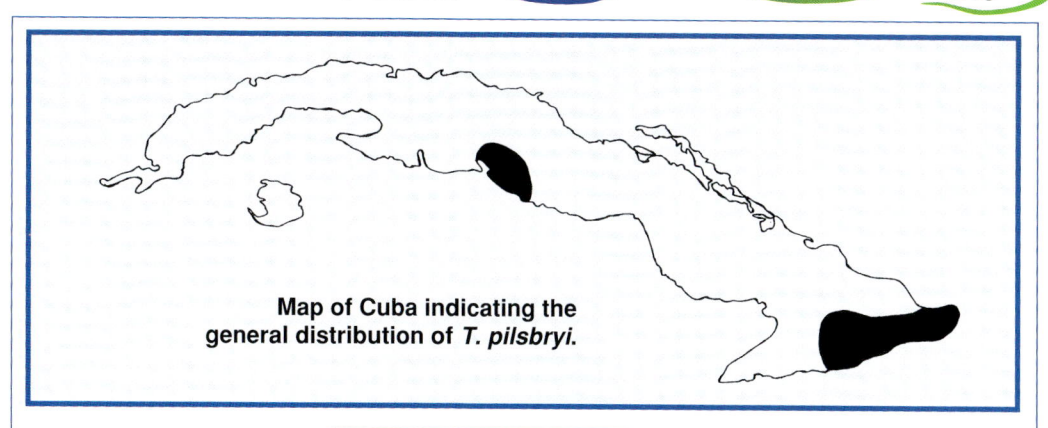

THE DWARF BOAS: TROPIDOPHIIDAE

Map of Cuba indicating the general distribution of *T. pilsbryi*.

be two large pale occipital spots that fuse into a whitish collar behind the head (the source of the common name). There is a blackish stripe back from the eye, strongly contrasting with the yellowish lower jaw and throat. The belly is mostly pale except for the usual brown blotches. The tail is mostly yellowish below, pale above.

Adults are fairly large, often over 35 cm, with a record of almost 46 cm total length.

The two recognized subspecies are separated by hundreds of kilometers, but the rarity of the species in collections makes it hard to accept that the forms are actually isolated. *T. p. pilsbryi* occurs in extreme eastern Cuba; it has the scales in 23 to 25 rows, 160 to 166 ventrals, and 36 to 47 paravertebrals along the back. It was first described by Bailey in 1937 (*Proc. New England Zool. Club*, 16: 42). *T. p. galacelidus* Schwartz and Garrido, 1975 (*Proc. Biol. Soc. Washington*, 88: 81), comes from Cienfuegos and Sancti Spiritus Provinces in central Cuba; in this form the scales are in 25 or 27 rows at midbody, and there are 177 to 183 ventrals

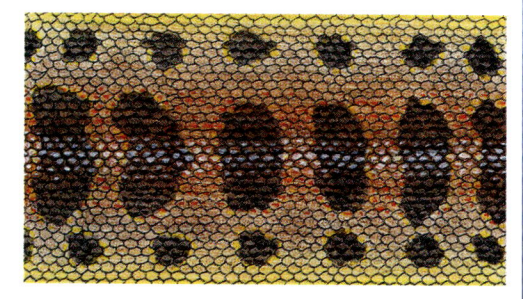

Head and midbody views of *T. pilsbryi*.

and 44 to 50 paravertebrals along the back. The ventral count completely separates the two subspecies, and if they are truly isolated they should be considered full species.

Little is known about this species, and it is considered to be rare. Like other Cuban *Tropidophis* it is nocturnal and terrestrial; its habitats are relatively dry.

TROPIDOPHIS SEMICINCTUS

Two-spot Dwarf Boa

Another strongly spotted species of western Cuba, it is one of the three species of the Semicinctus Group defined in part by the elongate, graceful form and protuberant eyes. It differs from the other species by being distinctly yellow to reddish with two rows of large oval blackish blotches that may be irregularly fused. In *T. feicki* the background color is very pale gray (almost cream) with wide blackish saddles extending over the entire back. *T. wrighti* is yellowish cream or grayish yellow with four series of large blackish spots distinguishable though often partially fused.

There are 8 to 11 supralabials and 9 to 12 infralabials. The dorsal scales are smooth to weakly keeled and in 21 to 25 rows at midbody; the middorsal scale row may be enlarged. There are 201 to 214 ventrals and 34 to 40 subcaudals.

This striking dwarf boa is bright reddish brown on the head, becoming paler reddish or yellowish over the body, with a cream belly. Often there is a strongly marked brighter reddish band down the middle of the back. The back is marked with 19 to 26 large oval black blotches, with very even edges, in two distinct series. The blotches often fuse on the neck and may be partially fused or very narrowly separated at the middorsal line.

This species exceeds 40 cm in adults, the record being 46 cm.

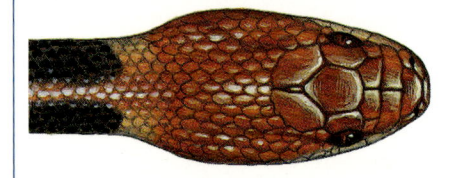

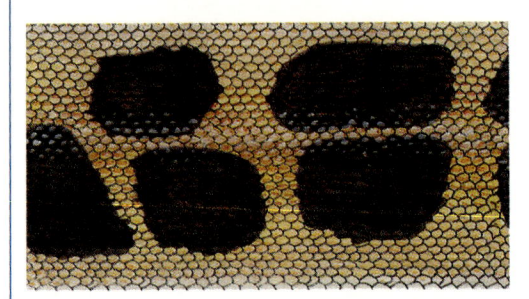

upper left: Head and midbody views of *T. semicinctus*.

below: Map of Cuba showing the general distribution of *T. semicinctus*.

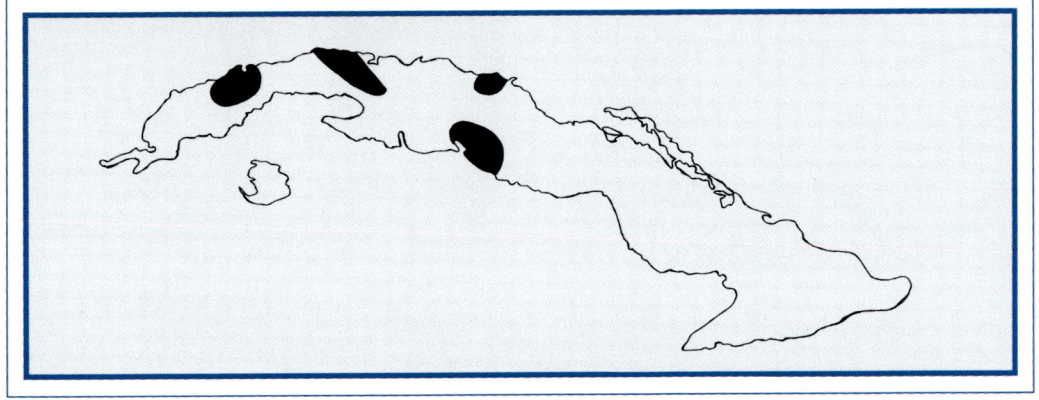

THE DWARF BOAS: TROPIDOPHIIDAE

T. semicinctus seems to be a rare snake in nature, but it may be overlooked due to small size and nocturnal habits. It is unavailable to hobbyists. This photo is of a preserved specimen. Photo by P. J. Stafford.

The Two-spot Dwarf Boa is known from western and central Cuba, where it occurs in dry areas under rocks and logs. It was described by Gundlach and Peters in 1864 (*Montab. Preuss. Akad. Wiss. Berlin*, 1864: 388) as *Ungalia maculata* var. *semicincta*. *T. moreleti* Bocourt, 1885 (supposedly from Guatemala) is a synonym.

Little is known of this bright-colored boa in nature, but it is assumed to be nocturnal and is a good climber. It probably feeds on anoles and other lizards plus frogs. The newborn young are about 16 cm long.

TROPIDOPHIS STEJNEGERI

Grant's Dwarf Boa

Normally considered a subspecies of the Hispaniolan *T. haetianus*, *stejnegeri* is here elevated to specific rank on the basis that it shows distinctions from both the Hispaniolan snakes and the other Jamaican species (*T. jamaicensis*) and there are no signs that it presently is exchanging genes with either taxon. It is isolated in northern Jamaica and separated by a mountain range from the southern Jamaican *T. jamaicensis*.

Like *T. jamaicensis*, it differs from *T. haetianus* in having a pale tail tip in most adults and in having the parietals in contact. It has 181 to 190 ventrals, similar to *T. haetianus* and unlike *T. jamaicensis*. It has keeled dorsal scales (smooth in both other species) in 27 rows at midbody

Midbody view of *T. stejnegeri*.

(25 in *T. jamaicensis*). There are 10 supralabials and 11 infralabials. Typically it is slate gray in color with just traces of about 10 rows of small spots around the body, but it also can be paler; large occipital spots may be present (usually absent in the other species). Adults reach about 42 cm.

T. stejnegeri is found over the northern third of Jamaica. The species was first described as *T. pardalis stejnegeri* by Chapman Grant in 1940 (*Jamaica Today* [London]: 157) from Boston Bay, between Port Antonia and Manchioneal. As far as known, its natural history is similar to other species of the genus and probably much like *T. haetianus*.

TROPIDOPHIS TACZANOWSKYI

Cordillera Dwarf Boa

The Cordillera Dwarf Boa is a South American mainland member of the Pardalis Group with strongly keeled dorsal scales in 23 rows at midbody. There are only 25 subcaudals, some occasionally divided.

There are 8 or 9 supralabials (2 entering the eye) and 10 or 11 infralabials. The parietals are fairly large but sometimes split into two. There are 149 to 160 ventrals and 25 subcaudals. The dorsal scales are in 23 rows at the midbody, all but the three lower rows on each side keeled.

The Cordillera Dwarf Boa is brownish to violet-brown above, yellowish below. On the back are six series of indistinct dark spots, the lower ones large and sometimes edged with yellow. There may be short dark lines in the pattern as well as spots. The pattern may be indistinct and ragged in appearance, and the species has been compared with *T. melanurus* in appearance.

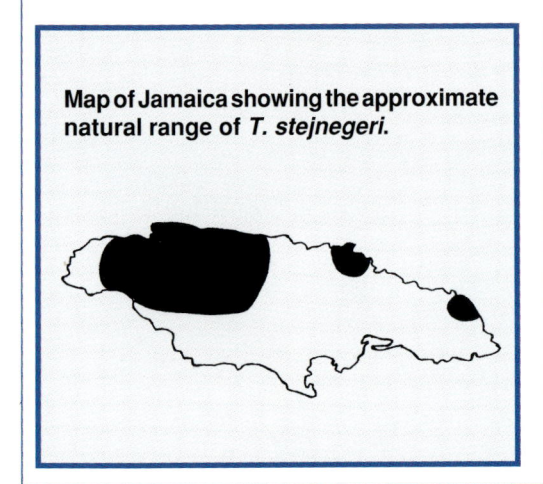

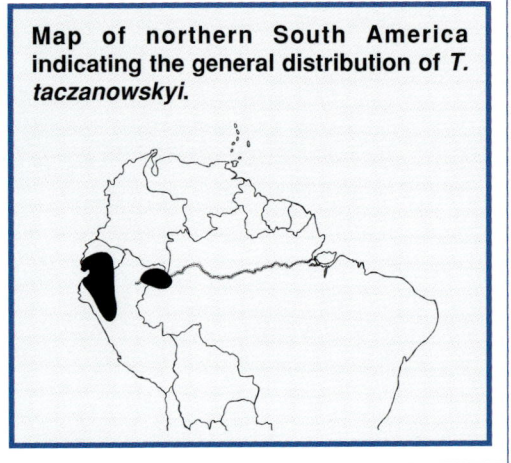

Map of Jamaica showing the approximate natural range of *T. stejnegeri*.

Map of northern South America indicating the general distribution of *T. taczanowskyi*.

THE DWARF BOAS: TROPIDOPHIIDAE

Midbody view of *T. taczanowskyi*.

There are large black spots at the edges of the belly, these sometimes joining into irregular cross-bars; the undertail is similarly patterned. There may be dark flecks on the head and a dark line back from the eye.

Adults are at least 34.5 cm long, the tail over 10% of the total length.

This appears to be a species restricted to the Cordillera Oriental of Ecuador and the Cordillera Central of Peru. The types came from Tambillo, Peru, and there are specimens from Guyaquil (a shipping point?) and the upper Rio Pastaza, Ecuador, as well as the Loreto area of Peru. There is a doubtful record from Brazil (which might make sense if it were from the Amazon). This species was described as *Ungalia taczanowskyi* by Steindachner in 1880 (*Sitz. Ak. Wein.*, 80: 552, plate). The name sometimes is spelled *taczanowski*.

Steindachner said that one of his types contained five well-developed embryos about 75 mm long that already had keeled scales and dark spots on the belly.

TROPIDOPHIS WRIGHTI

Wright's Dwarf Boa

Wright's Dwarf Boa is the third of the trio of heavily spotted snakes comprising the Cuban Semicinctus Group, graceful snakes with protuberant eyes. Of the three it is the only one where four rows of large dark spots or blotches can be distinguished.

There are 10 supralabials, 3 entering the eye, and 10 infralabials. The dorsal scales are smooth and in 21 or 23 rows at midbody (the middorsal row may be weakly keeled and enlarged). The ventrals number 193 to 222, the subcaudals 36 to 45.

Not as attractively colored as the other Semicinctus Group species, this is a pale gray or dull creamy yellow species with 17 to 37 very irregular rows of large

Head and midbody views of *T. wrighti*.

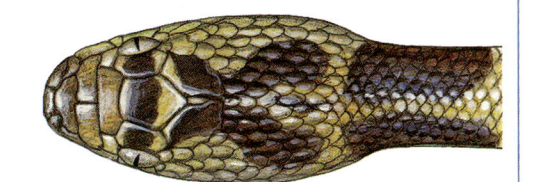

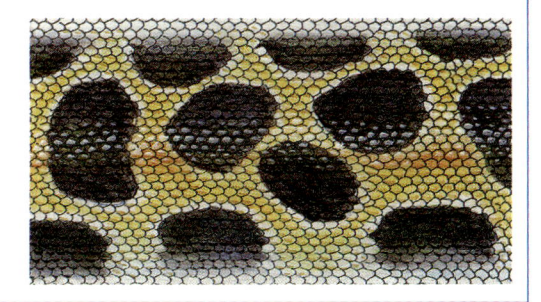

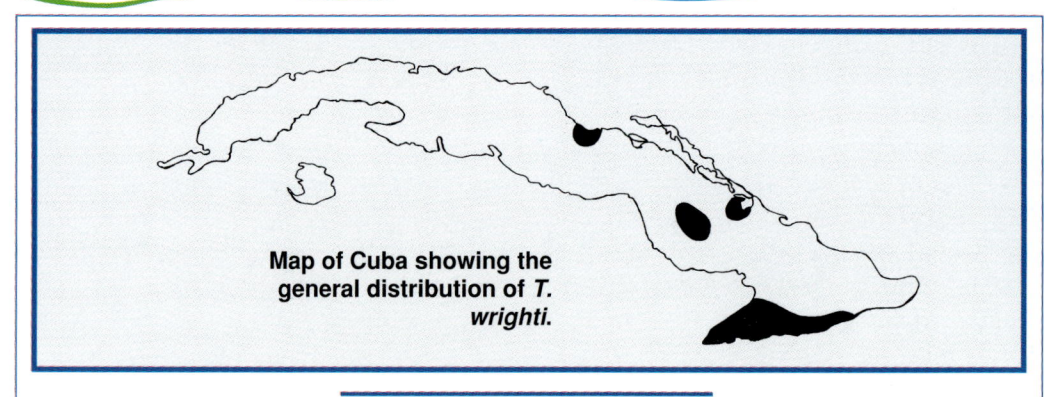

Map of Cuba showing the general distribution of *T. wrighti*.

oval blackish spots along the back. Counted from side to side, there are up to four rows of spots, though they often are variably fused into larger blotches. The coloration is quite iridescent. The top of the head is grayish and may have a large blackish trapezoid behind the eyes and a bar between the eyes. The belly is cream except where the lower spots extend onto its edges and where they run across the undertail.

The smallest species of the group, adults apparently do not exceed 40 cm in total length.

T. wrighti is a species of central and eastern Cuba. Its range almost touches but does not overlap that of *T. semicinctus*. The species was described by Stull in 1928 (*Occas. Papers Mus. Zool., Univ. Michigan*, No. 195: 38) from a single specimen of uncertain origin in eastern Cuba.

This is an uncommonly collected secretive nocturnal species that often is found 1 to 3 meters above the ground while foraging at night.

Genus Ungaliophis Mueller, 1882 (*Verh. Naturforsch. Ges. Basel*, 7: 142). Type species by monotypy *U. continentalis* Mueller, 1882.

Synonyms: *Peropodum* Bocourt, 1882 (not technically a new name; see Foart, 1951 for a discussion).

Small tropidophiid boas with smooth scales and the prefrontals fused into a large rounded shield before the frontal, which may be smaller than the prefrontal shield. Only males have external spurs. The nasal scale is divided into two scales, the nostril piercing the anterior scale. There is a single squarish loreal before a single large vertical preocular scale and a single large supraocular scale over each eye. Usually two or three supralabials enter the eye. The cloacal scent glands are strongly staggered, one much farther from the vent than the other.

Until recently these little boas have been very rare in collections and usually were seen only when random specimens were found in imported bunches of bananas and similar fruits. They are strongly arboreal and beautifully patterned though not colorful. Today one (or perhaps both) species has been bred in very small numbers by several zoos and a few specialist breeders, but they still are rare in the hands of the average hobbyist.

THE DWARF BOAS: TROPIDOPHIIDAE

Though the genus was reviewed by Bogert (1968a), that paper was based on examination of only a dozen specimens. Bogert sorted out two species from a very confused state, but it is not impossible that examination of larger series, especially from Mexico and northern Central America, might show that at least one other species is recognizable.

Key to the species of Ungaliophis

A. Dark spots on back oval; midbody scales in 25 rows; rostral separating internasals .... *continentalis*

AA. Dark spots on back triangular; midbody scales in 19 to 25 rows; rostral not separating internasals .... *panamensis*

UNGALIOPHIS CONTINENTALIS

Round-spot Banana Boa

The Round-spot Banana-Boa is the species of Mexico and northern Central America and the only one seen even occasionally in captivity. The new common name is suggested to emphasize the distinctive pattern that readily separates it from the southern species.

In addition to the large oval black spots distinguishing this species at a glance from *U. panamensis*, there are many differences in head scalation. The fused prefrontal shield is just a bit larger than the rather rounded frontal and usually is touched by the rostral shield, which separates the small internasals.

Supralabials 9 or 10, usually 2 entering the orbit; infralabials 10

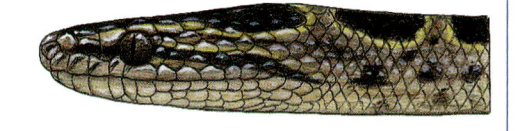

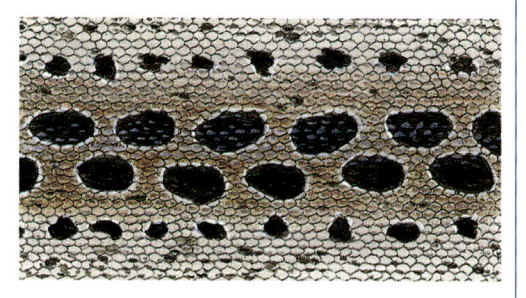

Head and midbody views of *U. continentalis*.

or 11. Scales smooth, the rows at midbody almost always 25, reduced to 15 near the vent. Ventrals 230 to 258 (with one record of 204 from an upland location in Chiapas, Mexico); subcaudals not divided, 39 to 47; anal scale single. There are about 12 maxillary teeth.

Though not colorful, these are strongly patterned snakes. They are grayish to brownish over the back, often quite glossy, with many scattered black flecks. The top of the head is black, as is a broad band back from the eye to behind the corner of the mouth; the black on top of the head often extends backward as two short or long arms over the nape. There are about 35 to 40 large oval black spots down the back, sometimes in a single row and sometimes partially in two alternating rows, becoming a single row on

THE LIVING BOAS

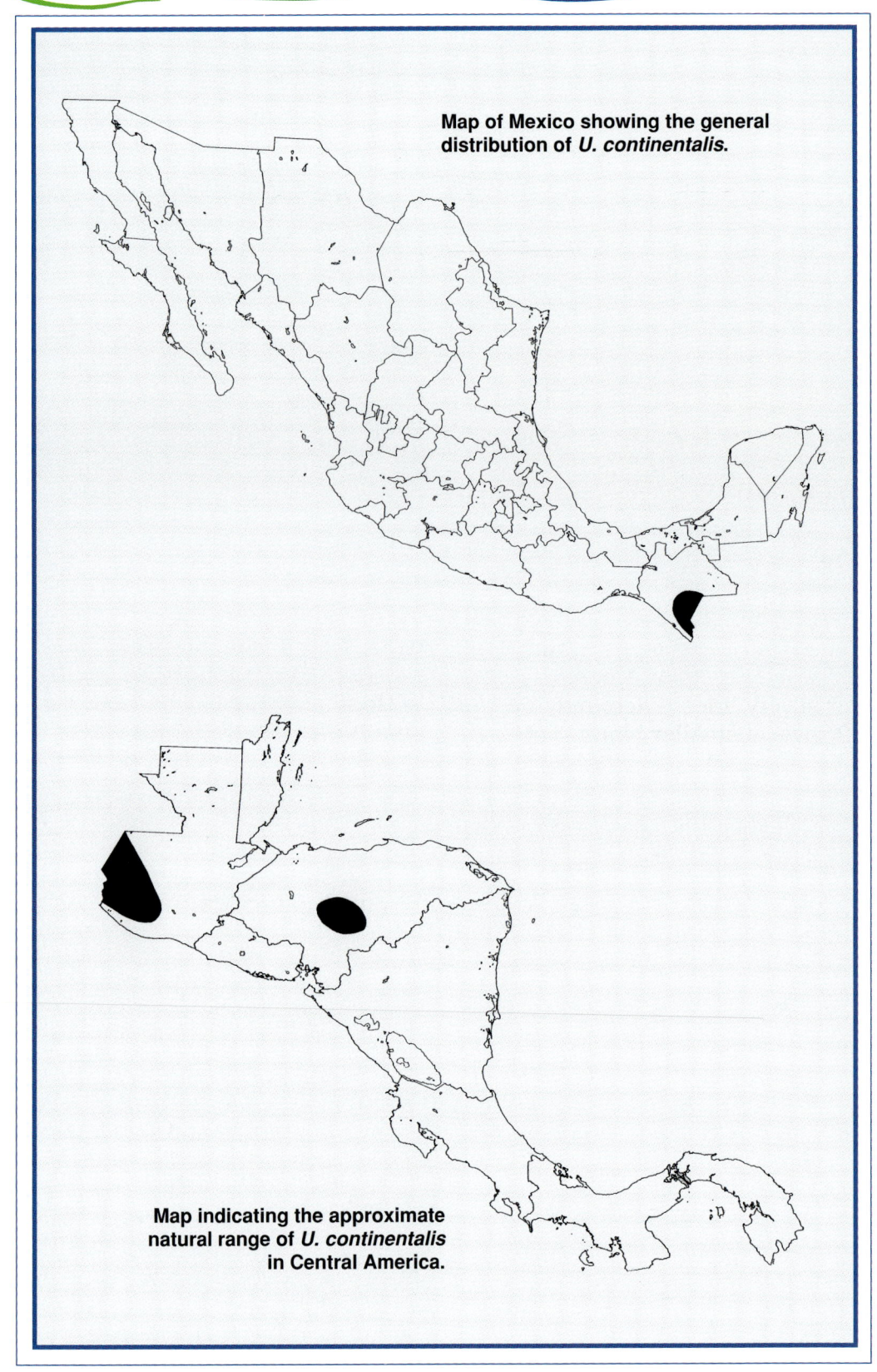

Map of Mexico showing the general distribution of *U. continentalis*.

Map indicating the approximate natural range of *U. continentalis* in Central America.

THE DWARF BOAS: TROPIDOPHIIDAE 251

U. continentalis is present, but rare, in the hobby. It is rather hardy once acclimated and does well in naturalistic, arboreal terraria. Photo by R. D. Bartlett.

top of the tail. The black of the head and the ovals is outlined by narrow but obvious cream, yellow, or silvery lines. There may be 1 or 2 rows of smaller black spots along the sides, the lower row often extending onto the belly, which is cream with variable black spots and blotches. Young often are darker than adults.

Adults often are 40 cm in total length and may approach 50 cm. The type specimen (from Guatemala) was 76 cm long. The tail is about 10% of the total length.

The Round-spot Banana Boa is found from the Pacific slope of southern Mexico (Chiapas) south to Honduras and possibly Nicaragua; it also occurs on the Carib-

Round-spot Banana Boas are nocturnal snakes that feed on frogs and anoles. Sometimes they refuse to switch over to rodents in captivity. Photo by R. D. Bartlett.

bean slope of Chiapas. It is found from low altitudes to over 2000 meters and from warm, moist habitats to drier, cool areas. Because of the great range of environments occupied and the variation in scale counts, it is not impossible that more than one species is confounded under this name.

on the ground. At one time the species apparently was common enough in banana plantations for specimens to reach the fruit markets in New York and other large cities in hands of bananas, but today pesticides and chemical treatment of harvested bananas make accidental importations unlikely.

Captive-breeding of Round-spot Banana Boas occurs sporadically. Although this species prefers cool temperatures, gravid females appreciate a basking light. Photo by R. D. Bartlett.

Little is known about this species in nature, but it appears to be associated with bromeliads and is arboreal. At high altitudes it has been found in Mexican pines, while at low altitudes it appears to be associated with many types of vegetation. It eats a variety of frogs and lizards, which it kills by constriction. Specimens are nocturnal and seldom are found

Round-spots have been kept and bred by several zoos and are relatively easy to maintain. They do well in small vertical terraria with branches for climbing and almost any type of substrate that holds some moisture. Bromeliads and other epiphytes are appreciated, as is a hide box affixed toward the top of the terrarium. Depending on origin of the specimens, they tolerate temperatures

THE DWARF BOAS: TROPIDOPHIIDAE

from about 20 to 25°C (68 to 77°F) well, often preferring the coolest part of the terrarium. Much of their day is spent in loose coils under cover, the boas coming out at night to feed if they have any preference in the matter.

Wild-collected specimens probably will insist on lizards and frogs as the preferred food, but many can be switched over to small mice by scenting the mice with lizards at first. Captive-bred specimens may already be adjusted to mice. Small specimens may require feeding with lizard and mouse legs or tails touched to the snout or worked into the front of the mouth.

Males have small but obvious spurs, while females generally are said to lack external spurs. Females may be 10 cm or more longer than males. During mating the male bites the female's tail and scratches his spurs along her back. Litters are small, usually six to ten young, and the babies are about 15 cm long. They look much like the adults. Though hard to feed at first, they may accept mouse tails and pieces of mice scented with lizards. Sexual maturity is reached in less than two years. It has been recorded as living over 17 years in captivity. For an account of keeping experiences, see Burger, 1995.

UNGALIOPHIS PANAMENSIS

Triangle Banana Boa

This very poorly understood species of banana boa is easily distinguished by the large triangular black spots running down

Head and midbody views of *U. panamensis*.

the back in two alternating series. The fused prefrontal shield is rounded and larger than the triangular frontal. The rostral shield is short and broad and does not separate the large internasals that are in contact at the midline.

Supralabials 8 or 9, 2 or 3 entering the orbit; infralabials about 9. The smooth dorsal scales are in 19 to 23 rows at midbody, rarely in 25 rows. There are 13 to 15 maxillary teeth.

This is an intensely patterned boa, the brownish to grayish back covered with two alternating rows of large black triangular spots that are nearly in contact and surrounded by distinct creamy or yellowish lines. The chains of triangles continue over the tail. The belly is creamy with many black blotches. The top of the head is largely dark and usually puts out two long black stripes

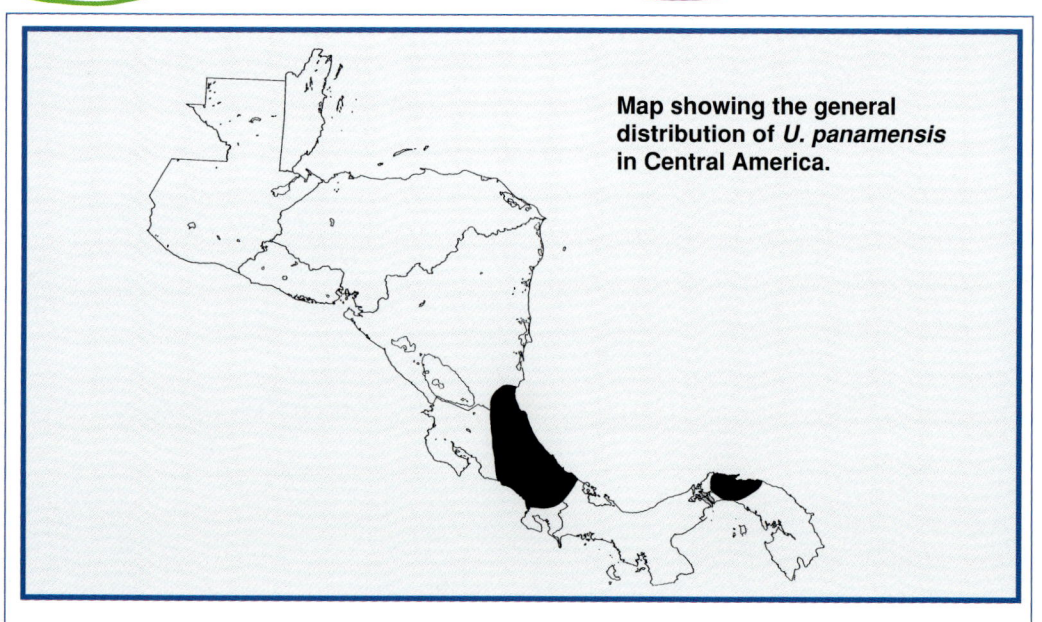

Map showing the general distribution of *U. panamensis* in Central America.

that connect with the rows of triangles. There may be one or two series of smaller black spots low on the sides or they may be fused into a continuous narrow black strip.

Adults appear to seldom exceed 50 cm in total length.

Ungaliophis panamensis is known from southern Nicaragua, Costa Rica, Panama, and Colombia but only a few specimens have been collected at any one spot. The species was described from Panama by Schmidt in 1933 (*Smithsonian Misc. Coll.*, 89[1]: 12). In 1940, Prado described a juvenile from near Antioquia, Colombia, as *U. danieli* (*Mem. Inst. Butantan*, 14: 35); this name now is considered a synonym.

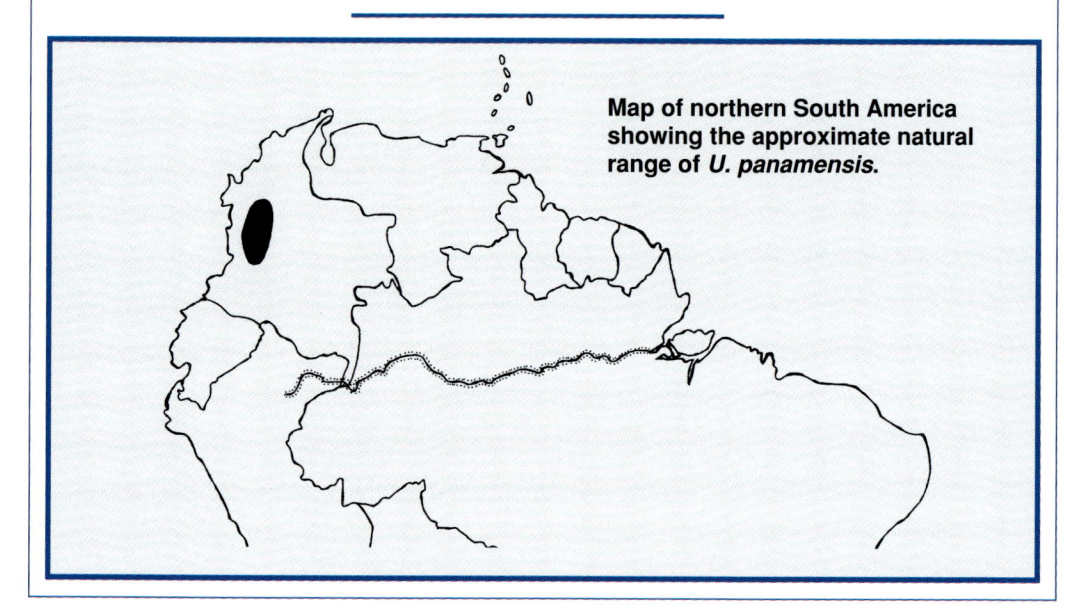

Map of northern South America showing the approximate natural range of *U. panamensis*.

THE DWARF BOAS: TROPIDOPHIIDAE

This *U. panamensis* is giving birth, but, unfortunately, the young were stillborn. Breeding of this species is very rare, and it is certainly possible the proper parameters are not understood fully. Photo by P. Freed.

Preserved specimen of *U. panamensis*. Suitable mountain habitat for this species and *U. continentalis* is disappearing, threatening both species. Photo by P. J. Stafford.

As far as known, this species is arboreal, living in bromeliads and other epiphytes and seldom coming to the ground. It usually has been collected by accident or as a result of felling of trees. Like the Round-spot, it frequents banana plantations (or at least it did) and has reached large cities in hands of bananas. Few specimens are in collections, but it seems to be keepable and breedable much like *U. continentalis*.

As a rule of thumb, handling snakes periodically keeps them from becoming aggressive. Over-handling, however, will cause stress to the snake. This is a Red-tailed Boa. Photo by I. Francais.

BOA CARE

Unlike the pythons, most boas are rather small animals, only a few species greatly exceeding 2 meters in length. They cover a variety of habitats, however, and though most are terrestrial to moderately arboreal, a few are strongly aquatic, strictly arboreal, or total burrowers. Most are sedentary animals that like to just loll about the cage in a favorite warm corner, under or on a piece of bark or a branch, occasionally soaking in their water bowl and feeding mostly at night. Almost all feed on small birds and mammals, with the occasional lizard or snake thrown in. The tropidophiids are more likely to feed on insects and even worms, but even they adapt to mice in the terrarium. In the earlier chapters I've discussed the essentials for keeping most of the species in some detail, so this chapter is just a summary of basic techniques for keeping the "average" boas, such as a Red-tailed Boa or a Rainbow Slender Boa in the terrarium.

PRECAUTIONS

If you keep a large boid, anything from the common Red-tail to a Green Anaconda, you probably will be bitten. Many large boas are quick to react to movements of all types and assume that anything that comes at them is either a predator or prey. In the case of smaller boas the bite, though painful, is no more serious than that of a kingsnake or Corn Snake; you will bleed a bit for a few minutes and then forget about it. As a precaution, it is best to clean any boa bite carefully with hydrogen peroxide and a general antiseptic such as povidone-iodine. A bandage may be necessary to keep the wound clean. Many boas have dirty

When removing a snake, particularly a large one, from its hide box, be slow and cautious. If startled, the snake may bite in defense. Even docile Red-tailed Boas can be aggressive if frightened. Photo by I. Francais.

some *Epicrates*, the anacondas, *Acrantophis*, and larger *Corallus*) can be a serious or even deadly danger. The front teeth of most boas are large and very sharp and can penetrate deeply. A bite often is accompanied by bruising and crushing as well as the usual puncture wounds and bleeding. Deep puncture wounds easily may become infected, sometimes dangerously so, and the bruising may actually crush cartilage in the finger joints. Some boas instinctively go for the face, and the bite of even a rather small Redtail to the nose or cheek may require medical attention. Some breeders grow full beards to help prevent such serious accidents, but obviously this solution is not a very satisfactory one.

For large and/or temperamental animals, many keeper use snake hooks or tongs to move their boas during cage maintenance. Pictured is the Jamaican Slender Boa. Photo by I. Francais.

mouths and may have large numbers of amoeba in the tissues of the jaw, so beware of infections; consult a doctor if pain and redness continue or if you notice the bluish streaks typical of infections.

Large boas are more dangerous and a matter of concern to all hobbyists. Any boa 2 or 3 meters long (Red-tails and other *Boa*,

If you are bitten by a large boa, it might be best to have a doctor check the wound and give you a course of antibiotics. The doctor also should check for the presence of amoebas in the wound and perhaps keep an eye out for blood-carried infections at a later date. Also, the doctor should look for broken teeth in the wound that may slow healing and serve as centers for infection. Your tetanus immunization should be kept up to date to ease your peace of mind.

Most boas are ambush predators, lying in wait along a game trail and quickly striking at suitable prey as it passes within reach. The snake then throws one or several coils over the prey and constricts it until it stops breathing because the ribs and diaphragm (of bird and mammal prey) cannot move. Almost all boas have heat-sensing areas under the jaw scales even if there is no external pit visible. They help measure small differences between the body temperature of warm-blooded prey and the atmosphere or ground, allowing the snake to strike without actually seeing the prey in detail. The vision of most boas is poor and adapted more to detect movement than actually visualize the animal. When constricting prey, boas respond to the struggling of the animal by applying more pressure; thus more muscle movement results in tighter coils.

What all this means is that a large boa is attracted to warm surfaces of a keeper's body, such as the neck and arms, and will attempt to coil there, especially if it has struck you and gotten you confused with food. Your neck is especially warmer because of the large blood vessels just under the skin. If you let a large boa coil around your neck, you are asking for trouble and may very well get it. Boas have a tendency to become tangled in long head hair and may require two people to untangle them, something to remember when you take your Red-tail for a walk.

It is doubtful if any boas have ever killed a human, though a large Green Anaconda certainly could easily drown an adult human just by throwing a few coils and retreating into deeper water. Fortunately, large anacondas are shy and sluggish snakes and accidents are unlikely to happen either in nature or in captivity. Red-tailed Boas and their relatives, as well as a few large *Epicrates*, are large enough to at

Most boas are powerful constrictors adapted to kill and consume rather large prey. This Madagascan Boa is constricting a wild rodent. Photo by K. H. Switak.

Tall cages made of screen and wood are probably the best enclosures for arboreal boas such as these Emerald Tree Boas. Photo by I. Francais.

nance. It may take two people to get it in and out of its cage. If you are bitten, it may take a second person to drive you to the hospital or to clean and bandage the would. Always have a support person to help you in case of trouble.

Large boas are a danger to pets, and they seem to especially enjoy stalking and eating cats. Their cages must be sturdily built and be able to latch securely. If you have children, the cages should be kept locked. Never give a large boa the free run of the house. Boas also have been known to bend the bars of bird cages and squeeze inside.

Always follow the local laws and permitting procedures that apply to keeping large snakes in your particular country, state, province, or city. No matter how much you feel that your big boa is completely tame and predictable, it is a dangerous animal to everyone else. You cannot hide a large boa, and you probably cannot afford the fines if your neighbor turns you in. Some areas may simply prohibit the keeping of all snakes over a certain size (usually

least in theory injure or kill a child, but such accidents are quite rare even in captivity. However, any boa over 2 meters can be dangerous through its bite and may cause a great deal of stress if you have to try to uncoil one from around your neck. If your boa is over 3 meters in length, it should never be handled by only one person. It will take two people to uncoil it if there is an accident during feeding or cage mainte-

BOA CARE

about 2 meters), in which case you may have to consider moving to a more favorable locality. If you try to go underground you are certainly headed for trouble. Notice, also, that many homeowner's insurance policies will not cover homes or apartments with large snakes, a matter of growing concern in some areas.

CAGING

Cages for boas can be relatively simple as long as they are sturdily constructed and can be securely covered. Though glass aquaria work well for small animals such as the erycinids and smaller boas, larger specimens will require specially built cages of wood, plastic, and Plexiglas. Fortunately, the inactive lifestyles of most boas mean that you don't need a cage much longer than the length of the snake for it to be comfortable. Boas don't need exercise.

As a general rule, a terrarium for a small to medium boa should be 1 to 2 meters long and about half that in width; for the climbing species it should be a meter or so high as well. The lid should be partially screened to allow air flow and also to allow the rays of a heat bulb to penetrate easily. Different keepers prefer different bedding materials, but aspen litter, small smooth pebbles, washed sand, and newspaper all have been recommended by keepers and breeders and work under a variety of circumstances. Obviously a boa that prefers it dry (as do most erycinids) should not be kept in a cage with a moisture-holding substrate, while one that is thin-skinned and needs lots of moisture (anacondas, small *Corallus*) may like to have at least part of the cage bottom covered with sphagnum so there always is a moist area to retire to.

A hide box always should be

A humidified shelter like the one pictured will help keep rainforest-dwelling boas healthy. This is a Rainbow Boa. Photo by R. Sacha.

available. Snakes like to relax with their bodies touching a solid object, and they like cramped hide boxes. An overly large hide box may make your boa uncomfortable. Many different styles of hide boxes can be purchased at your pet shop, and large curved slabs of cork bark or split logs serve well. Moisture-loving species may

Sand makes a good substrate for burrowing boas from arid areas, like the Central Asian Sand Boa. Photo by K. H. Switak.

like having the hide box partially filled with sphagnum that is kept a bit moist; this also may help them have smooth molts without the problem of adhering pieces.

Almost all true boas (the erycinids being the exception) like a large water bowl in their terrarium, and many will drink from it, defecate in it, and bathe in it. Obviously the water must be kept clean at all times to prevent possible reinfection from intestinal parasites passed in the feces.

The erycinids often are very sensitive to excess humidity both in the substrate and in the air, so they usually are kept without a water bowl. Many hobbyists put a small bowl of water in for one day each week and remove it after they have seen the snake drink. The water bowl should not be left in the cage for more than two days at a time.

Species that are partially or mostly arboreal (specifically the tree boas) will need several large and sturdily anchored branches on which to relax. Some species, such as the Emerald Tree Boa, will spend the entire day on a branch, coming down at night to feed. Be sure that branches are not placed directly over each other if more than one boa is in the terrarium, or they will shortly become covered with feces and will have to be removed and cleaned.

Though arboreal species such as the tree boas and some *Epicrates* need large, vertically oriented terraria, others (such as the erycinids, tropidophiids, and even small Red-tailed Boas) do very well in small quarters and can be kept in rack systems using plastic boxes such as those used for breeding colonies of kingsnakes and Corn Snakes.

Heat and Light

Most boas do not need artificial light to prosper. They are nocturnal and normally are not active during the day. They do respond to sunlight in the way of day length (photoperiod), however, and if at all possible their terrarium should be exposed indirectly (as through an open window) to normal day lengths during most of the year. Many boas seem to do best if exposed to about 14

Aspen bedding is a good substrate for species that don't require high humidity, like Red-tailed Boas. Photo by I. Francais.

BOA CARE

Emerald Tree Boas and other arboreal boids will kill and eat their prey right from their perches. Their enlarged anterior teeth most likely evolved to prevent them from dropping their prey. Photo by K. H. Switak.

hours of light most of the year, reduced to about ten hours during the winter months. If you use artificial lights (most hobbyists like to have full-spectrum fluorescent bulbs as a back-up for sunlight), they should be positioned outside the terrarium to prevent burns. Full-spectrum fluorescents, though recently considered of questionable value by some hobbyists, will do no harm and may improve the snake's outlook on life in some indefinable way.

Almost all boas like to have a basking light over one corner of the terrarium. The erycinids from dry habitats may require a basking light to keep one part of the terrarium dry and warm most of the day. Pregnant females often like to bask for hours each day, as may juveniles. A warm corner also helps promote a thermal gradient from warmest to coolest temperatures in the terrarium. The basking light should be placed over a favored branch or rock, not over the water bowl or hide box. The snake must always be able to move away from the warm corner.

Almost all boas do well at temperatures between 24 and 30°C (75 and 86°F) during the day, with

Anacondas, big Red-tails, and other large adult boas are often fed rabbits. Photo by M. Gilroy.

Pinkie and fuzzy mice are the standard food for newborn boas. Photo by M. Walls.

a corner a few degrees warmer. Under-tank heaters work well in helping maintain such temperatures most of the year, especially when the basking light is on for several hours a day. Almost all boas seem to do better if the temperature is allowed to drop a few degrees at night. Constant temperatures are not necessary and are not desirable, especially for species from desert-like habitats. Also, boas seem to live longer and breed better if the temperature is dropped by about 5°C for two or three months during the winter months in the Northern Hemisphere.

Most keepers feed full-grown rats to their adult boas. Photo by S. Shore.

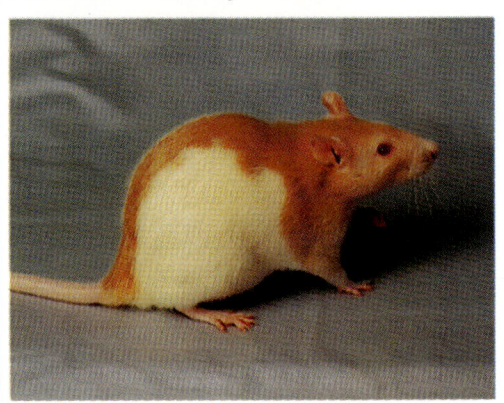

FEEDING

The most popular boas feed on rodents, rabbits, and chicks of appropriate size. Tropidophiids may take insects, lizards, and even fish in nature, but most adapt to mice in captivity. Hatchlings of most common boas are started on mice and then moved on to rats, hamsters, gerbils, guinea pigs, and rabbits, depending of course on adult size and age. Large boas may need increasingly larger and more expensive foods, a fact to be remembered when you make your initial purchase of that cute baby.

Adult mice can be taken by the neonates of larger boas and the adults of some smaller species. Photo by I. Francais.

Recently the life of the boa keeper has been made easier by a blooming of companies supplying frozen mice and rats of all sizes. Such frozen foods are convenient and relatively inexpensive and do not smell like living rodent colonies. Most boas accept completely thawed rodents without much trouble once they have gotten used to them. Also available now are so-called mouse sausages, which basically are chopped rodents packed in a thin skin, frozen, and in a conveniently stored and fed form.

BOA CARE

Garden Tree Boas and other arboreal species feed largely on anoles and geckos in the wild. Wild-caught and newborn specimens may insist on these as food for a period before taking rodents. Photo by A. Winstel.

Quail chicks may tempt some reluctant eaters. Common finches also work for this purpose. Photo by M. Walls.

Wild-caught imported boas may be too heavily stressed to feed on their own and may have to be force-fed at first. Forced-feeding is an art that should be learned from a practiced hand because it is stressful to the snake and may be dangerous to the handler(s) as well. Newborns that do not feed on their own for several weeks after birth also may have to be force-fed, an even more delicate operation.

Frogs of the genus *Eleutherodactylus* are common in the Neotropics and eaten by many boas. Tropidophiids and *Epicrates* may refuse other foods entirely. Photo by M. Bacon.

How much you feed and how often obviously will depend on the species, the season, and the size of the boa. As a general rule, young boas feed more often than older ones, and very large boas feed at long intervals. Never try to get your boa to swallow food items that cause it a great deal of effort and excessive jaw distention. Like most animals, boas prefer smaller prey that is easily overcome and swallowed. Excessively large prey items may cause jaw damage and stress the snake, completely throwing it off its feed.

Rule one of feeding, of course, is that living rodents able to move around on their own must never be left with any snake, regardless of size, overnight. A mouse can gnaw deeply into the body of even a large boa and cause horrendous scars and occasionally even death. Snakes that have been bitten by rodents often avoid such food items from then on.

GENERAL HEALTH

I've long held that the recognition and treatment of even the most basic ills of reptiles are beyond the capabilities of the average hobbyist. By this I do not mean to imply that hobbyists are stupid or uneducated, just that diagnosis and treatment of almost all illnesses require very specialized education and experience as well as generally unavailable equipment. In England it is illegal for a non-veterinarian to give

Dysecdysis, a failure to shed properly, is usually caused by keeping a snake in a terrarium that is too dry. Emerald Tree Boas and other species needing humid enclosures frequently suffer from this condition in captivity. Photo by I. Francais.

veterinary advice or attempt to treat any but the most common conditions of pets, and perhaps this would be sound policy in the United States as well.

With a few exceptions (mostly wild-caught specimens), boas are moderately to very expensive animals to purchase and maintain, and it is to your best interest to make arrangements with a qualified reptile veterinarian the moment you begin to seriously consider purchasing a boa. Once rarities, reptile vets today can be found in or near most large cities, and many advertise in reptile magazines and even in the yellow pages. Veterinary organizations recently have realized the growing importance of reptiles in the pet industry, and some now offer their members special seminars and courses to improve their knowledge of reptile medicine. Your pet shop probably has an agreement with a local vet to handle their reptile problems, and they may be happy to refer you to their vet. Just be sure the veterinarian you use is interested in reptile medicine, is qualified to treat boas, and is willing to handle the problems that go along with specimens of the larger species.

The best way to be sure you have a healthy snake is to purchase a captive-bred specimen that is guaranteed to be feeding on a food you can supply. Wild-caught imports have intestinal parasites that will have to be treated by your vet immediately (unless your dealer can provide you with proof that the specimen already has been wormed) and will be stressed. They may be dehydrated, scarred, and have badly damaged snouts and broken tails. Any major purchase should be vetted immediately after you obtain it.

The eyes of healthy boas always are bright and glossy, never dull and sunken (unless before a shed). No boa should have cheesy white material in the mouth or be blowing bubbles through the nostrils. Boas do not breathe with their mouths open unless they are sick, and they never rasp when they breathe. Never purchase a boa that may be ill—it will cause you no end of troubles and may infect any other specimens in your collection. Beware obese boas. They may not be able to reproduce and may have shortened lives.

You can detect and treat mites and ticks in boas. Ticks often are abundant on imported specimens. They may appear as the usual blood-inflated sacks between scales almost anywhere on the body or as small black spots wedged under the free edges of the ventrals. Ticks can be removed by using pointed tweezers (forceps, the term I prefer) to grasp them firmly as close to the skin as possible, twisting a bit, and then pulling. To prevent infection, put a dab of povidone-iodine on each tick bite site. Small ticks may be difficult to remove by hand but usually can be killed by following the treatment for mites. Ticks almost never can reproduce in the terrarium, and once all are removed your problems should be finished. I know of no reported incidents of snake ticks carrying Lyme's disease, but I guess it is possible, so never use your fingers

The jaws of this Boa Constrictor are greatly distended due to a serious case of mouth rot. Even mild cases of this illness require prompt veterinary care. Photo by W. P. Mara.

BOA CARE

to remove a tick and always drop the tick in a small bottle of alcohol for safe disposal.

Mites can be treated in many different ways, but the use of synthetic pyrethrums in the form of sprays and rinses work well. Mites are tiny blackish red spider-like animals that often can be seen crawling in the corners of the cage at night or recognized by the silvery sheen of their feces on the snake's body. Mites lay eggs in the cage, usually in tiny crevices in bark or in the substrate, so any treatment has to be repeated at least twice at intervals to be sure the next generation is killed. Follow the instructions on the product label for most efficient use of any mite remedy.

Recently a simple manual removal method for mites has been suggested that might work in terraria containing small boas. Mites tend to climb up the sides of a terrarium and accumulate near the upper frame at night. If a strip of folded double-sided sticky tape is applied along the upper frame of the terrarium, the mites will climb up to the folded crease in the tape and get stuck, soon dying. All stages of the mites will be caught in the tape, from young nymphs to gravid females. The tape is removed and disposed of weekly and new tape installed. This method may work in problem cases where it is not possible to completely clean out and sterilize all the cage furnishings after a treatment with a spray or rinse.

Never be afraid to ask your dealer for help if you have a problem. Never be afraid to visit a qualified vet (with an appointment) if your boa appears to be out of sorts, even if you don't see anything really wrong with it. Vets won't work for free, but they may be the best friend your snake will ever have. Be prepared to pay a fair price for a worthwhile service.

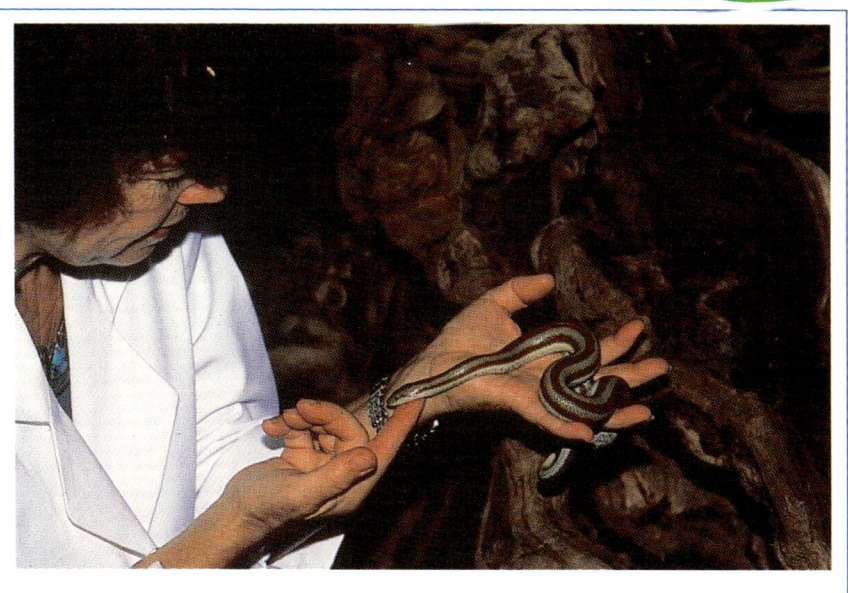

Reptile veterinarians are becoming easier to find. It is best to establish a relationship with one before an emergency ensues. Here, a vet examines a Rosy Boa. Photo by J. Balzarini.

BREEDING BOAS

To many hobbyists the proof that they are successful is the breeding of their boas. In fact, almost all hobby literature features this as the main or perhaps only thrust of keeping snakes in captivity. Personally, I feel that this is a passing aberration of hobby literature. Not every keeper can be a breeder, nor should they try. Breeding most boas requires access to at least two or three specimens in excellent condition and of the proper age for breeding. They must be properly housed, and there must be sufficient room and equipment to maintain the newborns.

If you are a lucky and careful breeder, you may be able to recoup your investment in the parents by selling the young. However, at the moment there are literally dozens, perhaps hundreds, of small breeders of boas in the United States, plus a few dozen large-scale commercial breeders. There also are many importers that can supply specimens at lower cost per head than any breeder. If you successfully breed a species that is common, you may never be able to sell the young. This is the problem at the moment with the Red-tailed Boa, where undistinguished specimens with little color are difficult to dispose of. It costs a breeder more to maintain adult boas of the larger species than Corn Snakes or other colubrids, yet the young of some boas sell for only as much as young Corns. The only real money in breeding is to be made either in mass production in commercial quantities of common species or being among the first to successfully breed and sell a rare

This is a pair of wild Rosy Boas engaged in courtship. In this species, the males do not engage in combat prior to mating. Births normally take place in the fall after about six months of gestation. Photo by K. H. Switak.

BREEDING BOAS

species or variety before everyone else is doing it.

Hobbyists must begin to consider the possibility that breeding is not everything. My suggestion would be to buy your boas as pets, handle them, and learn to understand them. Don't breed unless you have a carefully considered plan of how to get rid of young if you cannot sell them, and by that I don't mean abandoning them in the local park.

BASICS

Most common boas, including the members of the Boidae and the Erycinidae, are being bred in captivity by someone. Unlike the pythons, which lay eggs that must be carefully incubated and produce young that often feed only on lizards, the boas all give live birth after a gestation period of several months. The young of most true boids take mice from birth without complications, though the tiny young of erycinids may be difficult to get to feed at first.

To be breedable, boas must be sexually mature. In most species boas are adult by an age of about three, with some females not maturing until five years of age. Many boas are long-lived and able to successfully produce young for ten or more years, making them quite productive in the hands of a capable breeder. The adults must be in excellent condition and able to survive a cooling period for several weeks or months with little or no food. Females must have sufficient fat reserves to withstand the rigors pregnancy.

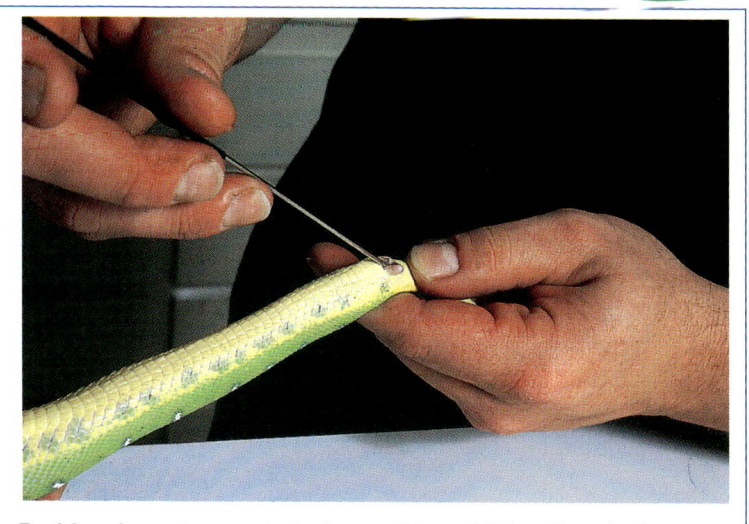

Probing, here demonstrated on an Emerald Tree Boa, is the most accurate way to determine the sex of a snake. Photo by I. Francais.

The males of many boa species have large spurs that can be used to accurately sex them. The spurs are not always visible in juveniles. Pictured is Fischer's Slender Boa. Photo by T. Dodd.

Of course you have to determine the sexes correctly. Few boas can be sexed correctly by external appearance. Often female are stouter and longer than males of equal age, but this seldom is reliable. In true boas (Boidae) and the burrowing boas (Erycinidae), both sexes have well-developed spurs, the external claw of a reduced pelvic girdle. In the Tropidophiidae the spurs may be quite small, though they are present in males of all (or at least almost all) species and present as small remnants in females (occasionally absent). In true boids the male's spurs often are distinctly larger than those of the females, but it takes a very experienced eye to correctly guess sex by spur development.

Correct sexing requires probing of the pouches at the base of the cloaca and noting the depth of penetration of the probe. Females have shallow scent glands behind the cloaca that seldom extend more than four or five subcaudals, while the invaginated hemipenes of a male almost always probe at least eight to ten or more subcaudals. Rough probing may damage the hemipenes or caudal glands of a specimen, so be sure that you see probing done by an experienced hand before you try it. Your pet shop should be able to give you some guidance on purchasing the correct size of probes for your boa species and how to handle the probe. Probing almost always takes two people, by the way.

Tails of copulating Rough-scaled Sand Boas. This species is easy to breed in captivity. Photo by J. Merli.

BREEDING BOAS

When albino boas are crossed with boas lacking red pigments (anerythristic), normal babies result. If these offspring are bred together, some of their progeny will be close to pure white. Photo by W. P. Mara.

Very young male boas, only a few days old, often have the hemipenes partially exposed. This temporary condition should be looked for in litters of new-born young and any males noted by sketches or photography for future reference. Of course, the lack of a partially exposed hemipenis is not proof that a specimen is a female.

All breeding stock must be wormed before the breeding season and should be free of mites and ticks. Specimens showing any signs of respiratory disease may not survive a cooling period.

COOLING

It is hard to generalize about when boas breed because they come from so many different types of habitats and climatic conditions. Additionally, only a few species have been extensively studied in nature. The majority of the *Epicrates* are poorly known as living animals, while the Tropidophiidae include some of the most poorly known snakes in the Americas. The true boas, Boidae, are fairly well known, however, and often are bred in captivity, with captive-bred Red-tailed Boas now being fairly common. Of the Erycinidae, the Rosy Boa is the only species bred in large numbers, though several species of *Eryx* are being bred in increasing numbers.

As a very broad generalization, boas mate during the cooler months (the dry season in the tropics). Though captives often breed without any special efforts on the part of the hobbyist, most breeders feel that boas reproduce more successfully and consistently if they are cooled for about two months each year. The cooling period is equivalent to the incomplete hibernation or brumation given to many colubrid snakes to promote breeding, but it does not have to be as extreme.

Typically the temperature is gradually reduced at about the same time that the days begin to shorten. Feeding is reduced and usually stopped when the temperature reaches its lowest point. Breeders disagree on the temperatures that are best for boas, but typically they suggest a daytime high of about 24°C (75°F) and a nighttime low of about 19 or 20°C (66 to 68°F). Unlike most cooling schemes for pythons, the sexes typically are left together during the cooling period because mating actually occurs during the low-temperature period rather than when the animals are warmed up again after the cooling.

The yellow color of this *C. carinata* may be due to a xanthic mutation, but that can only be discovered through a few generations of careful breeding. Photo by M. Walls, courtesy of J. Tracy.

PREGNANCY AND BIRTH

It is difficult to know exactly how long pregnancy (from fertilization of the eggs to birth) lasts in boas because the period between mating (copulation) and fertilization is variable. Females appear to be able to store sperm for at least a month or two. One female may mate with more than one male, further complicating measurements.

It seems likely that fertilization typically occurs one or two months after copulation, and pregnancy lasts four to ten months, depending on species, temperature, age of the mother, and just individual variation. In nature the litters are born at the beginning of the wet season or in late spring when prey for the young snakes is most likely to be abundant.

Pregnant females may not be obviously gravid in some species, merely appearing well-fed. They tend to bask quite a bit, perhaps more than for non-pregnant females of the same size and age, and in most cases they continue to hunt and eat throughout pregnancy. Some breeders believe that females stop eating a few weeks before giving birth, but others strongly disagree, so what we probably are seeing is individual variation in snakes and in keeping protocols among breeders.

Litter sizes vary greatly in the boas, though as a rule larger females of a species have more and often somewhat larger young than smaller females. Common litter sizes range from four or five young to 30 to 40. Each young is

BREEDING BOAS

Amelanism and most of the other color variations of boids are caused by recessive mutations. This means normal appearing snakes can sometimes carry these mutations hidden in their genes. Pictured is an albino Rosy Boa. Photo by G. and C. Merker, courtesy R. Limburg.

enclosed in a transparent to translucent membrane that represents the membrane found just below the shell of the egg of a python. The young snake breaks the membrane almost as soon as it leaves the female's body and before the membrane can dry up. Almost all larger litters of young are accompanied by several stillborn young and also unfertilized eggs (called slugs by many breeders). In nature the young break the membrane, dry off a bit, and then leave the vicinity of the mother to find a secure hiding place. Cannibalism by both the mother and litter-mates is not unheard of in the boas.

The young snakes or newborns (sometimes called neonates for the first week or so of life) typically do not feed until after their first molt. This may be just one or two days after birth or as much as two weeks. Almost all true boas and erycinids will take small mice (pinkies or fuzzies, depending on size) as a first meal.

For some reason many hobbyists often think that live-bearing snakes are more advanced than egg-layers and that live-bearing is a great advantage to a snake. This probably represents just mammalian thinking and is not a realistic appraisal. Regardless of philosophy, breeding live-bearers often is considered to be less complicated than for egg-layers because there are none of the problems associated with incubating eggs under somewhat tricky conditions. If you keep a pregnant female warm and happy, you have a good chance of getting a good litter.

Further Reading

The following bibliography obviously is merely an introduction to the literature on the boas. Because of their familiarity since early times, their importance in exploration and adventure literature, and their present popularity in the terrarium, the boas have a massive amount of paper and ink devoted to them. There has not been a comprehensive review, even at the introductory level of this book, since Boulenger's catalog of 1893, but there is a large amount of taxonomic literature on the families here considered to be boas.

If you look at the titles listed below and also check the references in their bibliographies (the secondary bibliography) and so on, you have access to a large percentage of the important references on the families.

Abalos, J. W., E. C. Baez and R. Nader. 1964. "Serpientes de Santiago del Estero," *Acta Zool. Lilloana*, 20: 217-223 (*Epicrates*).

Amaral, A. do. 1927. "Studies of Neotropic Ophidia. VIII. *Trachyboa* Peters, 1860," *Bull. Antivenin Inst. Amer.*, 1(3): 86-87.

Amaral, A. do. 1954. "Contribuicao ao conhecimento dos ofidios neotropicos. XXXVII. Sub-especies de *Epicrates cenchria* (Linne, 1758)," *Mem. Inst. Butantan*, 26: 227-247.

Anderson, S. C. and A. E. Leviton. 1969. "Amphibians and reptiles collected by the Street Expedition to Afghanistan, 1965," *Proc. Calif. Aca. Sci.*, 37(2): 25-56.

Andreotti, F. 1993. "Notes on captive propagation and husbandry of the red-tail boa constrictor, *Boa constrictor* ssp.," *Bull. Chicago Herp. Soc.*, 28(5): 98-102.

Auffenberg, W. 1958. "The trunk musculature of *Sanzina* [sic] and its bearing on certain aspects of the myological evolution of snakes," *Breviora, Mus. Comp. Zool.*, No. 82: 1-12.

Bailey, J. R. 1937. "A review of some recent *Tropidophis* material," *Proc. New England Zool. Club*, 16: 41-52.

Bannikov, A. G., I. C. Darevskiy and A. K. Pustamov. 1971. *Amphibians and Reptiles of the Soviet Union (CCCP)*. Moscow.

Barker, D. and T. Barker. 1994. "Boas in the spotlight," *The Vivarium*, 6(2): 39-41.

Bartlett, R. D. 1986. "An incidental interest in '*intermedia*'," *Notes from NOAH*, 13(5): 3-6.

Bartlett, R. D. 1987. "Oh no! Not rosies again! (The final (?) word)," *Notes from NOAH*, 14(8): 4-6.(*Lichanura*)

Belluomini, H. E., A. F. Maranhao Nina and A. R. Hoge. 1959. "Contribuicao a biologia do genero *Eunectes* Wagler, 1830. (Serp. Boidae). Estudo de seis ninhadas de 'sucuris'," *Mem. Inst. Butantan*, 29: 165-174.

FURTHER READING

Bogert, C. M. 1968a. "The variations and affinities of the dwarf boas of the genus *Ungaliophis*," *Amer. Mus. Novitates*, No. 2340: 1-26.

Bogert, C. M. 1968b. "A new genus and species of dwarf boa from southern Mexico," *Amer. Mus. Novitates*, No. 2354: 1-38.(*Exiliboa*)

Boulenger, G. A. 1893. *Catalogue of the Snakes in the British Museum (Natural History)*. Vol. 1. British Museum (Nat. Hist.); London. (Last full survey)

Branch, W. R. 1981. "Hemipenes of the Madagascan boas *Acrantophis* and *Sanzinia*, with a review of hemipeneal morphology in the Boinae," *J. Herpetology*, 15(1): 91-99.

Branch, W. R. 1986. "Hemipenial morphology of African snakes: A taxonomic review. Part 1. Scolecophidia and Boidae," *J. Herpetology*, 20(3): 285-299.

Branson, B. A. 1993. "American boa constrictors," *Reptile & Amphibian Mag.*, No. 24: 48/55.

Brongersma, L. D. 1951. "Some notes upon the anatomy of *Tropidophis* and *Trachyboa* (Serpentes)," *Zool. Mededelingen*, 31(11): 107-124.

Burger, R. M. 1995. "An arboreal burrower: The dwarf boa *Ungaliophis*," *The Vivarium*, 7(2): 46-49.

Burt, C. E. and M. D. Burt. 1932. "Herpetological results of the Whitney South Sea Expedition. VI. Pacific island amphibians and reptiles in the collection of the American Museum of Natural History," *Bull. Amer. Mus. Nat. Hist.*, 63(5): 461-596. (*Candoia*)

Bustard, H. R. 1969. "Defensive behavior and locomotion of the Pacific boa, *Candoia aspera*, with a brief review of head concealment in snakes," *Herpetologica*, 25(3): 164-170.

Butner, A. 1963. "An addition to the boid snake subfamily Tropidophinae," *Copeia*, 1963(1): 160-161.

Campbell, H. W. 1978. "Observations on a captive Mona Island boa, *Epicrates monensis monensis* Zenneck," *Bull. Maryland Herp. Soc.*, 14(2): 98-99.

Campbell, J. A. and J. L. Camarillo R. 1992. "The Oaxacan dwarf boa, *Exiliboa placata* (Serpentes: Tropidophiidae): Descriptive notes and life history," *Caribbean J. Sci.*, 28(1-2): 17-20.

Carpenter, C. C., J. B. Murphy and L. A. Mitchell. 1978. "Combat bouts with spur use in the Madagascan boa (*Sanzinia madagascariensis*)," *Herpetologica*, 34(2): 207-212.

Cei, J. M. 1986. *Reptiles del centro, centro-oeste y sur de la Argentina*. Mus. Regionale de Scienze Naturali; Torino, Italy.

Chippaux, J.-P. 1986. "Les serpents de la Guyane francaise," *Faune Tropicale*, 27: 1-165.

Christie, B. 1994. "Husbandry and reproduction of the Amazon tree boa (*Corallus e. enydris*)," *Captive Breeding*, 2(2): 20-24.

Conant, R. 1966. "A second record for *Ungaliophis continentalis* from Mexico," *Herpetologica*, 22(2): 157-160.

Crawford, D. 1990. "Tongue coloration as a luring device in Haitian boas," *Notes from NOAH*, 17(10): 12-14.

Cunningham, J. D. 1966. "Observations on the taxonomy and natural history of the rubber boa, *Charina bottae*," *Southwestern Naturalist*, 11: 298-299.

Deschanel, J. P. and N. Chason. 1977. "Reproduction d'anacondas (*Eunectes murinus*) au Jardin Zoologique de Lyon," *Aquarama*, No. 39: 37-40.

Dixon, J. R. and P. Soini. 1986. *The Reptiles of the Upper Amazon Basin, Iquitos Region, Peru*. Milwaukee Publ. Mus.; Milwaukee, WI.

Dowling, H. G. 1975. "The Nearctic snake fauna," *Yearbook of Herpetology, 1974*: 190-202.

Dunn, E. R. and R. Conant. 1936. "Notes on anacondas, with descriptions of two new species," *Proc. Acad. Nat. Sci. Philadelphia*, 88: 503-506.

Edwards, P. F. 1988. "Successful captive reproduction of the emerald tree boa (*Corallus canina*)," *Notes from NOAH*, 16(1): 11-13.

Erwin, D. B. 1964. "Some findings on newborn rubber boas, *Charina b. bottae*," *Copeia*, 1964(1): 222-223.

Erwin, D. B. 1974. "Taxonomic status of the southern rubber boa, *Charina bottae umbratica*," *Copeia*, 1974(4): 996-997.

Focart, L. 1951. "Nomenclature remarks on some generic names of the snake family Boidae," *Herpetologica*, 7: 197-199.

Fogel, D. 1988. "Captive care of the emerald tree boa constrictor (*Corallus canina*)," *Notes from NOAH*, 16(3): 18-21.

Fogel, D. 1994. "Boa constrictors in captivity: with notes on subspecies," *Captive Breeding*, 2(4): 4-8.

Frazzetta, T. H. 1959. "Studies on the morphology and function of the skull in the Boidae (Serpentes). Part 1. Cranial differences between *Python sebae* and *Epicrates cenchris*," *Bull. Mus. Comp. Zool.*, 119(8): 453-472.

Gamow, R. I. & J. F. Harris. 1973. "The infrared receptors of snakes," *Scientific American*, 228(5): 94-100.

Gasperetti, J. 1988. "The snakes of Saudi Arabia," *Fauna of Saudi Arabia*, 9: 205-210. (*Eryx* only)

Gibson, F. W. 1970. "The 'quadrifurcate' hemipenis of *Tropidophis*," *Herp. Review*, 2(4): 29-30.

Gilmore, R. M. 1993. "On large anacondas, *Eunectes murinus* (Serpentes: Boidae), with special reference to the Dunn-Lamon record," *Bull. Chicago Herp. Soc.*, 28(9): 185-188.

Glaw, F. and M. Vences. 1994. *A Fieldguide to the Amphibians and Reptiles of Madagascar*. (2nd Ed.) Vences & Glaw Verlag; Koln, Germany.

Gorman, G. C. 1965. "The distribution of *Lichanura trivirgata* and the status of the species," *Herpetologica*, 21(4): 283-287.

Gray, J. E. 1842. "Synopsis of the species of prehensile-tailed snakes, or family Boidae," *Zool. Misc.*: 41-46.

Guibe, J. 1949. "Revision des boides de Madagascar," *Mem. Inst. Sci. Madagascar*, (A) 3: 95-105.

Hanlon, R. W. 1964. "Reproductive activity of the Bahaman boa (*Epicrates striatus*),"

FURTHER READING

Herpetologica, 20(2): 143-144.

Hardy, L. M. 1989. "The karyotype of *Exiliboa placata* Bogert (Tropidopheidae), and comparisons with the family Boidae (Reptilia: Serpentes)," *Proc. Biol. Soc. Washington*, 102(4): 1045-1049.

Harlow, P. and R. Shine. 1992. "Food habits and reproductive biology of the Pacific Island boas (*Candoia*)," 26(1): 60-66.

Hedges, S. Blair and O. H. Garrido. 1992. "A new species of *Tropidophis* from Cuba (Serpentes: Tropidophiidae)," *Copeia*, 1992(3): 820-825.

Henderson, R. W. 1990. "Correlation of environmental variables and dorsal color in *Corallus enydris* (Serpentes: Boidae) on Grenada: Some preliminary results," *Caribbean J. Sci.*, 26(3-4): 166-170.

Henderson, R. W. 1991. "Distribution and preliminary interpretation of geographic variation in the Neotropical tree boa *Corallus enydris*: A progress report," *Bull. Chicago Herp. Soc.*, 26(5): 105-110.

Henderson, R. W. 1993a. "On the diets of some arboreal boids," *Herpetological Nat. Hist.*, 1(1): 91-96.

Henderson, R. W. 1993b. "*Corallus enydris*," *Cat. Amer. Amph. Rept.*: 576.1-576.6.

Henderson, R. W. 1994. "A splendid quintet: the widespread boas of South America," *Lore (Milwaukee Pub. Mus.)*,: 44(4): 2-9.

Henderson, R. W. and G. Puorto. 1993. "*Corallus cropanii*," *Cat. Amer. Amph. Rept.*: 575.1-575.2.

Henderson, R. W. and A. Schwartz. 1984. *A Guide to the Identification of the Amphibians and Reptiles of Hispaniola.* Milwaukee Publ. Mus.; Milwaukee, WI.

Henderson, R. W., et al. 1995. "Ecological correlates and patterns in the distribution of Neotropical boines (Serpentes: Boidae)," *Herpetological Nat. Hist.*, 3(1): 15-27.

Henderson, R. W. and R. A. Winstel. 1992. "Activity patterns, temperature relationships, and habitat utilization in *Corallus enydris* (Serpentes: Boidae) on Grenada," *Caribbean J. Sci.*, 28(3-4): 229-232.

Hoffstetter, R. 1955. "Sur les Boides fossiles de la sous-famille des Eyrcines," *Comptes Rendus Seances l'Academie Sci.*, 240: 644-645.

Hoge, A. R. 1953. "A new genus and species of Boinae from Brazil, *Xenoboa cropanii*, gen. nov., sp. nov.," *Mem. Inst. Butantan*, 25(1): 27-34.

Hoyer, R. F. 1974. "Description of a rubber boa (*Charina bottae*) population from western Oregon," *Herpetologica*, 30(3): 275-283.

Hudelson, S. and P. Hudelson. 1992. "Case report of gentamicin toxicity in a captive common boa (*Boa constrictor*)," *The Vivarium*, 3(5): 24-26.

Joy, W. D. 1992. "World record boa constrictor "de-discovered"," *Notes from NOAH*, 19(10): 21.

Kend, B. and S. Kend. 1993. "The rough-scaled sand boa in captivity," *Reptile & Amphibian Mag.*, No. 22: 14-18.

Klauber, L. M. 1943. "The subspecies of the rubber snake, *Charina*," *Trans. San Diego Soc. Nat. Hist.*, 10(7): 83-90.

Kluge, A. G. 1988. "Parsimony in vicariance biogeography: A quantitative method and a Greater Antillean example," *Syst. Zool.*, 37(4): 315-328. (*Epicrates*)

Kluge, A. G. 1989. "A concern for evidence and a phylogenetic hypothesis of relationships among *Epicrates* (Boidae, Serpentes)," *Syst. Zool.*, 38(1): 7-25.

Kluge, A. G. 1991. "Boine snake phylogeny and research cycles," *Misc. Publ., Mus. Zool., Univ. Mich.*, No. 178: 1-58.

Kluge, A. G. 1993. "*Calabaria* and the phylogeny of erycine snakes," *Zool. J. Linnean Soc.*, 107: 293-351.

Kurfess, J. F. 1967. "Mating, gestation, and growth rate in *Lichanura r. roseofusca*," *Copeia*, 1967(2): 477-479.

Langhammer, J. K. 1983. "A new subspecies of boa constrictor, *Boa constrictor melanogaster*, from Ecuador (Serpentes: Boidae)," *Tropical Fish Hobbyist*, 32(4): 70-76, 78-79.

Lanza, B. 1983. "A list of the Somali amphibians and reptiles," *Monitore zool. italiano*, N.S. Suppl. 18(8): 193-247.

Laurent, R. 1949. "Notes sur quelques reptiles appartenant a la collection de l'Institut Royal des Sciences Naturelles de Belgique. III. Formes americaines," *Bull. Inst. roy. Sci. nat. Belgique*, 25(9): 1-20.

Lazell, J. D., Jr. 1964. "The Lesser Antillean representatives of *Bothrops* and *Constrictor*," *Bull. Mus. Comp. Zool*, 132(3): 245-273.

Lehmann, H. D. 1993. "Observations on the husbandry and reproduction of *Trachyboa boulengeri* (Serpentes, Boidae)," *Bull. Chicago Herp. Soc.*, 28(2): 25-31. (trans. and reprinted from *Salamandra*, 6(1/2): 32-42, 1970)

Lehmann, H. D. 1993. "*Trachyboa boulengeri* (Serpentes, Boidae) eats fish," *Bull. Chicago Herp. Soc.*, 28(2): 30-31. (trans. and reprinted from *Salamandra*, 10(3/4): 132-133, 1974)

Machado, O. 1944. "Observacoes sobre ofidios do Brasil," *Bol. Inst. Vital Brazil*, No. 27: 61-64.

MacDonald, L. 1973. "Attack latency of *Constrictor constrictor* as a function of prey activity," *Herpetologica*, 29(1): 45-48.

Matsuda, B. 1992. "Colombian rainbow boa birth at Vancouver Aquarium," *Captive Breeding*, 1(1): 8-11.

Matz, G. 1978. "Les boides ou serpents constricteurs. 5," *Aquarama*, No. 41: 40-41.

Matz, G. 1981. "Les boides ou serpents constricteurs. 7. *Eunectes* Wagler," *Aquarama*, No. 61: 37-39.

Matz, G., J. Matz, and M. Vanderhaege. 1982. "Les boides ou serpents constricteurs. 8. Reproduction de deux boines: *Epicrates c. maurus* Gray et *Acrantophis dumerili* Jan," *Aquarama*, No. 63: 49-51, 66-67.

McCoy, M. 1980. *Reptiles of the Solomon Islands*. Wau Ecology Inst., Handbook No. 7. Wau, Papua New Guinea.

McDowell, S. B. 1979. "A catalogue of the snakes of New Guinea

FURTHER READING

and the Solomons, with special reference to those in the Bernice P. Bishop Museum. Part III. Boinae and Acrochordoidea (Reptilia, Serpentes)," *J. Herpetology*, 13(1): 1-92.

McGinnis, S. M. and R. G. Moore. 1969. "Thermoregularion in the boa constrictor *Boa constrictor*," *Herpetologica*, 25(1): 38-45.

McManaway, B. 1988. "Breeding the common boa (*Boa c. constrictor*)," *Notes from NOAH*, 16(1): 19.

McSherry, C. 1992. "Starting your babies on the fast track," *Notes from NOAH*, 19(8): 7-8. (*Epicrates cenchria*)

Medina, D. R. 1959. "Observations on the feeding behavior of a captive rosy boa, *Lichanura roseofusca*," *Copeia*, 1959(4): 336.

Merli, J. 1991. "Ontogenetic color change in the emerald tree boa, *Corallus caninus*," *The Vivarium*, 3(4): 19-21.

Mertens, R. 1972. "Madagaskars Herpetofauna und die Kontinentaldrift," *Zool. Mededelingen*, 46(7): 91-98.

Minton, S. 1966. "The Herpetology of West Pakistan," *Bull. Amer. Mus. Nat. Hist.*, 134: 118-120. (*Eryx* only)

Murphy, J. B., D. G. Barker and B. W. Tryon. 1978. "Miscellaneous notes on the reproductive biology of reptiles. 2. Eleven species of the family Boidae, genera *Candoia*, *Corallus*, *Epicrates* and *Python*," *J. Herpetology*, 12(3): 385-390.

Murphy, J. B., W. E. Lamoreaux and D. G. Barker. 1981. "Miscellaneous notes on the reproductive biology of reptiles. 4. Eight species of the family Boidae, genera *Acrantophis*, *Aspidites*, *Candoia*, *Liasis* and *Python*," *Trans. Kansas Acad. Sci.*, 84(1): 39-49.

Noble, G. K. and G. C. Klingel. 1932. "The reptiles of Great Inagua Island, British West Indies," *Amer. Mus. Novitates*, No. 549: 1-25.

Ottley, J. R. 1978. "A new subspecies of the snake *Lichanura trivirgata* from Cedros Island, Mexico, *Great Basin Nat.*, 38(4): 411-416.

Ottley, J. R. 1987. "Now hold on just a doggone minute there!." *Notes from Noah*, 14(10): 18. (Letter on Rosy Boa problem).

Ottley, J. R., R. W. Murphy and G. V. Smith. 1980. "The taxonomic status of the rosy boa *Lichanura roseofusca* (Serpentes: Boidae)," *Great Basin Nat.*, 40(1): 59-62.

Parker, H. W. and A. G. C. Grandison. 1977. *Snakes - A Natural History*. Brit. Mus. (Nat. Hist.); London.

Pendlebury, G. B. 1974. "Stomach and intestine contents of *Corallus enydris*: a comparison of island and mainland specimens," *J. Herpetology*, 8(3): 241-244.

Peters, J. A. 1957. "Taxonomic notes on Ecuadorian snakes in the American Museum of Natural History," *Amer. Mus. Novitates*, No. 1851: 1-13.

Peters, J. A. 1960. "The snakes of Ecuador. A check list and key," *Bull. Mus. Comp. Zool.*, 122(9): 491-541.

Peters, J. A. and B. Orejas-Miranda. 1970. "Catalogue of the

Neotropical Squamata: Part I. Snakes," *Bull. U. S. Natl. Mus.*, No. 297.

Peters, W. C. H. [1995]. *The Herpetological Contributions of Wilhelm C. H. Peters (1815-1883)*. Soc. Study Amph. and Reptiles; Ithaca, NY.

Pope, C. H. 1961. *The Giant Snakes*. A. A. Knopf; New York.

Price, R. M. and P. Russo. 1991. "Revisionary comments on the genus *Boa* with the description of a new subspecies of *Boa constrictor* from Peru," *The Snake*, 23: 29-33.

Puorto, G. and R. W. Henderson. 1994. "Ecologically significant distribution records for the common tree boa (*Corallus enydris*) in Brasil," *Herpetological Nat. Hist.*, 2(2): 89-91.

Raiti, P. and W. Cermak. "Anorexia in a Solomon Island ground boa," *Reptile & Amphibian Mag.*, No. 24: 80, 82-83.

Reichling, S. B. 1991. "The serpents of St. Lucia, *Bothrops caribbae* and *Boa constrictor orophias*," *The Vivarium*, 3(3): 7-9, 22.

Rendahl, H. and G. Vestergren. 1941. "On a small collection of snakes from Ecuador," *Arkiv for Zoologi*, 33A(5): 1-16.

Rieppel, O. 1978. "A functional and phylogenetic interpretation of the skull of the Erycinae (Reptilia, Serpentes)," *J. Zool., Lond.*, 186: 185-208.

Rieppel, O. 1979. "A cladistic classification of primitive snakes based on skull structure," *Z. Zool. Syst. Evolut.-forsch.*, 17: 140-150.

Rooj, N. d. 1917. *The Reptiles of the Indo-Australian Archipelago. II. Ophidia*. E. J. Brill; Leiden. (Boidea: 14-33)

Ross, R. A. and G. Marzec. 1990. *The Reproductive Husbandry of Pythons and Boas*. Inst. Herpetol. Res.; Stanford, CA.

Schuett, S. P. 1994. "Captive maintenance and propagation of the Brazilian rainbow boa (*Epicrates cenchria cenchria*)," *Reptiles*, 1(6): 32-34.

Schulz, W. 1995. "New marine station benefits people and environment," *Smithsonian Inst. Research Reports*, No. 81: 1, 6. (Hog Island, Belize)

Schwartz, A. 1957. "A new species of boa (genus *Tropidophis*) from western Cuba," *Amer. Mus. Novitates*, No. 1839: 1-8.

Schwartz, A. 1963. "A new subspecies of *Tropidophis greenwayi* from the Caicos Bank," *Breviora, Mus. Comp. Zool.*, No. 194: 1-6.

Schwartz, A. 1975. "Variation in the Antillean boid snake *Tropidophis haetianus* Cope," *J. Herpetology*, 9(3): 303-311.

Schwartz, A. and O. H. Garrido. 1975. "A reconsideration of some Cuban *Tropidophis* (Serpentes, Boidae)," *Proc. Biol. Soc. Washington*, 88(9): 77-90.

Schwartz, A. and R. W. Henderson. 1985. *A Guide to the Identification of the Amphibians and Reptiles of the West Indies Exclusive of Hispaniola*. Milwaukee Publ. Mus.; Milwaukee, WI.

Schwartz, A. and R. W. Henderson. 1991. *Amphibians and Reptiles of the West Indies*. Univ. Florida Press; Gainesville, FL.

Schwartz, A. and R. J. Marsh. 1960. "A review of the *pardalis-*

FURTHER READING

maculatus complex of the boid genus *Tropidophis* of the West Indies," *Bull. Mus. Comp. Zool.*, 123(2): 1-89.

Scortecci, G. 1939. "Spedizione Zoologica del Marchese Saverio Patrizi nel Basso Giuba e Nell Oltregiuba. Giugno-Agosts 1934. XII. Rettili Ofidi," *Ann. Mus. civ. Stor. nat. Giacomo Doria, Genova*, 58: 267-270. (*Eryx* only)

Sharp, B. 1986. "Notes on husbandry and breeding of *Corallus caninus*," *Notes from NOAH*, 13(5): 13-15.

Sheplan, B. R. and A. Schwartz. 1974. "Hispaniolan boas of the genus *Epicrates* (Serpentes, Boidae) and their Antillean relationships," *Annals Carnegie Mus.*, 45(5): 57-143.

Smith, C. and K. Wintin. 1993. "Captive husbandry and reproduction of the rosy boa (*Lichanura trivirgata trivirgata*)," *Captive Breeding*, 1(3): 12-15.

Smith, H. M. 1969. "The nomenclature of certain taxa of higher categories in snakes," *J. Herpetology*, 3(1-2): 19-25.

Smith, H. M. and D. Chiszar. 1992. "A Mexican genus of tropidopheine snakes," *Bull. Maryland Herp. Soc.*, 28(1): 19-28. (*Boella tenella* = *Epicrates inornatus*, see Wallach & Smith, 1992)

Sorensen, D. 1989. "[Breeder's Corner: *Eryx conicus*, *Eryx miliaris*]," *Notes from NOAH*, 17(1): 10.

Speer, R. J. 1992. "Birth of an emerald tree boa, *Corallus caninus*," *Notes from NOAH*, 19(12): 1-2.

Spiteri, D. G. 1987. "I hear hearsay," *Notes from NOAH*, 14(11): 19. (Letter on Rosy Boa problem)

Spiteri, D. G. 1993. "The current taxonomy and captive breeding of the rosy boa (*Lichanura trivirgata*)," *The Vivarium*, 5(3): 18-21, 27, 34.

Stafford, P. J. 1986. *Pythons and Boas*. T.F.H. Publ.; Neptune, NJ.

Stafford, P. J. (MS, 1994). *Tree Boa Manual*. Natural history, care and maintenance. (Unpublished manuscript)

Stewart, G. R. 1977. "*Charina*," *Cat. Amer. Amph. Rept.*: 205.1-205.2.

Stickel, W. H. and L. F. Stickel. 1946. "Sexual dimorphism in the pelvic spurs of *Enygrus*," *Copeia*, 1946(1): 10-12.(*Candoia*)

Stimpson, S. and A. Ellis. 1989. "The hardy and prolific sand boa, *Eryx jaculus jaculus*," *The Vivarium*, 2(4): 20-24.

Stimson, A. F. 1969. "Liste der rezenten Amphibien und Reptilien. Boidae (Subfam. Boinae, Bolyeriinae, Loxoceminae et Pythoninae)," *Das Tierreich*, 89: 1-49.

Stoops, E. D. and A. T. Wright. 1993. *Boas & Pythons. Breeding and Care*. T.F.H. Publ.; Neptune, NJ.

Strimple, P. 1993. "Overview of the natural history of the green anaconda (*Eunectes murinus*)," *Herpetological Nat. Hist.*, 1(1): 25-35.

Strimple, P. 1995. "A Venezuelan adventure," *Reptiles*, 2(4): 68-84. (*Eunectes*)

Stuart, L. C. 1954. "Further notes on the status of the generic names *Peropodium* and *Ungaliophis*," *Herpetologica*, 10: 79-81.

Stull, O. G. 1928. "A revision of the genus *Tropidophis*," *Occas. Papers Mus. Zool., Univ. Mich.*, No. 195: 1-49, 3 pls.

Stull, O. G. 1932. "Five new subspecies of the family Boidae," *Occas. Papers Boston Soc. Nat. Hist.*, 8: 25-30.

Stull, O. G. 1933. "Two new subspecies of the family Boidae," *Occas. Papers Mus. Zool., Univ. Mich.*, No. 267: 1-4.

Stull, O. G. 1935. "A check list of the family Boidae," *Proc. Boston Soc. Nat. Hist.*, 40(8): 387-408.

Stull, O. G. 1938. "Three new subspecies of the family Boidae," *Occas. Papers Boston Soc. Nat. Hist.*, 8: 297-300.

Stull, O. G. 1956. "Description of a new subspecies of the boid snake, *Enygrus carinatus*," *Copeia*, 1956(3): 185-186. (*Candoia*)

Tanner, V. M. 1933. "A study of the variation of the dorsal scale rows of *Charina bottae* (Blainville)," *Copeia*, 1933(2): 81-84.

Tanner, V. M. and W. W. Tanner. 1939. "Notes on *Charina bottae* in Utah: Reproduction," *Great Basin Nat.*, 1(1): 27-30.

Thomas, M. E. 1974. "Bats as a food source for *Boa constrictor*," *J. Herpetology*, 8(2): 188.

Thomas, R. 1963. "Cayman Islands *Tropidophis* (Reptilia, Serpentes)," *Breviora, Mus. Comp. Zool.*, No. 195: 1-8.

Tokar, A. A. 1989. "[Revision of the genus *Eryx* based on osteological characters]," *Vestnik Zoologii*, No. 4: 46-55. (in Russian)

Tolson, P. J. 1987. "Phylogenetics of the boid snake genus *Epicrates* and Caribbean vicariance theory," *Occas. Papers Mus. Zool., Univ. Mich.*, No. 715: 1-68.

Tolson, P. J. 1994. "The reproductive management of the insular species of *Epicrates* (Serpentes: Boidae) in captivity," in Murphy, J. B., K. Adler, and J. T. Collins (eds.), *Captive Management and Conservation of Amphibians and Reptiles*. Soc. Study Amph. and Rept.; Ithaca, NY. (Contrib. Herp., Vol. 11)

Tolson, P. J. and R. W. Henderson, 1993. *The Natural History of West Indian Boas*. R & A Publishing; Taunton, England.

Trutnau, L. 1979. *Schlangen I.* Ulmer GmbH & Co.; Stuttgart, Germany.

Underwood, G. 1976. "A systematic analysis of boid snakes," in A. d'A. Bellairs & C. B. Cox (eds.), *Morphology and Biology of Reptiles*, Linnean Soc. Symp. Ser., No. 3: 151-175.

Vanzolini, P. E. 1986. "Addenda and corrigenda to the *Catalogue of Neotropical Squamata*," *Smithsonian Herp. Inform. Serv.*, No. 70.

Villa, J. D. and L. D. Wilson. 1990. "*Ungaliophis*," Cat. Amer. Amph. Rept.: 480.1-480.4.

Wallach, V. and H. M. Smith. 1992. "*Boella tenella* is *Epicrates inornatus* (Reptilia: Serpentes)," *Bull. Maryland Herp. Soc.*, 28(4): 162-170.

Walls, J. G. 1994. *Boas: Rosy & Ground*. T.F.H. Publ.; Neptune, NJ.

FURTHER READING

Walsh, T. 1994. "Husbandry of long-term captive populations of boid snakes (*Epicrates, Corallus,* and *Chondropython*)," in Murphy, J. B., Adler, K., and Collins (eds.), *Captive Management and Conservation of Amphibians and Reptiles.* Soc. Stud. Amph. and Rept.; Ithaca, NY. (Contrib. Herp., Vol. 11)

Wiley, E. O. 1978. "The evolutionary species concept reconsidered," *Syst. Zool.*, 27(1): 17-26.

Wilson, L. D. and J. R. Meyer. 1985. *The Snakes of Honduras.* (2nd Ed.). Milwaukee Publ. Mus.; Milwaukee, WI.

Winstel, A. 1988. "The Amazon tree boas' amazing colors," *The Vivarium*, 1(3): 5-7.

Winstel, A. 1989. "Herpetoculture of the Amazon tree boa, *Corallus enydris enydris* (Linnaeus)," *The Vivarium*, 1(4): 12-14.

Winstel, A. 1995. "Tree boas on a tropical isle," *Reptiles*, 2(5): 16/22.

Wright, K. 1992. "The Solomon Island ground boa," *Reptile & Amphibian Mag.*, No. 16: 25-29.

Yingling, R. P. 1982. "*Lichanura*," *Cat. Amer. Amph. Rept.*: 294.1-294.2.

Zaher, H. 1994. "Les Tropidopheoidea (Serpentes: Alethinophidia) sont-ils reellement monophyletiques? Arguments en faveur de leur polyphyletisme," *Comptes Rendus l'Acad. Sci.* (III), 317(5): 471-478.

INDEX

Abaco Slender Boa, 116-117, **116**, **117**
Acrantophis, 40-48,
   definition, 40-41,
   specific key, 41
Acrantophis dumerili, **5**, **33**, 41-46, **42**, **43**, **44**, **45**
Acrantophis madagascariensis, 46-48, **46**, **47**, **48**, **259**
Anacondas, **see** *Eunectes*
Arabian Sand Boa, 180-182, **181**, **182**
Argentine Boa, **16**, **49**, **56**, 60
Argentine Rainbow Boa, **105**, 110, **110**
Bahaman Dwarf Boa, 223-225, **224**, **225**
Battersby's Dwarf Boa, 222-223, **223**
Bimini Boa, **see** *Epicrates striatus*
Birth, 274-275
Bites, 257-259
Black-bellied Dwarf Boa, 239-240, **239**
Boa, 48-64,
   definition, 48-49,
   specific key, 50
Boa constrictor, **9**, **10**, **16**, **39**, **49**, 50-61, **50**, **51**, **53**, **55**, **56**, **57**, **58**, **59**, **60**, **256**, **257**, 259, **262**, **268**, **273**
Boa constrictor amarali, **55**
Boa constrictor imperator, **59**, 60
Boa constrictor melanogaster, **55**
Boa constrictor occidentalis, **16**, **49**, **56**, 60
Boa constrictor ortoni, **50**
Boa nebulosa, 61-62, **61**, **62**
Boa orophias, 62-64, **63**
Boidae, 37-151,
   description, 37-38,
   generic key, 40
Brazilian Dwarf Boa, 241-242, **241**, **242**
Brazilian Rainbow Boa, **1**, **17**, **101**, **105**, 111, **112**, 113, **261**
Breeding, 270-275
Brown Dwarf Boa, 228-229, **229**
Brown Sand Boa, **29**, **161**, 182-187, **182**, **183**, **184**, **185**, **186**
Caging, 261-264
Caicos Dwarf Boa, 229-231, **230**, **231**
Candoia, 64-75,
   definition, 64,
   specific key, 64-65
Candoia aspera, **38**, 65-68, **65**, **66**, **67**
Candoia bibroni, **19**, 68-71, **68**, **69**, **70**, **71**
Candoia carinata, 72-75, **72**, **73**, **74**, **75**, **274**
Caymans Dwarf Boa, 225-226, **225**

Central Asian Sand Boa, **163**, 187-190, **187**, **188**, **189**, **190**, **262**
Charina, 155-160,
   description, 155-156
Charina bottae, **153**, **155**, 156-160, **156**, **157**, **158**, **159**
Colombian Rainbow Boa, **108**, 111, 113
Conant's Anaconda, 134-135, **134**
Cooling, 273-274
Corallus, 76-100,
   definition, 76,
   specific key, 76
Corallus annulatus, **36**, 78-81, **78**, **79**, **81**
Corallus caninus, **6**, 81-86, **82**, **83**, **84**, **85**, **86**, **87**, **260**, 262, **263**, **267**, **271**
Corallus cooki, 96
Corallus cropani, **21**, 86, 88-90, **88**, **89**, **90**
Corallus enydris, **see** *Corallus hortulanus*
Corallus grenadensis, 96
Corallus hortulanus, **77**, 90-100, **90**, **91**, **93**, **94**, **95**, **96**, **97**, **98**, **99**, **265**,
   revision by Henderson, 96-97
Corallus ruschenburgeri, 96
Cordillera Dwarf Boa, 246-247, **247**
Cryptic Slender Boa, 119-120, **119**, **120**
Cuban Dwarf Boa, **206**, **218**, **219**, 235-238, **236**, **237**, **238**
Cuban Slender Boa, 102-104, **102**, **103**, **104**
Dominican Boa, 61-62, **61**, **62**
Dumeril's Boa, **5**, **33**, 41-46, **42**, **43**, **44**, **45**
Elegant Sand Boa, 174-176, **175**
Emerald Tree Boa, **6**, 81-86, **82**, **83**, **84**, **85**, **86**, **87**, **260**, 262, **263**, **267**, **271**
Epicrates, 100-132, 259,
   definition, 100,
   specific key, 100, 102
Epicrates angulifer, 102-104, **102**, **103**, **104**
Epicrates cenchria, **1**, **17**, **101**, 104-113, **105**, **106**, **107**, **108**, **109**, **110**, **111**, **112**, **113**, **261**,
   subspecies of, 110-112
Epicrates cenchria alvarezi, **105**, 110, **110**
Epicrates cenchria assisi, **105**, **106**, 110-111, **112**
Epicrates cenchria cenchria, **1**, **17**, **101**, **105**, 110, **112**, 113, **261**
Epicrates cenchria crassus, **105**, **107**, 111
Epicrates cenchria gaigei, 111, **111**
Epicrates cenchria maurus, **108**, 111, 113
Epicrates cenchria polylepis, 111-112, **113**

Rosy Boa, **8**, **15**, **196**, 197-205, **197**, **198**, **199**, **200**, **201**, **202**, **203**, **204**, **205**, **269**, **270**, **275**
Rough-scaled Sand Boa, **162**, 171-174, **171**, **172**, **173**, **174**, **272**
Round-nosed Island Boa, **19**, 68-71, **68**, **69**, **70**, **71**
Round-spot Banana Boa, **209**, 249-253, **249**, **251**, **252**
Rubber Boa, **153**, **155**, 156-160, **156**, **157**, **158**, **159**
Saddled Dwarf Boa, 226-228, **226**, **227**
Sanzinia, 144-151,
   definition, 144-145
Sanzinia madagascariensis, **13**, **23**, **145**, 146-151, **146**, **147**, **148**, **149**, **150**, **151**
Scalation,
   body, 28-30,
   head, 25, 28, **26**,
   ventral, **29**
Sexing, 272-273
Six-spot Dwarf Boa, 240-241, **240**, **241**
Skull, 24-25, **24**, **25**
Snake hook, **258**
Somali Sand Boa, 191-192, **191**
Species, 18-20,
   definition, 18,
   checklist, 34-36
Spurs, **271**, 272
Square-nosed Island Boa, 72-75, **72**, **73**, **74**, **75**, **274**
St. Lucian Boa, 62-64, **63**
Subspecies, 20-22
Tan Slender Boa, 114-116, **114**, **115**
Tartar Sand Boa, 192-195, **193**, **194**, **195**
Ticks, 268-269
Tortola Slender Boa, 120-122, **121**
Trachyboa, 212
Trachyboa boulengeri, **12**, 212-215, **213**, **214**, **215**
Trachyboa gularis, 215-217, **216**, **217**
Triangle Banana Boa, 253-255, **253**, **255**
Tropidophiidae, 207-255, 264,
   description, 207,

   generic key, 209
Tropidophis, 217-248,
   description, 218,
   husbandry, 219-221,
   identification, 221-222
Tropidophis battersbyi, 222-223, **223**
Tropidophis canus, 223-225, **224**, **225**
Tropidophis canus barbouri, 224
Tropidophis canus androsi, 224
Tropidophis canus canus, 224
Tropidophis canus curtus, 224, **224**
Tropidophis caymanensis, 225-226, **225**
Tropidophis feicki, 226-228, **226**, **227**
Tropidophis fuscus, 228-229, **229**
Tropidophis greenwayi, 229-231, **230**, **231**
Tropidophis haetianus, 231-233, **231**, **232**, **233**
Tropidophis jamaicensis, 233-234, **234**
Tropidophis maculatus, 234-235, **235**
Tropidophis melanurus, **206**, **218**, **219**, 235-238, **236**, **237**, **238**
Tropidophis nigriventris, 239-240, **239**
Tropidophis pardalis, 240-241, **240**, **241**
Tropidophis paucisquamis, 241-242, **241**, **242**
Tropidophis pilsbryi, 242-243, **243**
Tropidophis semicinctus, 244-245, **244**, **245**
Tropidophis stejnegeri, 245-246, **246**
Tropidophis taczanowskyi, 246-247, **247**
Tropidophis wrighti, 247-248, **247**
Two-spot Dwarf Boa, 244-245, **244**, **245**
Ungaliophis, 248-255,
   description, 248,
   specific key, 249
Ungaliophis continentalis, **209**, 249-253, **249**, **251**, **252**
Ungaliophis panamensis, 253-255, **253**, **255**
Viper Boa, **38**, 65-68, **65**, **66**, **67**
West African Sand Boa, 190-191, **190**
Wright's Dwarf Boa, 247-248, **247**
Xenoboa, 14, 76, 86, 88
Xenoboa cropani, **see** *Corallus cropani*
Yellow Anaconda, **27**, **134**, 140-144, **141**, **142**, **143**, **144**

INDEX

Epicrates chrysogaster, 114-116, **114**, **115**
Epicrates exsul, 116-117, **116**, **117**
Epicrates jordi, **20**, 117-119, **117**, **118**, **119**
Epicrates gracilis, 119-120, **119**, **120**
Epicrates granti, 120-122, **121**
Epicrates inornatus, 122-124, **122**, **123**
Epicrates monensis, 124-125, **124**, **125**
Epicrates striatus, 125-130, **125**, **126**, **127**, **128**, **129**, **271**
Epicrates striatus fosteri, **128**
Epicrates striatus strigulatus, **129**
Epicrates subflavus, **129**, **130**, 130-132, **131**, **132**, **258**
Erycinidae, 153-205, 262,
    description, 153-154,
    generic key, 154
Eryx, 160-195,
    description, 160-161,
    specific key, 162-163
Eryx colubrinus, **22**, 163-170, **164**, **165**, **166**, **167**, **168**, **169**, **170**
Eryx conicus, **162**, 171-174, **171**, **172**, **173**, **174**, **272**
Eryx elegans, 174-176, **175**
Eryx jaculus, **152**, 176-180, **176**, **177**, **178**, **179**, **180**
Eryx jayakari, 180-183, **181**, **182**
Eryx johni, **29**, **161**, 182-187, **182**, **183**, **184**, **185**, **186**
Eryx miliaris, **163**, 187-190, **187**, **188**, **189**, **190**, **262**
Eryx muelleri, 190-191, **190**
Eryx somalicus, 191-192, **191**
Eryx tataricus, 192-195, **193**, **194**, **195**
Eunectes, 133-134, 259,
    definition, 133-134,
    specific key, 134
Eunectes "*barbouri*," **136**, 138
Eunectes deschauenseei, 134-135, **134**
Eunectes murinus, **35**, **133**, 135-140, **135**, **136**, **137**, **138**, **139**, **140**, 259
Eunectes notaeus, **27**, **134**, 140-144, **141**, **142**, **143**, **144**
Exiliboa, 209-212,
    description, 210
Exiliboa placata, 210-212, **211**
Families, 12-13
Feeding, 264-266
Fischer's Slender Boa, 125-130, **125**, **126**, **127**, **128**, **129**, **271**
Freckled Dwarf Boa, 234-235, **235**
Garden Tree Boa, **77**, 90-100, **90**, **91**, **93**, **94**, **95**, **96**, **97**, **98**, **99**, **265**,
    revision by Henderson, 96-97
Genera, 13-18,
    in Boidae, 14, 38-40,
    in Erycinidae, 14,
    in Tropidophiidae, 13-14
Grant's Dwarf Boa, 245-246, **246**

Green Anaconda, **35**, **133**, 135-140, **135**, **136**, **137**, **138**, **139**, **140**, 259
Haitian Boa, **see** *Epicrates striatus*
Haitian Dwarf Boa, 231-233, **231**, **232**, **233**
Haitian Vine Boa, **see** *Epicrates gracilis*
Health, 266-269
Heating, 262-264
Hemipenes, 30-31, **30**, **31**, **32**
Hispaniolan Slender Boa, **20**, 117-119, **117**, **118**, **119**
Hog Island Boa, **57**, 60
Hoge's Boa, **21**, 86, 88-90, **88**, **89**, **90**
Horned Spiny Boa, **12**, 212-215, **213**, **214**, **215**
Hybridization, 19-20
Jamaican Dwarf Boa, 233-234, **234**
Jamaican Slender Boa, **129**, 130-132, **130**, **131**, **132**, **258**
Javelin Sand Boa, **152**, 176-180, **176**, **177**, **178**, **179**, **180**
Keeled Spiny Boa, 215-217, **216**, **217**
Kenyan Sand Boa, **22**, 163-170, **164**, **165**, **166**, **167**, **168**, **169**, **170**
Labial pits, **23**, 87
Lichanura, 195-205,
    description, 195-197
Lichanura trivirgata, **8**, **15**, **196**, 197-205, **197**, **198**, **199**, **200**, **201**, **202**, **203**, **204**, **205**, **269**, **270**, **275**
Lichanura trivirgata arizonae, **199**, 202
Lichanura trivirgata gracia, **199**, 202
Lichanura trivirgata myriolepis, **201**, 202, **203**
Lichanura trivirgata roseofusca, **197**, **200**, 202, **202**, **203**, **275**
Lichanura trivirgata trivirgata, **199**
Lighting, 262-263
Madagascan Boa, 46-48, **46**, **47**, **48**, **259**
Madagascan Tree Boa, **13**, **23**, **145**, 146-151, **146**, **147**, **148**, **149**, **150**, **151**
Mites, 268-269
Mona Slender Boa, 124-125, **124**, **125**
Oaxacan Cloud Boa, 210-212, **211**
Pale-spot Dwarf Boa, 242-243, **243**
Paraguayan Rainbow Boa, **105**, **107**, 111
Precautions, 257-261,
Pregnancy, 274
Probing, **271**, 273
Puerto Rican Slender Boa, 122-124, **122**, **123**
Rainbow Boa, **1**, **17**, **101**, 104-113, **105**, **106**, **107**, **108**, **109**, **110**, **111**, **112**, **113**, **261**,
    subspecies of, 110-112
Rearing, 275
Red-tailed Boa, **9**, **10**, **16**, **39**, **49**, 50-61, **50**, **51**, **53**, **55**, **56**, **57**, **58**, **59**, **60**, **256**, **257**, 259, **262**, **268**, **273**
Ringed Tree Boa, **36**, 78-81, **78**, **79**, **81**